3 ~~ONE~~ WEEK LOAN

Reading *Six Feet Under*

TV TO DIE FOR

edited by
Kim Akass & Janet McCabe

I.B. TAURIS

LONDON · NEW YORK

Published in 2005 by I.B.Tauris & Co Ltd
6 Salem Road, London W2 4BU
175 Fifth Avenue, New York NY 10010
www.ibtauris.com

In the United States and Canada distributed by Palgrave Macmillan, a
division of St. Martin's Press, 175 Fifth Avenue, New York NY 10010

ISBN 1 85043 809 9
EAN 978 1 85043 809 0

A full CIP record for this book is available from the British Library
A full CIP record for this book is available from the Library of Congress
Library of Congress catalog card: available

Typeset in Goudy by Dexter Haven Associates Ltd, London

CONTENTS

ACKNOWLEDGEMENTS

The editors would first like to thank the authors – Mark Lawson, David Lavery, Mark W. Bundy, Rob Turnock, Lucia Rahilly, Mandy Merck, Dana Heller, Robert Deam Tobin, Ashley Sayeau, Peter Wilson, Erin MacLeod, Joanna di Mattia, Brian Singleton, Samuel A. Chambers, Peter Kaye and Thomas Lynch – for turning in such fascinating contributions, adhering to strict deadlines and changing the way we see this series.

Special thanks go to Philippa Brewster. Once again, her wise counsel, warm friendship and outrageous humour have helped us enormously through this project. Thanks also to Susan Lawson, for holding the reins when Philippa was away, Deborah Susman and Isabella Steer, as well as those who have supported the project at I. B. Tauris and Palgrave Macmillan. Thanks to Robert Hastings for being an excellent project manager and guiding the project through its final stages.

The editors would like to acknowledge the following libraries: Trinity College, Dublin; London Metropolitan (especially Crispin Partridge); the British Film Institute library; and the Billy Rose Theater Collection, at the New York Public Library for Performing Arts. Special thanks goes to Eydie Wiggins and Idelsa Peña at the Billy Rose Theater Collection whose sterling work on the photocopier saved the day before a flight home to London. Their good humour and willingness to help is much appreciated.

Additional thanks go to David Lavery for giving invaluable advice and Ashley Sayeau for sending us the 'Stiffs of the Week'. We would like to thank Richard Marvin for taking time out of his busy schedule to speak to Peter Kaye and to Anne Hogan for the introduction. We would also like to pass on our appreciation to T. Cribb and Sons, especially John Harris and Marcus for giving generously of their time and taking the trouble to show us around their funeral home. Gratitude for letting us use their images as well as allowing us to take photos. Thanks to Neil Dutton for help with the photos. Heartfelt thanks go to Tamméé Greeves for her wonderful drawings and continued friendship and support.

Janet McCabe would like to thank the Arts and Social Sciences Benefaction Fund at Trinity College, Dublin, for supporting this project, and awarding her a grant to travel and research in New York. Kim Akass extends her thanks to the Research Committee at London Metropolitan University for awarding her the same.

As always, we have to say thank you to our families for supporting us through this project. Thanks to Mike Allen for offering invaluable suggestions and advice, and for alcohol and food, which just appeared during writing sessions. Thanks to Jon Akass for keeping the children amused and the home fires burning, and to Daryl and Caitlin for being patient.

We dedicate this book to our husbands, Mike and Jon, with love.

CONTRIBUTORS

KIM AKASS is a senior lecturer in film studies at London Metropolitan University. She has written articles on motherhood in American TV, and (with Janet McCabe) co-edited and contributed to *Reading Sex and the City* (I. B. Tauris, 2004). She is currently researching representations of the mother and motherhood in American TV drama. She is a member of the editorial board for *Critical Studies in Television*.

MARK W. BUNDY lives in Southern California, where he is completing work on a Ph.D. in English as a Chancellor's Distinguished Fellow, with emphases in lesbian and gay studies, the Gothic genre and contemporary American poetry. Most recently, he has published an article in *Reading Sex and the City* (I. B. Tauris, 2004), and his writing will be featured in a collection of critical and creative pieces on the influence of Gloria Anzaldúa's groundbreaking theoretical discourse, which is due for release in 2005.

SAMUEL A. CHAMBERS teaches political theory in the Department of Political Science at Penn State University. His work has appeared in journals such as *Political Theory*, *American Journal of Political Science*, *Theory & Event*, *Angelaki* and *Contemporary Political Theory*, and his first book is *Untimely Politics: Taking on the Political* (Edinburgh and New York University Presses, 2003). He is currently working on a manuscript on the political theory of Judith Butler.

JOANNA DI MATTIA received her Ph.D. from the Centre for Women's Studies and Gender Research, Monash University, Australia in 2004. Her thesis, *The Hard Body Goes Soft: Anxious Men and Masculinity in the Films of the Clinton Era*, explores the trouble with masculinity in the nineties. She has recently published an essay in *Reading Sex and the City* (I. B. Tauris, 2004), and two entries for *Men and Masculinities: A Social, Cultural, and Historical Encyclopedia* (ABC-Clio Press, 2004). When she isn't watching television, she is developing a research project that examines the challenge posed to hegemonic masculinity by the increasing visibility of queer men in the mainstream.

DANA HELLER is Professor of English and Director of the Humanities Institute at Old Dominion University. She is author of *The Feminization of Quest-Romance: Radical Departures* (University of Texas, 1990), *Family Plots: The De-Oedipalization of Popular Culture* (University of Pennsylvania Press, 1995), *Cross Purposes: Lesbianism Feminists and the Limits of Alliance* (Indiana University Press, 1997) and editor of *The Selling of 9/11: How a National Tragedy Became a Commodity* (Palgrave Macmillan), which will be released in spring 2005.

PETER KAYE has been professionally pottering around the music business for 35 years, including performing, songwriting, record production, music editing and mostly composing for film and television. But, as his career plunged from the tee-hee of Paul Morrisey and yuk-yuk of Cheech & Chong to the most banal of television, he started becoming more interested in the medium itself. In the last few years he has been researching modern common practice of music and moving image, hoping to develop new didactic tools for aspiring – or perspiring – composers.

DAVID LAVERY is Professor of English at Middle Tennessee State University, where he teaches courses on American literature, science fiction, modern poetry, popular culture and film. He is the author of over 60 published essays and reviews and author/editor/co-editor of six books: *Late for the Sky: The Mentality of the Space Age* (Southern Illinois University Press, 1992); *Full of Secrets: Critical Approaches to Twin Peaks* (Wayne State University Press, 1994); *'Deny All Knowledge': Reading The X-Files* (Syracuse University Press, 1996); *Fighting the Forces: What's at Stake in Buffy the Vampire Slayer* (Rowman and Littlefield, 2002); *Teleparody: Predicting/Preventing the TV Discourse of Tomorrow* (Wallflower Press, 2002); and *This Thing of Ours: Investigating The Sopranos* (Columbia University Press, 2002). He co-edits the e-journal *Slayage: The Online International Journal of Buffy Studies*, has spoken on television in Australia, Germany, Ireland and the UK, is a member of the editorial board of *Studies in Popular Culture*, *Refractory: A Journal of Entertainment Media*, *Intensities: The Journal of Cult Media*, and *Critical Studies in Television*. To learn more about him, visit his home page at www.mtsu.edu/~dlavery/.

MARK LAWSON is a journalist, broadcaster and author. He presents BBC Radio 4's arts magazine *Front Row*. He has been a freelance contributor to numerous publications since 1984 and a *Guardian* columnist since 1995. In the mid-nineties he presented *The Late Show* on BBC 2, and he has presented *The Late Review* since 1994. He has twice been voted TV Critic of the Year and has won numerous awards for arts journalism.

THOMAS LYNCH is an essayist, poet and funeral director. He is the author of three collections of poetry: *Skating with Heather Grace* (Knopf, 1987); *Grimalkin & Other Poems* (Jonathan Cape, 1994); and *Still Life in Milford* (W.W. Norton, 1998). His first collection of essays, *The Undertaking – Life Studies from the Dismal Trade* (Norton, 1997), won the Heartland Prize for non-fiction, The Society of Midland Authors Award and the American Book Award, and was a finalist for the National Book Award. It is translated into eight languages. His second book of essays, *Bodies in Motion and at Rest* (W.W. Norton, 2000), won the Great Lakes Book Award. A third book of non-fiction, *Booking Passage – We Irish & Americans,* will be published in 2005. In 2001 Thomas Lynch was named Michigan Author of the Year by the Michigan Library Association and was awarded an Honorary Doctor of Humanities by Oakland University. He is the recipient of fellowships from the National Endowment for the Arts, the Michigan Council for the Arts and the Irish Arts Council. He is a regular contributor to radio on the BBC, RTE and NPR. His BBC Radio 4 series, *Colloquies,* won the Sony Gold Award in 2001. He has appeared on *The Today Show,* CNN, the PBS-Bill Moyers series, *On Our Own Terms* and *Religion & Ethics Newsweekly.* His work has appeared in *Poetry, Harper's, Esquire, The New Yorker, The Paris Review, Time, Newsweek, The Christian Century, The U.S. Catholic, The New York Times, The Los Angeles Times, The Times of London* and *The Irish Times.* Thomas Lynch has read and lectured throughout Europe, North America, Australia and New Zealand. Described by *The New York Times* as 'a cross between Garrison Keillor and William Butler Yeats', he is a regular presenter to health care, hospice, medical ethics, clergy, funeral service, academic and literary conferences, and is an adjunct professor with the Graduate Department of English at the University of Michigan, Ann Arbor. He lives in Milford, Michigan, where – since 1974 – he has been the funeral director, and in West Clare, Ireland, where he keeps an ancestral cottage.

ERIN MacLEOD is a Ph.D. student in communications at McGill University. She is also an instructor in the English Department at Vanier College, Montreal, Quebec, teaching courses in West Indian, Canadian and cyberpunk literature. Combining an expansive knowledge of popular culture with an interest in issues of identity formation, her scholarship has investigated a wide range of subjects – from Jamaican music to television and cyberfeminism.

JANET McCABE is a Research Associate at Manchester Metropolitan University. She has written several essays on American TV drama on British television, narrative form and gender, as well as co-authoring essays with Kim Akass on female narratives and narration in American TV drama. She is author of *Feminist Film Studies: Writing the Woman into Cinema* (Wallflower Press, 2004), and has co-edited (with Akass) and contributed to *Reading Sex and the City* (I. B. Tauris, 2004). She is currently researching a book on female narrative in contemporary American TV drama. She is a member of the editorial board for *Critical Studies in Television*.

MANDY MERCK is Professor of Media Arts at Royal Holloway, University of London. Her recent books include *In Your Face: Nine Sexual Studies* (New York University Press, 2000) and *The Art of Tracey Emin* (Thames and Hudson, 2002). Her current research is on ideas of 'American-ness' in US film.

LUCIA RAHILLY has done graduate work in film, TV and literature, and holds an MA from the Cinema Studies Department at New York University. Her other TV-related publications include 'Through a Glass, Malarkey' in *Reading Sex and the City* (I. B. Tauris, 2004) and 'WWF Wrestling as Popular Sadomasochism' in *Steel Chair to the Head* (Duke, 2005). She lives in New York City.

ASHLEY SAYEAU (formerly Nelson) received her MA in liberal studies in 2002 from the New School for Social Research, where she completed a thesis on single women and *Sex and the City*. She has written extensively on women, politics and popular culture for a variety of American publications, including *The Nation, Salon, Dissent* and *The Philadelphia Inquirer*. She has also contributed to *Reading Sex and the City* (I. B. Tauris, 2004) and *The W Effect: Bush's War on*

Women, edited by Laura Flanders (Consortium, 2004). Visit her website at: www.ashleysayeau.com.

BRIAN SINGLETON is Head of the School of Drama at Trinity College, Dublin. For the past three years he has been editor of *Theatre Research International* (Cambridge University Press), and he is currently the Vice-President for Publications of the International Federation for Theatre Research as well as series editor of *Studies in International Performance*, published by Palgrave. He has published two books on the life and work of Antonin Artaud and edited two journal collections on Irish theatre, and his most recent monograph is entitled *Oscar Asche, Orientalism and British Musical Comedy* (Praeger, 2004).

ROBERT DEAM TOBIN is a Professor of German at Whitman College in Washington State, where he also teaches courses in film and gender studies. Besides his two books, *Warm Brothers: Queer Theory and the Age of Goethe* (University of Pennsylvania Press, 2000) and *Doctor's Orders: Goethe and Enlightenment Thought* (Bucknell University Press, 2001), he has published essays on masochism, German film and the series *Queer as Folk*. He is completing a book on the emergence of modern discourses of sexuality in Germany.

ROB TURNOCK is a lecturer in media theory at Bournemouth University. He is currently completing a book on British television and culture in the 1950s and 1960s, which is to be published by I. B. Tauris in 2005, and is co-editing a book on the history of ITV. He is also author of *Interpreting Diana: Television Audiences and the Death of a Princess* (BFI Publishing, 2000).

PETER WILSON is a principal lecturer in English and creative writing at London Metropolitan University. His main teaching and research interests are in modernist poetry, stylistics and creative writing. These are reflected in his publications, such as *A Preface to Ezra Pound* (Longman, 1997) and *Mind the Gap: Ellipsis and Stylistic Variation in Spoken and Written English* (Pearson Education, 2000). Peter is a practising poet whose main focus is collaborative work with artists and musicians, such as his poems for the CD-ROM, *Poems, Pictures, Music* (Ultralab, 1997).

REGULAR CAST LIST

Olivier Castro Stahl	Peter Macdissi
Keith Charles	Mathew St Patrick
Bernard Chenowith	Robert Foxsworth
Billy Chenowith	Jeremy Sisto
Brenda Chenowith	Rachel Griffiths
Margaret Chenowith	Joanna Cassidy
Russell Corwin	Ben Foster
Federico 'Rico' Diaz	Freddy Rodriguez
Vanessa Diaz	Justina Machado
Claire Fisher	Lauren Ambrose
David Fisher	Michael C. Hall
Lisa (née Kimmel) Fisher	Lili Taylor
Nathaniel 'Nate' Fisher, Jr	Peter Krause
Nathaniel Fisher, Sr	Richard Jenkins
Ruth (née O'Connor) Fisher (now Sibley)	Frances Conroy
Arthur Martin	Rainn Wilson
George Sibley	James Cromwell

foreword

Reading *Six Feet Under*

In a time when American confessional talk shows have featured almost every possible form of sexual behaviour – and paedophiles have been interviewed on peak-time documentaries in Britain – it's tempting to conclude that television no longer has any taboos.

Yet, well into the twenty-first century, one everyday human activity remains a subject of extreme sensitivity for television: death. Speaking to guests about the death of relatives, interviewers routinely use euphemisms such as 'loss' and 'passing away'. On 24-hour news channels, coverage of wars and catastrophes (Oklahoma, 9/11, Iraq) anchors frequently prefer to refer to 'casualties' or people being 'beyond help'.

It's true that two of the most popular dramatic genres at the turn of the millennium – series featuring detectives or pathologists – were predicated on death and usually involved a couple of cold bodies early in the plot. But even in shows based around the morgue – *Silent Witness* in the UK, *Diagnosis Murder* in the US – the corpses were incidental characters and bereavement was somehow redeemed by the solution to the murder. Death in such programmes was deliberate, rare and more or less conquered by the optimism of finding someone to blame in the final frame.

So the central distinction of *Six Feet Under*, produced by HBO (Home Box Office Entertainment) is to have created the first television drama to be underpinned at every moment by the point-lessness, indignity and finality of death.

SFU – the abbreviation nicely encapsulating its attitude towards social and television conventions – can now be seen as one of a number of circa-2000 series which marked a new darkening of tone, deepening of subject matter or complexity of structure in American television. The others are: *The Sopranos, The West Wing, Sex and the City, 24* and *Nip/Tuck*.

Though, as the essays here stress, much of the credit for the toughening of American television must go to HBO (producer of *The Sopranos, Sex and the City* and *Six Feet Under*), which saw that cable television had created a space in the medium for adult imagination, this opening of the box has also spread to networks such as NBC and Fox.

Each of the shows cited above was significantly innovative. *The Sopranos, The West Wing* and *Sex and the City* offered dialogue of a kind never previously heard on TV in terms respectively, of cynical profanity, political complexity and sexual explicitness. And *24* was unprecedented in its games with the shape and timing of television: the commercial hour, the week's wait for the next instalment.

Even so, the plots and content of Keifer Sutherland's race against time were familiar from a hundred movie thrillers, and *The*

Sopranos, The West Wing and *Sex and the City* all have clear ante-
cedents in cinema. Aaron Sorkin had first explored the presidency
in Rob Reiner's *The American President*, the White House sets of
which were recycled for the television series. *The Sopranos* has a
declared overlap with *The Godfather* and a more subliminal one with
Analyse This, while *Sex and the City*, if made as a movie, would join
a crowded shelf of spiky, sexy New York dating films from *Looking
For Mr Goodbar* to *Kissing Jessica Stein*.

This tendency for innovative television to borrow from originality
long ago established in cinema is also shown by *Twin Peaks*. That
series – perhaps TV's most daring piece until *Six Feet Under* – was a
formal import to the small screen of a movie style established by its
creator David Lynch in *Blue Velvet* and other films.

So what is most notable about *Six Feet Under* is not only that it
is bold and original within the context of television schedules but
also that it has no clear ancestry in any area of culture. Its only
significant debt to cinema is that it was the success of Alan Ball's
script for Sam Mendes's *American Beauty* which drove the first
publicity for *Six Feet Under*. And, while there are possibly subtle nods
to Evelyn Waugh's *The Loved One* and Robert Louis Stevenson's *The
Wrong Box*, no earlier undertaking on the subject of death had
so combined data with satire, progressive politics with traditional
domestic drama.

In 20 years as a television critic, I have only rarely felt myself
pulled forward on the sofa by the absolute shock of the new: *Boys
from the Blackstuff, Blackadder, Inspector Morse, Twin Peaks, One Foot
in the Grave, Talking Heads, Cracker, The Office* and *Nip/Tuck*. But
this feeling – that this programme has never happened before and
cannot actually be happening now – has never affected me as strongly
as while watching a press video of the pilot episode of *Six Feet Under*.

No previous series had ever dispensed so casually and callously
– in such a savagely choreographed accident – with someone who
the close-focus grammar of the opening had established as a likely
major character.

This pre-credits sequence of *SFU* – setting up the corpse that
will drive the story – is a brilliant subversion of the established
device in hospital dramas in which the opening scenes tease us with
the illness or injury of the week. Yet, while it has become accepted
for a patient to die at the end of *Casualty* in the UK or *E.R.* in the

US, *Six Feet Under* has the nerve to start with a cadaver every week – and one despatched with malicious wit: broken into 50 pieces by an industrial dough mixer, or electrocuted when the cat kicks the heated rollers into the bath.

It was also immediately apparent in that pilot that Alan Ball was challenging not only mainstream television's primary taboo – death – but a significant secondary sensitivity – gay sex – and, as a further declaration of adult intent in television, an inter-racial relationship between two men.

This concentration on a community ill-served by television, however, was placed within a universally impressive range of characterisation. As essays in this book make clear, the female characters – especially the matriarch Ruth and the adolescent Claire – are depicted with unusual psychological depth and narrative generosity.

By the time it became apparent that *Six Feet Under* included its own spoof ads (for embalming fluid and other restorative necessities) I was, as we were clearly led to believe the corpses probably weren't, in heaven.

Also present from the beginning was a political resonance. Whereas television's previous dealings with the body had involved saintly pathologists, their remit often extended to take in detective work and psychic healing, the staff of the Fisher & Sons Funeral Home have a much more practical and cynical attitude to corpses.

Their only aim is to achieve a trick of light and likeness that will survive the visitation of the open casket. For them, that fashionable piece of shrink-lingo, 'closure', refers only to the moment when the lid is closed and the body can begin its rot.

In this sense, the Fishers are spin doctors (professional siblings, in fact, of the cosmetic surgeons in *Nip/Tuck*). And the business, it's made clear, is going ever deeper into deceit. The corporation which is attempting to take them over in season one is even sneakier with euphemism: what the Fishers call 'the funeral business' has become 'the death care industry'. The process of 'embalming' is now to be called 'preparation for visitation'. George Orwell, who first spotted spin, would have treasured these examples.

At this level, *Six Feet Under* can be seen as a more topical and pointed series about politics than *The West Wing*. While that show inhabits a fantasy about Washington, depicting a sexually continent, Nobel-Prize-winning president during the actual incumbencies of the libidinous Clinton and the anti-intellectual Bush, *Six Feet Under* can be seen as a sardonic commentary on the dressing up and presentation which have become so central to American politics.

Since the Iraq War – and the decision by the Bush administration to prevent television coverage of the bodies of American soldiers being flown home – *SFU*'s focus on the presentation of death – and its insistence on keeping the body in shot – has taken on an even deeper meaning.

In discussing *Six Feet Under*, the essays collected here touch on a wider debate about how television should be discussed. As a civilian television critic, I am conscious of the linguistic gap between newspaper reviewing and academic consideration: we say 'programmes' they say 'texts', and so on.

This, however, is an inevitable result of television's struggle to be taken seriously as a critical subject. In British newspapers (commendably less so in America), TV is the only artistic discipline in which it has been common for reviewers to be appointed with a mission to dislike the form. While theatre and movie critics are essentially enthusiasts whose love of the subject sometimes induces disappointment, a TV critic can survive, and may even be admired for, an instinctive suspicion of the medium.

If this tendency to patronise television exists in the popular media, then imagine how much worse it has been in academia. As the stereotypical don was reluctant to watch television, the resistance to it being studied was considerable. In applying the language of academic analysis, these pieces are claiming for TV an equality of consideration with books, films and plays.

My regret about the proper attention paid to television in the colleges is that writers sometimes have a tendency to validate the upstart medium by invoking an older, more respectable one. I am always disappointed to be told that a piece of TV is good because it looks like a Vermeer or could easily have been confused with a Scorsese movie.

This cultural twin-towning comes from a defensiveness about the subject under discussion, but it seems to me a pity; television should be considered, for better or worse, as television.

In the same way, I am suspicious of those who avoid these landmark series on TV, waiting until the complete season is released as a box of DVDs, then consuming them through a weekend. While this approach can be allowed with *24* (adding a time game of our own to the ones the series plays), it must generally be wrong. The point about television programmes is that – unlike theatre or cinema – they live within a flow of other images: sports, commercials, wars. This significantly affects both their conception and their reception.

Television should be watched – and written about – as television. As this book makes clear, the importance of *Six Feet Under* is not that it is like anything else, but that it isn't.

introduction

'Why do people have to die?' 'To make contemporary television drama important, I guess.'

Dad died last year. Visiting the undertakers to arrange his funeral took me into a world with which I already have a morbid pre-occupation. Off the high street, nestled between the local chip shop and solicitors, the funeral home invites its trade with a display of dusty pink plastic flowers and a jolly snap of a buxom lady in tweeds releasing doves.

Hands parting. Desiring spiritual transcendence. Seeing only disem-bodiment and dissolution.

'Do you want him embalmed?' enquired the funeral director (*Rico draining bodily fluids from a cadaver – Dad, maybe*). Perhaps he sensed our unease. He changed tack. 'The body begins to decompose immediately after death. If you want to see him…' Mum stopped him. 'He looked so ghastly at the end – so unlike himself – best not,' she said. Cancer had taken him long before death did. I had sobbed his passing long before he shuffled off this mortal coil at 5.10 a.m. that Tuesday morning.

Perusing a catalogue of hearses and selecting a suitable coffin to take Dad to his final resting place – *the fake infomercials for cosmetic putty and deluxe caskets which punctuate the pilot of Six Feet Under* – returned me to safe consumer territory. It all seemed so eerily normal and mundane. Maybe I was just numb: orphanage masquerading as civilised restraint – that stiff-upper-lipped superego. Reaching into popular culture, as a means of understanding an experience I found so utterly incomprehensible and emotionally unbearable, was the best I could do.

Thomas Lynch: 'A death in the family is not a retail event. It is an existential one' (2000: 164).

So, there I was: Sunday evening, sitting at the kitchen table with my husband, reminiscing over our first meeting. We were laughing, gagging for breath at the thought of ourselves as two 15-year-olds scarily fucked up and attracted to our differences. We wandered off in opposite directions but, some 15 years later, met up again, and now 15 years together have made our own family. It was much later, lying in bed that night, that it occurred to me. I had been watching 'Life's Too Short' (1:9), where Ruth mistakenly takes Ecstasy, goes midnight wandering and asks her dead husband: 'What happened to us? We were so in love. Where did it go?' And here lies the rub. It is no small coincidence that it is not death that is now my big taboo – it is life, that liminal space between birth and the hereafter; it is what will happen to me when my children leave home and my husband and I look at each other, maybe as strangers, and wonder: 'What happened to us? We were so in love. Where did it go?'

We mention our experiences precisely because in a society like ours, so able to articulate empowering experiences (like finding romance, making love work, managing our careers and money, giving parental and marital guidance) and define who we are, talking about ageing, dying and death pushes us to the limits of our ability to articulate experience. The enigma of death and the packaging of its aftermath, getting older and pondering the passing of time, present us with skewed perspectives undercutting all certainties. *Six Feet Under* is no exception. It divided critics and proved difficult to classify with hard-to-pin-down pleasures, as TV critic, Linda Stasi, found: 'I don't even know what I'm watching, let alone why. I mean who wants to watch a dramatic show about a dysfunctional family of undertakers?' (2001). On one level *Six Feet Under* fits easily into HBO's agenda of challenging conventional television wisdom and representing that which has rarely before been seen on our screens. But even so. It is a show pushing HBO to its limits. It exposes the workings of liminality on many levels: it is difficult to place in institutional and generic terms; it walks a fine line between comedy and tragedy; it teeters on the edge of unbearable poignancy before tipping over into corny melodrama. Structurally it deals with the liminal space between death and burial; thematically it focuses on cultural taboos – homosexuality, mental illness, old age, sickness, drug addiction, adolescence, race and class – which, in turn, are used to revisit traditional cultural certainties such as religion, marriage and the family – and it questions who we are.

Six Feet Under debuted on HBO at 10 p.m., Sunday 3 June 2001. It was the first drama series launched by the channel since *The Sopranos* – and HBO felt under pressure to repeat its success. The story about a dysfunctional family running a funeral home in Los Angeles first aired to much fanfare, heralded as the next breakthrough, high-quality, award-worthy hit series for the cable channel. For all its high hopes, HBO knew the show would be a hard sell. Chris Albrecht, then HBO president of original programming (now CEO and chairman of HBO), admitted that *Six Feet Under* 'represented a marketing challenge compared to those series with their high-concept scenarios' like *The Sopranos*, *Sex and the City* and *Oz*' (Weinraub 2001: 21).

Judging by initial reactions, Albrecht was right to be concerned. For all the hype generated by the HBO marketing department, the show failed to gain 'the same kind of press frenzy or wildly enthusiastic word-of-mouth that *The Sopranos* commanded in its first year' (Carter 2001). Critics felt a certain pressure to love the show simply because it was an HBO product. Eric Mink verifies this by saying, 'I'm supposed to like *Six Feet Under*. I know this because it's on HBO' (2001). Furthermore, there was an expectation among TV commentators that, because HBO had earned a reputation for making groundbreaking and original TV series like *The Sopranos*, *Six Feet Under* should also look and feel special. 'But it's hard to imagine anyone watching Sunday night's plodding and pretentious pilot and coming back for more' (ibid.).

Bothering pundits most was the fact that there seemed less to the new show than its film pedigree and existentialist subject matter initially promised. *Six Feet Under* appeared somewhat derivative and decidedly pedestrian to many: 'It isn't as hilarious or scathing as Jessica Mitford's 1963 book on the funeral industry ... It isn't as ironic or viciously comedic as Evelyn Waugh's ... novel [*The*] *Loved One* ... It isn't as comedically tragic as Eric Idle's *Nearly Departed* updated *Topper* series ...' (Kitman 2001). Wendy Lesser concurs, saying that the show 'openly borrows from such recent and past successes as *Ally McBeal* (the fantasy-hallucination sequences), *The Singing Detective* (ditto, mixed with song-and-dance) and *Sex and the City* (titillation and lightweight malaise)' (2001). Despite dealing with weighty topics such as death, dying and making life meaningful, it felt unsatisfying to some, achieving 'distinction mainly by trying desperately to be much deeper than it actually is' (Rosett 2001). It all seemed a little too clever: 'I'm supposed to like *Six Feet Under* because its tone is dark and sardonic, because its characters are cleverly literate, miserable and spiteful, because it sometimes shows gay men kissing and cuddling in bed and because there are gross close-ups of corpses and wounds and stuff' (Mink 2001).

Compared unfavourably with *The Sopranos*, *Six Feet Under* failed to measure up. Being scheduled to fill the slot recently vacated by the family saga about a crime boss and his dysfunctional family did not make it any easier, as where comparisons could not help but be made. 'Both shows combine gore, sex and bizarre incidents with much delving into the psyche' (Lesser 2001). But whereas *The Sopranos* was 'a rich and intriguing story', according to Lesser, 'in *Six Feet Under* there's so much self-conscious effort to be weird that the effect is simply waxen' (ibid.). Graphic depictions of sex and brutal mob aggression may have looked hip on *The Sopranos* but in *Six Feet Under* images of death, violence and sexuality came across as attention grabbers to keep the audience going while the Mafioso drama took a break. 'This show is slathered so thick (and slick) with gimmicks that its take on death remains largely cosmetic – more burlesque than black comedy' (Rosett 2001).

Judging by the immediate dip in ratings after the pilot, audiences were not quite sure either. But ratings did improve. 'It got a 10.7 rating a week ago, just under 5million viewers,' reported Bill Carter just a month later, in July (2001). And by August fans felt compelled to defend the show from critical opprobrium. Responses to Lesser's criticism of the 'sleazily mendacious' (2001) show and its troubled family prove instructive here. '*Six Feet Under* is first-rate entertainment: great writing, great acting and plot twists and turns that make this viewer long for the next instalment,' wrote Michael Cummings; another viewer from Manhattan said: 'The surprisingly blunt and humourless attempt to bury *Six Feet Under* by the usually subtle Wendy Lesser reveals a critic utterly at odds with a show's sensibility and seriocomic premise'; while Seth Fortin from Stone Mountain states: 'It may not be great tragedy but it hardly deserves Ms. Lesser's pasting' (Letters 2001).

Not all critics dismissed *Six Feet Under*. Kathryn Flett called it a 'genuinely entertaining and intelligent black comedy' (2002), while Linda Stasi confessed to an initial reluctance to engage with the programme before finding herself watching six hours' worth – 'by choice' (2001). David Bianculli observed that *Six Feet Under* may have started a 'little too smugly and self-consciously' but by the fourth week it had 'kicked into high gear, and for the rest of its 13 episode run delivered some gloriously rich characters, situations and ruminations on life and death' (2002). Season two found critics re-evaluating initial misgivings. Marvin Kitman, for example, stated that he would now like to bury his original review. 'The show is very good, totally addictive, worthy of all the acclaim and Emmy nominations' (2002). Moved to confess that all her doubts disappeared as she viewed the second season led Joy Press to declare that '*Six Feet Under* has been transformed into TV's most ravishing experience' (2003). Another convert was David Blum, who claimed that 'in its third season [*Six Feet Under*] now ranks alongside *The Sopranos* as one of the great family dramas of our time' (2003).

HBO, Quality and Changing TV

Viewers and TV journalists have come to expect difficult subject matter and thought-provoking television from HBO. Although drama series like *Six Feet Under* may prove innovative and groundbreaking, they also represent how the institution of television is changing. HBO has come a long way since it first transmitted a Vancouver–New York hockey game to 365 homes in Wilkes-Barre, Pennsylvania, back in 1972. In 1976 came the inclusion of live concerts, and five years later the cable channel started 24-hour broadcasting, filling its schedules with live sporting events and television premieres of uncensored and uninterrupted feature films (hence the title Home Box Office). Widespread dissemination of the VCR, whereby viewers could rent a movie and watch it at their convenience, meant that HBO had to diversify (Rogers et al. 2002: 50). Made-for-TV movies like *Stalin* and *Murrow* and original programming with adult content like *Dream On* and *The Larry Sanders Show* became increasingly important for HBO. Michael Fuchs took over at the helm in 1984, as the new chairman and CEO; he 'made a public pledge to produce mature and provocative original programming…and…saw an opportunity to turn HBO into a purveyor of adult-oriented content' (Rogers et al. 2002: 50, 51). Even though Fuchs pushed the envelope with sexually provocative dramas such as *And the Band Played On*, as well as those comedy series mentioned above, he failed to create a strong enough identity for the channel at a time when brand marketing was becoming integral to economic survival. Jeff L. Bewkes replaced him in 1995. Under Bewkes' leadership, according to Mark C. Rogers, Michael Epstein and Jimmie L. Reeves, 'HBO found itself on the front lines of yet another television revolution: the development of channel branding as a means of combating audience fragmentation…[and]…HBO [began producing] programmes that upped the ante on violence, sexuality, and the macabre' (51).

Today HBO reaches over 28 million homes; it airs almost a hundred uncut Hollywood movies a month and increasingly depends on original programmes like *Six Feet Under* to woo its subscribers. With the recent rise of DVD as well as the proliferation of movie channels with staggered viewing times, these new dramas have become much more important to HBO; as Albrecht is quoted as saying, 'Nobody is going to buy the service to see *Gladiator* one more time' (Carter 2001). Selling directly to the customer means that HBO is free from network constraints, and neither does it have to appease advertisers (Friend 2001: 82). Instead, 'HBO is eager to produce shows that confirm its audacious marketing claim [It's Not TV. It's HBO] that – contrary to every rule laid down since *The Beverley Hillbillies* went one way and PBS [Public Broadcasting Service] the other – television can be both profitable and of high quality' (ibid.).

The question of what we mean by 'quality' television is key here: more importantly, how does a television institution like HBO understand the term? While commercial television edges ever closer towards inexpensive reality TV like *Survivor*, HBO markets itself on selling a quality brand product to customers that is not regular TV. As 'the strongest possible counterpoint to network television', HBO desires *Six Feet Under* – like *The Sopranos* – to be different (Friend

2001: 82). The series is proof of the subscription channel's antipathy to the mainstream approach. 'This show is unlike anything that has ever been on network television,' Albrecht declares, 'noting that HBO actually ordered a second season before the series even went on the air. "No network would ever do that," he said' (Carter 2001). Not having to appease advertisers and network executives allows for creative integrity (more on this later), contentious subject matter and edgy scripts which include levels of sex and nudity, violence and profanity rarely, if at all, seen on US TV. Such criteria are intrinsic to the HBO brand identity and key to its appeal. No wonder HBO owns Sunday night.

Quality TV on HBO is also about telling the audience that they have made a wise consumer decision. By purchasing HBO rather than settling for mediocre network fare, programmes like *Six Feet Under* are designed precisely to make 'HBO subscribers feel good about their choices' (Friend 2001: 84). Flattering the audience is important to the company's marketing strategy. It is predicated on the notion that the subscription channel must attract punters for its commercial survival; yet they use the economic imperative to their promotional advantage. 'Because HBO likes to be seen as a grassroots phenomenon,' writes Tad Friend, 'the network plans to sell *Six Feet Under* by word of mouth' (2001: 89). The recent water cooler commercial (http://slate.msn.com/id/2102442) advertising HBO's Sunday night line-up with its group of office workers gathering to discuss the latest episode of their favourite 'must-see' TV show plays up this notion. Promoting the 'what the customer wants' idea enables HBO to trade on the fact that it is offering a unique product – something that audiences cannot get elsewhere, and will take time out to watch. Scheduling is tailored to allow for flexible viewing (*Six Feet Under* is first shown on Sunday evenings and then repeated throughout the week) as well as recognising that busy lifestyles must be accommodated. Even this works to the benefit of HBO, as it takes the cumulative rating into account when calculating viewing figures, which means the series compares favourably to a network show like NBC's *E.R.* that is only shown once a week. The ideas of customer choice, branding and niche audiences are increasingly becoming important indicators of television quality.

Another feature of quality relates to product differentiation in a diverse market place. Despite heavily promoting original programming (and any visit to the website confirms this notion), and

HBO executives endlessly talking about 'its riskier, artier ventures, emphasising just how different it is' (Friend 2001: 90), it is surprising to find a lot of regular TV on the cable channel. After *The Sopranos* it is not *Six Feet Under* (as one might expect) but boxing and salacious documentaries like *G-String Divas* and the *Real Sex* series (dealing with sexual fantasies) that prove ratings winners and fill the schedules. It would seem that HBO might not be so different after all – especially considering HBO is a branch of the Time Warner Inc. empire, which also includes Warner Bros. Television, producers of *E.R.* and *The West Wing*. Free from competition, it gives us an insight into why HBO can be patient with its shows and explains why Albrecht can say: '[with] a dark ironic show like [*Six Feet Under*] unless it's a creative or critical disaster you've almost got to give it two years for it to have a chance to build an audience' (Friend 2001: 88). These kinds of strategies allow HBO to be seen as cutting edge, yet 'HBO is not a band of artistic guerrillas who occasionally hijack the airwaves but an elite alternative to the parent company's mass-market brands' (Friend 2001: 89). HBO can dare to be different and push itself into new and often controversial television territory precisely because it is part of a vast economic conglomerate diverse enough to speculate and wait for a return on its investment.

Alan Ball, TV Auteurship and *Six Feet Under*

Central to HBO's definition of original programming is its promotion of the TV auteur and top-notch writing. Any survey of the original publicity for *Six Feet Under* reveals an emphasis placed by HBO on the creative genius behind the show: Alan Ball, creator/ executive producer. Graduating from the University of Georgia and Florida State, Ball started out in theatre. He helped set up the General Nonsense Theatre Company in Sarasota, Florida, before moving to New York. Here he formed the Alarm Dog Repertory Company (1986–1994) with friends. Writing and producing Off Off Broadway black comedies, he eventually came to the attention of Tom Werner and Marcy Carsey, prominent television producers, who offered him a job. Writing for *Grace Under Fire*, starring Brett Butler, for one year and *Cybill* with Cybill Shepherd for three years, where he rose to executive producer, saw Ball move into network television. In 1999 he signed a three-year television development deal with the production company Greenblatt Janollari Studio – the company that now produces *Six Feet Under*. The first project back in 1999 was a sitcom written by Ball for ABC called *Oh Grow Up*, a quasi-autobiographical series about three men, two straight and one gay, living together in Brooklyn. The show received mixed reviews before the network cancelled it.

The experience proved discouraging for Ball. Like other HBO series creators Darren Star (*Sex and the City*) and David Chase (*The Sopranos*), he found working in network television a dispiriting and frustrating experience: 'When my last show, *Oh Grow Up*, was cancelled by ABC [after only 11 episodes], I thought if I have to do another four-camera laugh track sitcom I'll shoot myself' (Brown 2001). A detour into film would change his profile when, in 2000, he won an Academy Award for Best Original Screenplay with *American Beauty*; the film won five Oscars, including Best Picture, and grossed nearly $350 million around the globe. The success of *American Beauty* meant Ball was much in demand and could leave behind network television. 'I was offered everything, but I didn't want to become a hired gun,' he said. 'I didn't want to be hired to write other people's ideas. I had done one year of *Grace Under Fire* and three years of *Cybill*. That was enough. It's no mistake that *American Beauty* was about a man who was beaten down and lost interest in his life rediscovering his passion for living' (Weinraub 2001: 21).

Ball admits that had *American Beauty* not been such a commercial and critical success 'HBO would not have come along and offered him almost total freedom on *Six Feet Under*' (25). But had he not been so taken with *The Sopranos*, he would not have got 'so excited about the possibilities of television' (Hendrickson 2002: 114). Soon after the film's release, Ball met with Carolyn Strauss, senior vice-president for original programming at HBO, who told him that her favourite films were *Harold and Maude* (1971) and *The Loved One* (1965) – 'black comedies that take decidedly irreverent attitudes toward death' (Weinraub 2001: 21). Inspired by her interest in producing a show about running a funeral home, he wrote the pilot. HBO bought the concept and gave him a 13-episode commitment – and *Six Feet Under* was born (or so the story goes).

What proves intriguing about this story is that Ball turned his back on film and theatre *as well as* network television. Like other TV auteurs Star and Chase before him, and despite being an Oscar winner, Ball confirms that HBO is the place to work. 'I get notes from HBO saying, "You don't have to spell this out, it's clear what's happening,"' Ball has said. 'They actually say, "Give it more edge." That doesn't happen on network television. On network television, everything is explained. Nothing is ambiguous. Any kind of edge is removed' (Weinraub 2001: 21). But this is more than just differentiating itself from network television, despite what Ball is saying. HBO prides itself on producing television with a new and groundbreaking sensibility; it may be drawing on talent and conventions from elsewhere (independent film, Off Broadway theatre and even network television), but it remains first and always television.

Liminality, *Six Feet Under* and TV To Die For

Creating an awareness of what HBO is doing is vital to an understanding of how the institutional context produces *Six Feet Under*. Operating as it does in a wider industrial context of changing televisual narratives, transforming generic conventions and how television is watched and consumed means its tag-line – 'It's Not TV. It's HBO' – is more than a distinction for its original programming from regular TV fare; it is describing a transitional moment in television culture. Just as *Six Feet Under* explores and is about liminal states, might it not be argued that HBO gives additional meaning to this idea?

Victor Turner, who writes about socio-cultural moments of transformation, describes liminality as being about a culture contemplating its rules and conventions, often using performative or dramatic forms with which to do so (1977). *Six Feet Under*, on the surface at least, confirms what Turner describes as liminal: as related to thresholds, transitions and margins. If, as he argues, every society carves out spaces existing on the cultural periphery that are shaped by ambiguity and paradox, then what does *Six Feet Under* say about ours? It is a question that this collection seeks to address. There is a liminality to this anthology as it considers how the series challenges representation, lifts cultural taboos, says what normally cannot be said on regular TV – as Thomas Lynch points out later, placing a corpse in a room means you can pretty much say anything.

Each episode begins with a demise: a man suffers a heart attack while taking out the rubbish, a conman cracks his head on the bottom of his swimming pool while Dean Martin croons 'Ain't that a kick in the head', a young woman commits suicide, and a 14-year-old falls off the bed laughing and breaks her neck. Each death will bring the Fishers some business, and often it sets the tone for the episode. The first section of this anthology, 'Memento mori: spectacle, the specular and observing the dead', starts from this premise – the idea of death and what it means. David Lavery starts by placing the genre of magic realism within a cultural and tele-visual context. Arguing that death allows for a moment where normal rules are suspended and everything becomes topsy-turvy, Lavery investigates how this operates at a generic and formal level in the show. Next is Mark W. Bundy's lyrical piece. It offers a visceral engagement with the show through his own experiences of death and illness. Rob Turnock's chapter returns us to a more critical study of liminality and how it functions within *Six Feet Under*. He suggests that the structure of each episode, which begins with a death and concludes with a burial, makes visible a liminal space that allows for possibilities of change and transformation. Concluding this first section, Lucia Rahilly offers a close textual reading of the death of porn actress Viveca St John (Veronica Hart) in 'An Open Book' (1:5). Rahilly makes a case for suggesting a blurring between the 'money shot' (the physical shuddering of male ejaculation in porno-graphic films) and the moment of death.

Six Feet Under premiered only months before the terrorist atrocities of 9/11, and thus was well positioned to respond to the haunting elegiac-ness of a nation in mourning. Peter Krause (who plays Nate Fisher) mused that 'after Sept. 11, a lot of people who do TV went back to work and thought, "Oh, jeez. This is meaningless" but our show is now as meaningful as ever' (Zaslow 2002). He went on, 'the basic theme of our show is, you've got one singular life and that's it. It makes people think about themselves and their place in the world' (ibid.). Part two, entitled 'Mourning and melancholia: American cultural crisis and recovery', is grounded in this uneasy cultural zeitgeist obsessed with death and tragedy. Arguably American culture has long been obsessed with death – with guns, violence and killing. We may be able to bear the cause and effect logic of a mobster whacking a miscreant in *The Sopranos,* but are far more uncomfortable with what Christopher Moore called 'the cool quiet of actual death' (2002). The section thus considers strategies of coping and healing, which in turn enable authors to ponder what lies beneath this American preoccupation.

The first two pieces explore the American Gothic as an historical strategy and how it is used to understand the present in *Six Feet Under*. Mandy Merck surveys how it works at a thematic and formal level, reading the series through Sigmund Freud's essay 'The Uncanny' and the tradition of nineteenth century Gothic literature. For Dana Heller the American Gothic speaks about America's repressed traumas such as slavery. She goes further to suggest how *Six Feet Under* in turn uses these same strategies to re-evaluate contemporary struggles involving race, ethnicity and class. The final two chapters of this second section look to more modern methods of coping with tragedy and healing. Robert Deam Tobin identifies strategies of gay mourning in post-AIDS America, suggesting how camp aesthetics have now entered the cultural mainstream as a means of uniting the tragic with the political. He contends that *Six Feet Under* explodes the rhetoric of gay responses to AIDS while, at the same time, re-using the fragments of that discourse in a general discussion of death. Bringing this section to a close is Ashley Sayeau and her contribution on how *Six Feet Under* is saturated in America's cultural preoccupation with self-help. Interrogating this very middle-class obsession allows her to argue that beneath the self-help agenda lies 'an almost irrepressible by-product of middle-class American anxieties surrounding success, fear and narcissism'.

Just as the *Six Feet Under* characters are drawn from the post-Vietnam, post-feminist, post-civil-rights, post-Watergate eras of social upheaval, which rendered patriarchal authority suspect, the aftermath of 9/11 has led to another period of introspection and a questioning of American patriarchy – its foreign policy, the Bush administration and the Republican agenda. As if to confirm this, the series opens with the death of the patriarch when Nathaniel Fisher perishes in a tragic accident. The series thus, argues Tobin in an earlier article, 'attempts to provide a positive answer to the question of how society should develop without patriarchal guidance' (2002: 87). Sections three and four provide answers of sorts to this post-patriarchal dilemma.

The first, 'Making visible the female subject', explores how the questioning of patriarchal authority has affected three women: Ruth Fisher (now Sibley), Claire Fisher and Brenda Chenowith. The authors in section three explore how representation is now up for grabs and how the Six Feet Under women are trying to carve their own identity, for better or worse, without patriarchal interference. Kim Akass argues that Six Feet Under offers a rare opportunity for an exploration of the middle-aged, post-menopausal mother with adult children, to suggest that there is more to this positioning than meets the eye. Invisible to most, Ruth's narrative finds her embracing her liminal status and overturning expectations along the way. Janet McCabe charts the complex narrative territory negotiated by Claire as she searches for identity. Required endlessly to talk about who she is and justify her actions reveals the precarious processes Claire must negotiate in order to attain female subjectivity. The final chapter, by Erin MacLeod, deals with the complicated narrative world of Brenda. MacLeod's chapter maps out the shift from Charlotte Light and Dark to Brenda's own attempts at writing, to expose the difficulties confronting Brenda when speaking about experience beyond the established forms of patriarchal discourse.

Section four investigates masculinity, male sexuality and the men in Six Feet Under. Joanna di Mattia leads with her study of the Fisher brothers, Nate and David. She argues that Six Feet Under offers a groundbreaking portrait of male intimacy rarely before seen on our television screens. If the portrayal of this sibling relationship is innovative then the representation of the Church, argues Brian Singleton, is nothing short of revolutionary. Read through queer theological theory, he argues that there is something more than a little queer about the Church and religion in this show. If the Church contributes to David's unease about his sexuality, then what do we make of Claire's (ex) boyfriend Russell and his sexual orientation? Samuel A. Chambers concludes this section with a study of heteronormativity and heterosexual assumptions of sexuality in Six Feet Under. Focusing on Russell allows Chambers to interrogate and question the whole notion of heterosexuality as the norm, and he posits the question: do we now need to out ourselves as heterosexuals?

Section five investigates the use of music as well as giving poetic insight into death and mourning. Peter Kaye begins his chapter by contextualising the musical influences in Six Feet Under – Thomas

Newman's musical pedigree and the Hollywood connection. Offering two close textual readings allows him to reveal not only how the original score functions as a brand but also how licensed music works alongside the narrative to give additional meanings. An interview with Richard Marvin, musical supervisor and composer for the series, concludes his contribution. A personal response from the man who provided the main inspiration for the series, Thomas Lynch (an American poet, author and professional undertaker in Milford, Michigan), ends the anthology. Alan Ball asked the cast and his writing staff to read Lynch's award-winning books *Bodies in Motion and At Rest* (2000) and *The Undertaking* (1997), along with Jessica Mitford's *The American Way of Death* (1963), before starting work on the show (Ross 2003: 12). Lynch's contribution here weaves his personal experience of undertaking with a poetic reflection on *Six Feet Under*.

The last three sections prelude with poems written by Peter Wilson. Each directly responds to both the series and individual deaths: one ('S&D @ HBO (TR for *SFU*)') conveys an impression of the moods and themes that pervade the show, while the others ('Emily Previn, 1954–2001', and 'Nathaniel Samuel Fisher, 1943–2000') adopt the personae of those in the thralls of death. Adapting stanzaic patterns such as terza rima and triolet gives order to the poetic form. With these elegiac attempts to give voice to the melancholic we come full circle. We end where we began – with a death. How Ball describes his own experience of familial loss tells us much about the series. When he was 13 years old his sister Mary Ann was killed when a car ploughed into them as she was driving him to a piano lesson. He says of the tragedy (Ross 2003:11):

That separated my life into a life before and a life after. It was really my first experience of losing someone close to me in the worst possible way – out of the blue and in front of my eyes… nothing else in my life has affected me quite as profoundly as that.

That nothing is ever quite the same again after you put that dead body in the room is realised in the series and explored in this collection. Each article carves out a new direction, some by revising old debates and others by seeing culture and theory anew. It is hoped that this collection will go some way in addressing the absence in language and pauses in discourse identified by Lynch (2000: 227).

A good funeral, like a good poem, is driven by voices, images, intellections and the permanent. It moves us up and back the cognitive and imaginative and emotive register. The transport seems effortless, inspired, natural as breathing or the loss of it. In the space between what is said and unsaid, in the pause between utterances, whole histories are told; whole galaxies glimpsed in the margins, if only momentarily...Good poems and good funerals are stories well told.

Part 1

Memento mori: spectacle, the specular and observing the dead

one

'It's not television, it's magic realism': the mundane, the grotesque and the fantastic in *Six Feet Under*

Prologue: Getting Six Feet Under

The sequence to which I call attention at the outset of this examination of *Six Feet Under*'s generic allegiances is as baffling as it is unclassifiable. In 'Parallel Play' (4:3) Federico (Rico) Diaz, the Fisher family's Puerto Rican restorative artist, has a strange dream (confirmed at the sequence end), clearly the product of his dalliance with the stripper Sophia (Idalis DeLeon), who has just manipulated him into agreeing to pay for new breast implants. Working as usual in the basement of the Fisher and Diaz Funeral Home (at dream's end he will wake up at his desk), he is distracted by music and light, by a strange unfolding scene in which he sees himself sitting on a sofa in a forest tableau, a Christ-like Sophia crucified behind him, wrapped in a loincloth but naked from the waist up, blood streaming from below her soon-to-be-surgically-enhanced breasts.

A series of shots: Sophia stripping; her bleeding breasts (again); a priest, to whom Rico confesses his sins; his wife Vanessa, dressed like the Virgin Mary; Sophia's young daughter; the birth of Rico and Vanessa's son, Augusto (at the end of season one); Vanessa mopping Sophia's brow – an ever-present bottle of Tylenol (Sophia's daughter's only toy, a makeshift castanet, in an earlier scene) passing back and forth between the various dream personae. Together, Vanessa and

Sophia (come down from on high) join to service Rico's needs: the Tylenol bottle now contains oil, poured onto his feet, which Sophia begins to wash, but the act of cleansing turns into oral sex, and he awakens. One of the great dream sequences in a series known for its reveries (its only oneiric TV rivals are *Twin Peaks*, *The Sopranos* and *Buffy the Vampire Slayer*), Rico's vision draws on the Hispanic imagination, tapping the tradition of magical realist art exemplified in paintings by Mexican artist Frida Kahlo (1907–1954): imagery from paintings like 'A Few Small Nips' (1935), 'The Two Fridas' (1939) and 'Tree of Hope' (1948), each dealing with surgery and hospitalisation, informs the dream.

Take note that in order to describe what amounts to less than five minutes of TV I resorted to a vocabulary not common in televisual parlance: 'the grotesque', 'fantastic', 'magic realism'. Discourse about *Six Feet Under* does not always require such exotic language; these are not the only registers in which the series functions. Its detractors, after all, find it anything but generically extraordinary, calling it 'a sitcom with elephantiasis' (Carson 2002), or a soap opera (Nussbaum 2002; Buckman 2004). Even its staunchest defenders single out its greatest virtue as not the bizarre but 'the mundane catastrophes of day-to-day life' (Havrilesky 2002). Beginning with its opening credits, however, *Six Feet Under* invites – indeed, insists – that we understand it as something quite different.

Opening Credits

A bird crosses blue sky. The camera tilts down to reveal a single tree on the horizon, where a verdant hill meets the sky. Two hands break apart in slow motion. A man washes his hands. The camera tilts to reveal two feet on a gurney – the big left toe bears an ID tag. Open sky again. A gurney moves down an institutional hallway – light at the end of the tunnel. From what might be the point of view of the body it bears, the gurney enters the light. Seen through a bottle of fluid, a man in a white coat moves about. A beaker of liquid (embalming fluid?) slowly empties. The corpse head is turned away from the camera. In close-up, a ball of cotton held in a pair of tweezers mops the brow. A tilt moves up the cadaver from its feet, stopping before showing the head. A jump cut reveals a vase of flowers dying (wilting) in time-lapse. A hearse door opens, a coffin within. In close-up the mortician's hand grabs its handle. (In earlier versions a clearly visible skull ring can be seen on the mortician's finger, but the memento mori was digitally removed in the final cut.) The hearse seen from behind, its load door wide open. A still life of two framed photos. In close-up, a bird's claw feet move slowly off. A tombstone bears the words 'Executive Producer Alan Ball'. A crow perches on a tombstone. The sky again, crossed by the black bird. The hill and tree from earlier. The tree puts down roots, forming a box, in which the words 'Six Feet Under' appear.

When Six Feet Under creator and executive producer Ball first saw Digital Kitchen's storyboard for this enigmatic, metaphysical opening credit sequence, he recalls finding it 'so elegant... so cinematic... so unlike TV' (season one DVD commentary; emphasis added). Ball, of course, had become prime mover on Six Feet Under on the strength of his Academy-Award-winning screenplay for American Beauty (1999), and though he was not new to TV (he had written for Grace Under Fire, Cybill and Oh Grow Up prior to attaining auteur status in screenwriting), it should surprise no one, least of all his bosses at HBO, that from the outset he was anxious to distinguish, in the premium channel's tradition, his series from ordinary television. Even the best makers of television – Buffy the Vampire Slayer's Joss Whedon, or The Sopranos' David Chase – commonly assert their disdain for TV and dream of escaping to greener movie pastures (see Lavery 2002; Lavery and Thompson 2002).

And yet, as Ball readily acknowledges, the opening title sequence 'transports you into the world of the show...' (season one DVD commentary), which is precisely what the credit sequence of any television series, network or cable, is supposed to do. The 'Welcome to Twin Peaks' road sign, the falls, the lake beside which Laura Palmer's body is found, 'wrapped in plastic', transported us to the extraordinary diegesis of Twin Peaks. An eagle's cry and an inquisitive moose prepared the viewer every week for a visit to Northern Exposure's Cicely, Alaska. Tony Soprano's cigar-chomping drive from New York, past Satriale's Pork Store, past urban New Jersey, to the front door of his palatial suburban home, ritualistically relocates us for a visit with The Family. These and other memorable televisual opening credits, aided by signature music (Thomas Newman, 'Six Feet Under', David Schwartz, 'Northern Exposure', Angelo Badalamenti, 'Twin

Peaks', A3, 'The Sopranos'), have long summoned viewers to step out of their household flow and into one-of-a-kind television worlds (Altman 1986: 43–44). *Six Feet Under*'s opening credits may be superb, may be enthralling, may be cinematic, may be HBO, but they are still, at least functionally, TV.

Executive producer Alan Poul's understanding of the opening credits, however, takes the matter further. 'The theme music and title,' Poul notes, thinking like a producer – like an employee of HBO and not just a creator – 'encapsulate the show so well in *a kind of branding way* that all you need is the opening chords or the image of the tree and it's so evocative that *people know what you are talking about*' (emphasis added). Poul's choice of words is revealing. As Mark Rogers, Michael Epstein and Jimmie Reeves describe in an essay on *Six Feet Under*'s big brother *The Sopranos*, HBO is all about branding. (The eras can be distinguished by their dominant forms of marketing: TV I – 1948–1975 – was 'the age of mass marketing'; TV II – 1975–1995 – was 'the age of niche marketing'; and TV III – 1995 to the present – is 'the age of brand marketing' (2002: 48).)

Six Feet Under, extremely edgy, very profane, highly sexual, very adult (very much the beneficiary of expanded creative freedom), is designed to help HBO 'build its brand and attract new subscribers' (Rogers et al. 2002: 47). If *The Sopranos* lends itself more easily to brand marketing, bringing imaginitive life and economic power to its about-to-become-a-cliché slogan ('It's Not TV. It's HBO'), it does so as a representative of a readily identifiable genre: the gangster film; what can be made of the harder to classify *Six Feet Under*, a series which, like its opening credits, is a strange concoction?

> It's very abstract, and there's something kind of spooky about it but something kinda beautiful about it at the same time, and that sorta fits within the tone of the show in which there are things that are sad and upsetting and ugly and depressing about life but there's beauty in them as well (Ball, director commentary for 'Pilot', season one DVD).

What on earth (or beneath it) is *Six Feet Under*? Are we certain Poul knows what he is talking about when he insists that *Six Feet Under* viewers 'know what you are talking about', beginning with the opening credits? The sequence offers us the macabre (a corpse), the enigmatic (that crow might have flown right out of a Wallace Stevens poem), the mystical (the white light into which the gurney and its passenger move resembles the classic near-death experience), the self-referential (Ball's name on a tombstone carries on a cinematic tradition of auteur signature, like Hitchcock's cameos) and the naturally mysterious (that single tree, that verdant hillside). If HBO's brand is 'not TV', what *is* the trademark, the brand, 'the mission statement', if you will, of this, its 'not *The Sopranos*' series?

It's Not TV, It's the Grotesque...

One ready-to-hand designation for *Six Feet Under* might be 'grotesque'. Needless to say, much of the often scatological, frequently-immersed-in-bodily-fluids, always about bodies, both dead and alive, often ghoulish *Six Feet Under* clearly invites such a seemingly non-commercial branding. (HBO, after all, demonstrates a certain affinity for the grotesque, as *Carnivale* in its entirety and *The Sopranos*, *Deadwood*, *Real Sex*, *Taxicab Confessions* upon occasion confirm.)

David Fisher rebukes his brother: 'You want to get your hands dirty? You sanctimonious prick. Talk to me when you've had to stuff formaldehyde-soaked cotton up your father's ass so he doesn't leak' ('Pilot', 1:1). A corpse displays an erection (a phenomenon known as 'angel lust') and later defecates ('The Will', 1:2). A man is accidentally sliced to pieces in a huge bread dough mixer ('The Foot', 1:3). A lawyer dies from autoerotic asphyxiation while masturbating ('Back to the Garden', 2:7). Blood erupts (twice) from the Fisher and Sons Funeral Home plumbing system – 'It's like *The Shining* in here!' Claire Fisher proclaims ('Parallel Play', 4:3). Claire steals a corpse's foot in order to get back at her boyfriend for labelling her a 'toe slut' at school ('The Foot', 1:3). A grossly fat corpse falls to the floor when the gurney collapses ('Making Love Work', 3:6). Rico restores the flattened face of a woman smashed in by a traffic light ('Crossroads', 1:8). Funeral services for a porn star ('An Open Book', 1:5) and a biker ('It's the Most Wonderful Time of the Year', 2:8) turn into bizarre, over-the-top wakes. Claire does a portfolio of photographs of corpses ('The Secret', 2:10). In 'The Plan' (2:3), Rico excitedly begins to describe the effects of cancer on the body to a widow who has just lost her husband to the disease, until silenced by David. Claire's art teacher Olivier praises her work with the strange compliment that it 'instantly makes me want to throw up' ('The Eye Inside', 3:3). A visiting artist, Scott Philip Smith (Evan Handler) at LAC-Arts, describes one of his favourite works: a Reagan-era protest in which he 'spent two nights roaming the streets of New York City in the dead of winter asking [the homeless, mentally ill] to wipe their asses with [the American flag]' ('Nobody Sleeps', 3:4). Mysterious boxes of shit (or 'doo', as Arthur Martin refers to it) begin arriving at the Fisher house, addressed to Ruth Fisher's new husband George Sibley in season four. All these matters might be called grotesque. But is *Six Feet Under* itself grotesque?

The grotesque, as William J. Free (1978) reminds us, is multi-faceted. Its 'fanciful and sinister' nature is two-faced, exemplified for Free in the paintings by Pieter Brueghel and Hieronymous Bosch. Brueghel's grotesque is an essentially comic 'irreverent attitude toward his subject', conveying 'the artist's joy at contemplating the hurly-burly confusion of life which swallows up any attempt of history to impose meaning on it' (1978: 191). Bosch's grotesque, on the other hand, is 'terrifying', the manifestation of an 'insanely demonic world peeping from beneath the order of life and threatening to destroy it in disgusting violence' (ibid.). Philip Thomson agrees: 'Writers on the grotesque have always tended to associate the grotesque with either the comic or the terrifying. Those who see it as a sub-form of the comic class the grotesque, broadly, with the burlesque and the vulgarly funny. Those who emphasize the terrifying quality of the grotesque often shift it towards the realm of the uncanny, the mysterious, even the supernatural' (1972: 20). Our reaction to the grotesque is thus inherently complex, even contradictory. Not surprisingly, Thomson makes the grotesque's *unresolved clash of incompatibles in work and response* part of its very definition, and offers as a secondary, simplified definition *the ambivalently abnormal* (27).

Our cultural understanding of the grotesque has, however, been significantly altered by Mikhail Bakhtin's *Rabelais and His World* (1968) and its championing of the carnivalesque he finds operative in *Gargantua and Pantagruel*, the 'earthy', pre-'bodily canon' celebration of the 'grotesque body' of pre-Renaissance art in general and Rabelais in particular. The grotesque body, Bakhtin writes, unashamedly 'fecundates and is fecundated … gives birth and is born, devours and is devoured, drinks, defecates, is sick and dying' (1968: 319). (The 'bodily canon', as Bakhtin defines it, censors the grotesque body, 'assert[ing] instead that human beings exist outside the hierarchy of the cosmos. It stresses that we are finished products, defined characters, and in its reductionism attempts to seal off the bodily processes of organic life from any interchange with the external world' (320–21).) Thanks to Bakhtin we now see the artistic embrace of the grotesque not only as a pact with the devil but an expression of 'true … fearlessness' (335) in the face of the human condition, an anti-anal (in the Freudian sense) world-view that accepts embodiment as 'a point of transition in a life eternally renewed, the inexhaustible vessel of death and conception' (318).

Six Feet Under is hardly carnivalesque in Bakhtin's sense (for that matter, neither is HBO's *Carnivale*); its grotesqueness is too gross. But its infatuation with the grotesque is certainly shaded towards the comic pole of the axis. The grotesque body may not be exuberant or joyous in the series' ongoing narrative, but it is not exactly repressed either. Consider the following exchange between Nate and Rabbi Ari (Molly Parker), to whom he confesses his possibly fatal brain abnormality ('Back to the Garden', 2:7):

> Rabbi Ari: You must be really scared.
> Nate: Yeah. I'm going to die.
> Rabbi Ari: Yeah, me too.
> Nate: Really? What do you have?
> Rabbi Ari: A body.

Coming from a woman who earlier quoted in a funeral service the Talmudic proverbial wisdom 'Better one day in this life than all eternity in the world to come', the Rabbi's jest nevertheless blesses, on behalf of the series itself, the return of the repressed, and may well crystallise what Heather Havrilesky intuits (but does not identify) as the '*wisdom guiding this show that we may have never encountered on television before—and might not encounter again*' (2003; emphasis added).

It's Not TV, It's the Fantastic …

A series in which the dead are seldom really dead and routinely talk to the living, in which imagination and reality are difficult to distinguish, *Six Feet Under* is not only routinely grotesque but also fantastic. 'So long as we are uncertain whether we are witness to the natural or the supernatural,' Diane Stevenson writes in an essay on *Twin Peaks*, 'we are in the fantastic' (1994: 70). As the Russian writer Solovyev insists, the fantastic in its purest form as a genre 'must never compel belief in a mystic interpretation of a vital event; it must rather point, or *hint* at it' (quoted in Hawthorn 1998: 74). Drawing on Todorov's thesis that, historically, the fantastic as a genre functioned as a kind of pre-scientific form of imagination enables Stevenson to suggest that *Twin Peaks'* disturbing representation of child sexual abuse resorted to the fantastic – making Laura Palmer's molester and killer not really her father but a supremely evil, supernatural parasite named BOB – because of its unthinkable-ness.

If *Twin Peaks* resorts to the fantastic in order to come to grips with the incomprehensible, might it not be argued that *Six Feet Under's* use of it is inspired by a similar motive: in order to explore not the aberrant, unnatural inexplicable-ness of a father's abuse and murder of his daughter but the ordinary, natural unfathomable-ness of death? If death, as someone once observed, is to us as sex was to the Victorians; if, as radical sociologist Ivan Illich once observed, we live in a time in which obituaries should properly be written in passive voice ('David Lavery has been died today') – death being now routinely thought of not as an existential given but as a failure of medicine; then how could a television series about a family of funeral directors not resort to the fantastic?

In the pilot, at a dreary, subdued viewing of their father's body, Nate tells Claire of a memory from a long-ago backpacking tour of Europe, and in his mind-screen we see the story unfold. He had been on a boat in the Mediterranean that delivered a coffin to a beach in Sicily:

> And there were all these old Sicilians, dressed up all in black, waiting, just lined up on the beach. And when they got that coffin to the beach, they just went ape-shit: screaming, throwing themselves on it, beating their chests, tearing at their hair, making animals noises. It was just so…so real. I mean, I had been around funerals all my life, but I had never seen such grief, and at the time it gave me the creeps, but now I think it's probably so much healthier than this.

Here, and on a weekly basis, *Six Feet Under*, frequently going ape-shit (narratively speaking), puts death in active voice, makes death real. 'What's remarkable about *Six Feet Under*,' writes Carina Chocano, 'is that it takes something everybody knows (we're all going to die) and calmly repeats it, with a surprising lack of morbidity and next to no moralizing, until everybody understands (we're all going to die!)' (2002). The fantastic and the grotesque are as essential to this transaction as they are to *Six Feet Under*'s brand, but as genetic features they are simply not comprehensive enough to capture the series in its entire complexity.

It's Not TV, It's Magic Realism...

A case could be made for suggesting that *Six Feet Under*'s dominant tendencies may be found, in germ, in a scene from *American Beauty*. Mid-film, the darkly morose but clearly brilliant Ricky Fitts (Wes Bentley) shows his new love Jane Burnham (Thora Birch) unusual film footage he captured with his always-at-hand camcorder of a plastic bag and leaves blowing back and forth before a garage door. (We know from Ball's 'Afterword' to the film's screenplay that 'an encounter with a plastic bag outside the World Trade Center' was one of *American Beauty*'s seed crystals (1999: 113), and, on the DVD commentary, director Sam Mendes acknowledges that the plastic bag scene was the hook that convinced him to direct the project.) As a work of art Ricky's film appears at first glance to be simple realism of the minimalist variety, but he sees in the image (as do we) much more, as he explains: 'That's the day I realized that there was this entire life behind things, and this incredibly benevolent force that wanted me to know there was no reason to be afraid. Ever.' After a moment's pause, during which Jane turns away from the screen to look at him, he confesses poignantly, 'Sometimes there's so much beauty in the world I feel like I can't take it... and my heart is going to cave in.' When critics identified *American Beauty* as 'magic realism', the plastic bag scene being key to the designation, and when *Six Feet Under* is similarly identified, is it not because of its comparable recognition – sometimes grotesque, sometimes fantastic – of 'this entire life behind things'?

Latin American authors such as Gabriel García Márquez, Julio Cortazar, Isabel Allende and Jorge Luis Borges made 'magic realism' a literary household phrase. The term has not only created, in Borgesian fashion, 'its own precursors' (Borges 1999: 365) but also become an international phenomenon and bled into other media forms. According to Luis Leal, magic realism 'can be expressed in popular or cultured forms, in elaborate or rustic styles, in closed or open structures' (1995: 119). But can television, ever infatuated with various notions of the 'real', from *You Are There* to *Survivor*, be *magically* real? From its opening credit sequence, to those omnipresent ghosts, to its dream and NDE (near-death-experience) visions, to its first-season-only hyper-real mortuary ads, all coexisting with life in the Fisher household, with school, with work (of morticians, florists, a Shiatsu masseuse, a policeman) – with what is mundane – *Six Feet Under* encourages us to label its exploration of life and death 'magic realism'.

The pursuit of the 'marvellous' in art, writes Alejo Carpentier, 'had, of course, been attempted before – by the fantastic, by surrealism…– but magic realism's heuristic followed a different method, looked in a radically new direction: if [earlier art forms] pursued the marvellous, one would have to say that [they] very rarely looked for it in reality' (1995: 102–104). Magic realism's anything but sanguine world-view is by no means sweetness and light. As David Danow is careful to note, it is in fact grounded in 'a view of life that exudes a sense of energy and vitality in a world that promises not only joy, but a fair share of misery as well' (1995: 65ff.). In what Robert Scholes terms a form of 'metafiction', magic realist story-telling, according to J.A. Cuddon, is likely to recognise 'the mingling and juxtaposition of the realistic and the fantastic, bizarre and skilful time shifts, convoluted and even labyrinthine narratives and plots, miscellaneous use of dreams, myths and fairy stories, expressionistic and even surrealistic description, arcane erudition, the elements of surprise or abrupt shock, the horrific and the inexplicable' (Cuddon 1998: 488). In three plus seasons crowded with dreams, fantasies, time dislocations, esoteric knowledge (what the hell is fenugreek, anyway?), mysteries and secrets, and a great deal of misery, *Six Feet Under* lays claim to these traits, keeping it simultaneously real, especially on the emotional level.

In worlds that magic realists create, 'the supernatural is not a simple or obvious matter, but it is an ordinary matter, an everyday occurrence' (Zamora and Faris 1995: 3). In magic realism, Bruce Holland Rogers insists, '[if] there is a ghost…the ghost is not a fantasy element but a manifestation of the reality of people who believe in and have "real" experiences of ghosts. Magical realist fiction depicts the real world of people whose reality is different from ours. It's not a thought experiment. It's not speculation. Magic realism endeavours to show us the world through other eyes' (Rogers:2004). The fantastic offers us a world, as we have just seen, where 'we are uncertain whether we are witness to the natural or the supernatural' (ibid.). Magic realism is not agnostic. The supernatural exists; it is real, at least for a given subject. In a revealing scene in 'The Plan' (2:3), David and Nate talk of their father:

Nate: Sometimes I kinda feel like dad's around. Do you ever?
David: Nope.

But the viewer knows that neither Nate nor David is being quite honest: both Fisher boys communicate with their dead father. Plenty of ghosts are seen by others: Nathaniel, killed in the pilot, is a regular, appearing to the principal characters; many a loquacious corpse refuses to go gentle into that good night. With the exception of Dorothy Sheedy's delusional, fatal misreading of floating sex dolls ('In Case of Rapture', 4:2), *Six Feet Under* seldom debunks the alternate realities to which its characters are privy. '*Six Feet Under*,' Laura Miller observes, 'is remarkable precisely because it refuses to instruct us on how to feel about its characters, something no other TV show does' (2002).

If *Six Feet Under*'s narrative DNA, including the magic realism 'chromosome', is contained in its opening credits, its 'genetics' may be more than merely metaphorical. Can it be merely coincidental that the son of Gabriel García Márquez, Nobel Prize for Literature Laureate (1982) and magic realism's patriarch, is one of *Six Feet Under*'s directors? Rodrigo García has directed four episodes to date, including the second and third season premieres. It will come as no surprise that some of the series' most memorable, and most magical, moments are his. García directed 'The Room' (1:6), scripted by Christian Taylor, in which investigating a receipt he finds among his father's records leads Nate to a mysterious back room at a restaurant the owner provided Nathaniel as payment for funeral services rendered. Sitting in his father's sparsely furnished, tawdry hideaway, Nate discerns that it had evidently served as a refuge, a hang-out, a place for his dad to get away from it all, and he imagines what he might have done there. In mind-screen we share his reverie: Nathaniel smokes pot, dances and plays air guitar, hangs out with bikers, receives a blow job from a prostitute, fires repeatedly – Lee-Harvey-Oswald-style – a high-powered rifle with a sight out of the room's lone window. The unfolding montage is orchestrated to the words (sung by Ted Nugent) of the Amboy Dukes' 1968 acid rock classic 'Journey to the Center of the Mind': 'Leave your cares behind / Come with us and find / The pleasures of a journey to the center of the mind / Come along if you care / Come along if you dare / Take a ride to the land inside of your mind / Beyond the seas of thought / Beyond the realm of what / Across the streams of hopes and dreams where things are really not.' García succeeds in the difficult feat of taking us inside two minds, father and son, one imagining the other, each real in the eye of the beholder.

García directed from a script by Ball, 'In the Game' (2:1), in which Nate unwittingly takes Ecstasy before a dinner party at the Fisher house. Abandoned by Brenda and his family, who find his drugged high spirits hard to take, he finds himself late at night alone with his father, who introduces him to two friends: the Grim Reaper (Stanley Kamel), an urbane white man smoking a cigar, and Mama Life (Cleo King), a large, jovial African-American woman. Clearly old pals, the two play Chinese chequers. But Death cannot keep his hands off Life; and, as Nate looks on in amazement, she mounts him. Here García captures with gusto a scene simultaneously grotesque and comic.

And García – again working with a Ball script – helmed 'Perfect Circles' (3:1), the mind-blowing opening sequence of which begins where season two left off: with Nate under the knife, brain surgeons operating on his arteriovenous malformation (AVM). Things are not going well (the surgeon asks for aneurysm clamps), and on the screen appears:

NATHANIEL SAMUEL FISHER, JR.
1965–2002.

In rapid succession, with seamless editing reminiscent of the final sequence in Kubrick's *2001: A Space Odyssey*, we see the following: Rico sitting at the foot of Nate's corpse; Claire lying morosely on her bed; Ruth, dressed in a slip, ironing; David at his desk, weeping; Nate, worried he will be 'late for his own funeral', impatiently watching his father eat – he is wolfing down fenugreek (an ancient medicinal herb, used as an embalming agent, to enhance nursing mother's milk supply, and as an insect repellent), which he claims to be delicious with maple syrup (he counsels his son not to be in such a hurry, for he now has all the time in the world; 'Time doesn't exist anyway,' he adds). Nate stalks off and finds himself at his funeral, where he sees his family (including Lisa and their baby, Maya) and stares at his own bald corpse on display ('Damn it, David. I said I wanted to be cremated!'). Moving into a nearby room he watches David trying to teach a near-catatonic Nate to pronounce words like 'cat' and 'duck'. Moving on, he watches himself with Lisa as they play with Maya on the floor. Hearing another baby crying, he discovers – smiling broadly – himself entering the Fisher home with Brenda and *their* child. Following voices, he looks on as the Fisher family eats dinner and engages in lively conversation about how George W. Bush stole the election and Nate voted for Ralph Nader. At another, smaller, table, another Nate, his father, an almost unrecognisable mother (blonde and completely bitchy) and sister (not Claire) eat Christmas dinner until interrupted by a customer in need (a very competent, very involved, very conventional-looking Nate handles the call). Again following voices in another room, he finds a redneck version of himself wearing a baseball cap, smoking a cigarette, and slumped on the couch watching a strange television programme; though it has the look and feel of a soap opera, we hear a laugh track and find the characters talking about 'Dr Schrödinger' and *Copenhagen/* Copenhagen (the Michael Frayn play about quantum physics? The Danish capital?) and uttering lines like 'We always end up in a universe in which we exist' and 'Everything that can happen does'. When this last line is uttered, Redneck Nate proclaims, 'I've seen this one before.' Nate follows his clipboard-carrying father (passing a man obliterating a wall clock with a sledgehammer) into a room with a coffin, full of mourners (all Nate-on-the-operating-table lookalikes, all bald), where he begins to question his son (who wants desperately to know if he is alive or dead):

Do you believe that your consciousness affects the behaviour of subatomic particles?
Do you believe that particles move backward and forward in time and appear in all possible places at once?
Do you believe that the universe is constantly splitting into billions of different parallel universes?

Nathaniel avoids giving his son a straight answer, explaining instead that in another universe Nate never existed. His insistence that Nate 'open the box' (the coffin) causes the assembled audience to simultaneously don identical sunglasses. (The coffin becomes, in effect, the famous box of Erwin Schrödinger's *reductio ad absurdum gedanken* experiment, in which a cat, hidden in a box, may be either alive or dead, depending on whether or not light is a wave or a particle, but visually the 'box' recalls the case [perhaps containing a nuclear weapon] opened at the end of the classic *noir Kiss Me Deadly*.) When Nate lifts the coffin lid, radiant light engulfs the room. Once again the NATHANIEL SAMUEL FISHER, JR. / 1965–2002 title appears, but the '2002' fades and we see Nate, holding Maya, talking about his surgery to a male friend at a family barbecue. If there has been a more extraordinary sequence in the history of television, I have not seen it. García and Ball's collaboration here makes Cooper's dream from *Twin Peaks* seem tame by comparison.

Earlier, in my brief examination of the grotesque in *Six Feet Under*, I catalogued Claire's despicable/fascinating art professor Olivier's insistence that good art makes him want to vomit. But there is more to his postmodern aesthetic, as he goes on to explain ('The Eye Inside', 3:3)

> This drawing instantly makes me feel nauseous. You can tell if something is truthful, even if you don't understand it, if it affects your body. Your liver and your bowels are more important as an artist than your eyes, because they are so far away from your brain.

Six Feet Under's art, whether in the hands of García or Ball, would probably not quite meet Olivier's exacting standards. But in magic realist mode it rouses both body and mind, and we can tell it is true, even if it is beyond our comprehension.

Epilogue: The Magic Bus

At the end of the pilot, Nate, out jogging, finds himself at the same intersection where the city bus struck his father's hearse. At a bus stop across the street, Nate sees his father sitting, waiting. When the bus arrives, he boards, and waves – as the bus pulls away – to his son, who stands and stares, making eye contact with passing strangers before the closing credits roll.

At the end of the next episode, 'The Will' (1:2), Nate and David return to the same spot, arranged by Brenda to allow the brothers to confront and move on. This time they board the bus, and while Nate looks at David, hoping to read his reaction, David stares out of the window, captivated by what he (and he alone) can see: his young father carrying him as a child. As Nate reaches out to hold his brother's hand, David collapses sobbing on his brother's shoulder before the closing credits roll.

The end of season two finds Nate preparing to go under the knife to repair his AVM. As the anaesthetic takes effect, he imagines himself jogging on a country road, the city – 'the world capital of the denial of death' – far behind. A bus passes him and stops; its doors open. Nate looks inside; it is empty. With the sounds of the operating room clearly audible, especially Nate's breathing, a cut takes us to a long view of the bus, Nate still standing at its side.

'The propensity of magical realist texts to admit a plurality of worlds,' Lois Zamora and Wendy Faris observe, 'means that they often situate themselves on liminal territory between or among those worlds – in phenomenal and spiritual regions where transformation, metamorphosis, dissolution are common, where magic is a branch of naturalism, or pragmatism' (1995: 6). *Six Feet Under*'s magic bus moves between these worlds, crosses thresholds. Where it is bound, this early in such a 'long haul' (Vowell 2000) series, we cannot tell. For, in a sense, *Six Feet Under* is this bus; but it is still TV – and therein lies the magic.

two

Exquisite corpse: death as an odalisque and the new American gothic in *Six Feet Under*

> I hope the exit is joyful
> And I hope never to return.
>
> Frida Kahlo

Let's face a third certainty in our lives besides death and taxes: most, if not all, US graduate students juggle the exhaustion of scholarly work with equally draining 'side jobs' of some sort – store clerks, restaurant workers, retail employees. Along with my diehard effort and determination to climb the fragile ladder of a Ph.D. in English, I have been working in the field of pharmacy for over 11 years. How many confused eyes have glazed over in sticky puzzlement whenever I've mentioned that I am years into an English Ph.D. programme while also performing the dark, arcane witchery that occurs behind those tall and aloof pharmacy walls? Literature and pills? It's not that big a stretch, folks.

About two years ago I got my first job in an inpatient hospital pharmacy – a completely different set of modalities and configurations of practising pharmacy from those in an outpatient retail setting. And, yes – I worked the graveyard shift. It was difficult, tiring work, and the very old hospital was quite literally haunted (on at least three floors, including the basement pharmacy). Part of what got me through the weeks and months of crazy schedules and near-meltdown status was my becoming a devout fan and critic of the HBO phenomenon *Six Feet Under*. I have a magnetic connection to the show on many levels.

Another personal note: a few months before I began working at the hospital, I developed epilepsy, in one completely out-of-the-blue moment. I had a massive grand mal seizure that lasted for quite a few minutes, and my life and body have never been the same since that October afternoon. More recently, I was diagnosed with fibro-myalgia – an incredibly painful syndrome with symptoms similar to those of lupus. This is a significant aside, because both illnesses forced me to see my physiological vulnerabilities and to face my own sense of mortality. My limits.

And the ether mists of death's metaphoricities, which I used to harvest and adorn with the sleekest 'Gothic' romanticism, now enforce an abject trembling (as when one stares too long at a painting by Francis Bacon) that terrifies me to the point of dank and chronic insomnia. Rainer Maria Rilke (2002):

> There stands death, a bluish distillate
> in a cup without a saucer. Such a strange
> place to find a cup: standing on
> the back of a hand. One recognises clearly
> the line along the glazed curve, where the handle
> snapped. Covered with dust. And *HOPE* is written
> across the side, in faded gothic letters.
>
> The man who was to drink out of that cup
> read it aloud at breakfast, long ago.
> What kind of beings are they then
> who finally must be scared away by poison?
> Otherwise would they stay here? Would they keep
> chewing so foolishly on their own frustration?
> The hard present moment must be pulled
> Out of them, like a set of false teeth. Then
> They mumble. They go on mumbling, mumbling...
> O shooting star that fell into my eyes and through my
> body—:
> Not to forget you. To endure

For now, I shall endure: in pain. Huge chunks of memory lost to seizures. But enduring.

What is it, then, that might position an innovative television show such as *Six Feet Under* as a directive, driving idiom of the 'New American Gothic'? Certainly, director and creator Alan Ball and the stunning crew and cast all continually spin seductive, dazzling blue-black threads of loss, rage, loneliness and the immediate hurt of splintering hearts – lives sinking, blue pulse slowing, in a small hole at the centre of a dark, frozen lake. Hearts swollen with bottomless longing yet sheathed (desperate, frantic, scratching at the seams of protection) in thick, colourless metallics.

And we, as viewers, loom and huddle over the rough-hewn, murky hole in the ice to watch – perhaps to empathise or to rescue. Maybe we swoon over the turbulence of the show's dynamics because there are traces of a palpable set of disarticulate erotics belonging only to each of our own narratives of winter and of the broken heart – the stark silence and the pure white sheen and timelessness of a 'Gothic' scene; evocatively, *Six Feet Under* unveils an atlas of both familiar and bewildering territories. To become engaged with the show as a regular viewer is to flirt vicariously with our own inevitable end, and also to alchemically process and translate the mysterious spirit that infuses the show – a fascinating force that Edward Hirsch explores: 'Duende' (2002:11).

> Duende rises through the body. It burns through the soles of a dancer's feet, or expands in the torso of a singer. It courses through the blood and breaks through a poet's back like a pair of wings. It smokes through the lungs; it scorches the voice; it magnetizes the words. It is risky and deathward leaning. 'The duende does not come at all unless he sees that death is possible,' Lorca says (*Deep Song*). Duende, then, means something like artistic inspiration in the presence of death. It has an element of mortal panic and fear. It has the power of wild abandonment. It speaks to an art that touches and transfigures death, that both woos and evades it.

Duende. It is an immense obsidian angel that can pierce a needle's eye. And it brings not only darkness but also pleasure and an ambivalent, damaged spirit. It is a pleasure of utter otherness – this *duende* – that saturates *Six Feet Under*.

Roland Barthes suggests that 'what pleasure wants is the site of a loss, the seam, the cut, the deflation, the *dissolve* which seizes the subject in the midst of bliss. Culture thus recurs as an edge: in no matter what form' (1990: 7).

20 July 200_, 4:26 a.m. I am busily preparing I.V. bags for both the dying and the newborn when the intercom goes off: 'CODE BLUE... CODE BLUE.' I rush to the scene to meet the rest of the team that is working on the dying person. The room is crowded and hectic, and everyone is focused, intent, coldly sweating. The patient is long gone, however. After 30 minutes of resuscitation efforts the physician calls the time of death, and we all go back to our given workstations as if nothing major had just happened.

I have seen the dead, poised like an unspeakable word on the edge of a blunt, rusted knife; poised like a perfect still life of a gleaming cut-glass bowl full of overripe black cherries. Poised like an odalisque: one moment of unblemished stillness captured in a bath of brief but radiant warm light.

And I'll let you in on a little secret: there is nothing mysterious going on behind the high walls of the pharmacist's box. I cannot speak for mortuary experts, but perhaps part of the allure of *Six Feet Under* is that viewers have countless opportunities to both thrill and cringe as voyeurs of one of the most privatised, taboo and mysterious professions – the atmosphere, tools and challenges of the embalming room – without actually having to experience the actual panic, abjection and disorientation of standing two feet away from a body that has just expired. In her poem 'The Stroller', Jane Kenyon strikes a certain chord that could easily describe the experience of becoming a fan of *Six Feet Under*: watching it 'is like looking into a mirror/

by kind permission of T. Cribb and Sons

And seeing your own eyes and someone else's/ Eyes as well, strange to you/ But benign, curious, come/ To interrogate your wounds, the progress/ Of your beating heart' (1993).

Six Feet Under skilfully plies the many visual and emotive conceits of death, dying and mourning while urging its audience to turn themselves inside out to have a look, if only for a short while. Mark Doty: 'Interiority makes itself visible' (2001: 49).

The New American Gothic, then, is not only the elemental Barthesian recursive edge of a particular type of text or culture – one that yields resounding grief, a choking stasis and a fathomless obsession with the exquisite corpse – but also one that recasts and collapses a representation of a contemporary American family into that of one wherein lives are suspended in a heightened contemplative state: paradoxical longings, salvaged lives; thin veins of memory and many artefacts of dead or dying relationships.

And deliberate veils of silence, fiercely shimmering. *Six Feet Under* clearly defies any singular means of taxonomy; however, I maintain that it represents the 'New American Gothic' because it sustains the portraiture of a contemporary culture where the living and the dead are both separate and together at the same time – asserting the given properties of the iconographic power of each of them at the appropriate moments in the show (which, often, are the most pleasurable and unexpected moments for viewers). Its complexities are indeed blissful for an ill Ph.D. candidate who has seen the real thing far too many times. Georges Perec, in *Species of Spaces*, takes fragmented words and phrases and creates this heartbreaking whole – this mirror of my life, of every life – of which only the ending I include (1997: 36)

> going into raptures touching up botching scraping dusting manoeuvring pulverizing balancing checking moistening stopping up emptying crushing roughing out explaining shrugging fitting the handle on dividing up walking up and down tightening timing juxtaposing bringing together matching assessing pinning up arranging distempering hanging up starting again inserting spreading out washing looking for entering breathing hard

> settling in
> living in
> living

For John, always.

three

Death, liminality and transformation in *Six Feet Under*

Pervaded by an overwhelming aura of death, the opening credits of *Six Feet Under* draw on both romantic and Gothic images with shots of hands parting, a time-lapse sequence of wilting lilies, and images of gravestones intercut and framed by those of a black crow. These shots are counterpoised against more clinical and modernist representations of death. Hands are washed in prelude to a quasi-surgical procedure, shots foreground beakers of embalming fluid and a trolley carrying a cadaver is pushed towards a bright light. Not only does the sequence indicate that this is a series about death and dying, it signals that each episode's narrative concerns the journey of the body from death to its disposal. In these opening sequences the parting hands mark the moment of death, the embalming process signifies the clinical transformation of the dead body, and the hearse and gravestone images signify the laying of the corpse to rest. Put simply, it makes known that each programme is about the initial, transitory stages of death.

These images, and the articulation of this transitional period of death, herald the fact that the *Six Feet Under* narrative operates as a liminal space and about a liminal time. In anthropological terms liminality derives from the Latin word *limen*, meaning 'threshold'; it is a transitory place which is neither here nor there (Turner 1969). Following the death of an individual, liminality threatens to erode the separation between mortal, quotidian existence and a frightening 'other world', transcendental plane or immaterial existence. And it is in this transitional sphere in which *Six Feet Under* operates. This dimension is not just ritually framed by the structure of each episode, but is also visually articulated throughout the series in hallucinatory sequences where the dead come back to life, or in dream sequences where alternative realities are explored.

At the same time, liminality can become a dangerous place because the usual rules and codes governing our day-to-day existence suddenly become meaningless in the face of death. With everyday rules and beliefs temporarily suspended, people can speak or act in ways which might otherwise be socially inappropriate. As a result, each *Six Feet Under* episode offers a liminal space for exploring socially and culturally problematic themes and taboo subjects: it is a space for transformation where meaning collapses, and this is dramatically explored through the changes each character undergoes across the series. Yet it also articulates two specific forms of transformation concerning funerary ritual in contemporary Western society: the first about how the social and cultural transformations of the dead body are dealt with in the funerary process; and the second about the broader transition currently taking place in social and cultural attitudes towards death, dying and bereavement. It marks an ongoing shift from modern, secular and clinical attitudes towards a more postmodern one. This shift draws on a variety of traditional and humanistic sources to personalise funerary rites, and to help make death and grief more socially meaningful for the bereaved. *Six Feet Under*, for me, marks a radical intervention in these changes by both airing the subject of death in a television drama and by offering a range of potential contemporary cultural and personal responses to death and bereavement.

Death Pollution

In *Six Feet Under* the purpose of the Fisher business is the disposal of the dead body. In sociological terms the removal of the cadaver, which is both physically and metaphorically polluting, is a key function of funerary rites. Not only does the physical breakdown and decay of the corporeal body present aesthetic, aromatic and hygienic problems, but also the corpse is a symbolic reminder of the disruptive potency of death – both personal and social. Death happens to us all, and this is potentially terrifying in and of itself for the living. It also threatens the moral and social order by bringing into question daily codes and conventions. In such circumstances the recently bereaved can experience an existential crisis that leads them to break the rules of everyday propriety, say things that should not be said and violate systems of daily life. Furthermore, within the patterns of the socio-economic division of labour in contemporary capitalist societies, such an existential dilemma can prove threatening, for it brings into question the fundamental premise of selling one's labour for wages. If we are all going to die, and if we should live every day as though it might be our last, why bother going to work at all?

In the world of *Six Feet Under*, as in real life, the mortuary trade plays an important role in managing death pollution. One of the ways is to make the formal arrangements for having the body removed, and to organise the rituals and/or religious ceremonies accompanying its removal. Each week finds the Fishers, along with restorative artist/embalmer and later business partner Rico Diaz, as well as apprentice Arthur Martin, dealing with a corpse and its disposal; and David in particular has specialist knowledge of a range of funerary rites and burial customs. Managing death pollution is strongly articulated in *Six Feet Under* through the visual control these men have over the dead body. In the first instance, this is represented by the cosmetic and quasi-surgical procedures they use to halt the inevitable decay of the corpse and make it presentable for public exhibition. Most funerary sequences in *Six Feet Under*, the rituals and the mourning, take place in the euphemistically named 'slumber room', where the recently bereaved are able to view the deceased in an open casket. The process by which the rotting body is made fit to be seen is articulated in the opening credit sequence with the beakers of embalming fluid, and the shot of a dead woman's brow being wiped with a swab. Within individual episodes, scenes often take place in the prep room, where David and Rico work hard to make dead bodies acceptable for viewing. In cases where individuals have died in particularly gruesome circumstances – like Thomas Romano (John Capodice), who is chopped into pieces after a colleague accidentally switches on an industrial dough mixer he is cleaning ('The Foot', 1:3), or Chloe Yorkin whose skull is completely shattered after colliding with a cherry-picker platform ('Crossroads', 1:8) – Rico takes great professional pride in his artistic ability to reconstruct mutilated faces and bodies for public presentation. His wife Vanessa on several occasions compliments him on his restorative talents, and calls his faultless reconstruction of Chloe Yorkin his 'Sistine Chapel'. Chloe's friends (Lori Harmon and Pat Destrocs) are also impressed, seeming less concerned with grieving over their dead friend than inspecting her corpse, which now bears no marks of her traumatic demise.

The second way in which the pollution of death is visually and physically managed in *Six Feet Under* is in the separation of the unacceptable dead body from public space. In this sense the prep room is a place where the preparation of the abject body takes place away from the public gaze. For the most part, the Fishers adopt a professional attitude to the dead bodies in their care. It is this professional practice that manages death pollution by keeping the dead body separate from public space – hiding its grotesqueness, making it acceptable for public viewing, and finally arranging for its disposal. The visual control of the dead body, by its sequestration of its troublesome properties from public gaze, and by its ultimate cremation or burial, powerfully articulates a simple but significant cultural proposition: 'out of sight, out of mind'.

Such a space is subject to strict codes of professional and personal conduct. In 'The New Person' (1:10), for example, the Fishers fire their new mortician's assistant Angela (Illeana Douglas) because she wears revealing tops to work and has telephone conversations about sex while preparing dead bodies for viewing. As Nate tells her: 'You know, Angela. My brother likes a certain decorum when you're working with someone's loved one.' The Fishers must deal with spot inspections, such as in 'The Last Time' (2:13), when Inspector Gerson (Larry Drake) pays them an unexpected visit. Finding Rico and Vanessa eating their lunch in the embalming room, a full fridge and Aaron Buchbiner's decomposing body as well as blood oozing out from the drains, results in a written citation and the threat of closure if the drainage system is not replaced in two weeks. It confirms wider social beliefs that disrespectful behaviour towards (or around) the dead body constitutes a form of desecration. Revelations about an infestation of rats at a Los Angeles County morgue, for example, with bodies being 'nibbled', were considered the 'ultimate sacrilege' (Wade 2002: 3).

The inappropriate treatment of dead bodies violates taboos, often spilling over into humour. In the episode 'The Foot' (1:3), Nate has difficulty lifting Thomas Romano's dismembered body onto the trolley. Instead, it falls to the floor in pieces. When he manages to pick up the bits he realises that a foot is missing. It later turns up in Gabe's locker as retribution for telling his friends about Claire sucking his toes. At the Romano viewing later, Rico proudly confides to David and Nate that he substituted the missing foot with a leg of lamb stored in their freezer. The deception is almost revealed when the grief-stricken Mrs Barbara Romano (Sandra Purpuro) turns into a 'casket climber' – someone so overcome with grief that they try to clamber into the coffin. Thankfully, Rico and David manage to pull her back before she dislodges the foot. Such absurdity, at the expense of the bereaved and their desire to see the body complete and bearing no trace of the terrible tragedy which befell them, reflects a wider anxiety that the dead should go into the 'afterlife' with an unmarred physical body (Wade: 2002).

Dead bodies can be troublesome in other ways. In *Six Feet Under* the presence of ghosts heckling from beyond the grave suggests that the deceased might still walk among us. While death represents separation and the loss of loved ones, and grief an emotional coming to terms with that loss, the idea that the deceased might remain here on earth in some ghostly or judgemental form is something that induces anxiety (Wade: 2002). Reflecting this anxiety that the recently deceased can see and judge us, Ruth suffers an emotional breakdown in 'Pilot' (1:1) because she believes that Nathaniel now knows of her infidelity. 'I'm a whore,' she cries out to a stunned Nate and David. 'I was unfaithful to your father for years. And now he knows.' Such ghostly apparitions express liminal erosion between mortal and deathly spheres. Throughout the series, the dead 'come to life' and confront individual members of the Fisher family about their attitudes or failings. In season one, for example, the ghosts of Paco (Jacob Vargas), the gang member shot in 'Familia' (1:4), Viveca St John (Veronica Hart), the electrocuted porn actress in 'An Open Book' (1:5), and Marcus Foster (Brian Poth), the victim of a homophobic attack in 'A Private Life' (1:12), taunt David about his sexuality. They often appear in the prep room, still bearing the physical scars of their death. Furthermore, being dead, they are freed from conventional propriety and the politeness of everyday life, and thus can utter uncomfortable truths. Challenging Paco for calling him a 'born bitch', David says, 'You're speaking like this at your funeral?' Paco replies: 'Damn straight. I say whatever I goddamn please.' The dead cease to reappear once the funerary rites for their character have been completed, thus complementing the anthropological view that the death ritual brings an end to periods of liminality.

An important exception, of course, is Nathaniel Fisher Sr, who appears to the characters throughout the series despite his funeral in the first episode. Although Nathaniel's continued presence contradicts the idea that the funerary rites exorcise the recently deceased, his appearance works as a narrative device to link the liminal experiences together and help articulate the dramatic transformations that the characters experience. As a dead person, he can speak difficult truths – utter what cannot otherwise be said – which the living are often reluctant to admit, even to themselves. Yet, unlike the deceased that the Fishers encounter in their professional lives, Nathaniel's reappearance signifies a longer grieving process – that the Fishers miss him and wish he were there to support and guide them.

Significantly, although Fisher and Sons (and later Fisher and Diaz) are professional practitioners, their personal experience of grief erodes their separation and detachment from the business of caring for the dead. Within the liminal space of the series, and shaped by personal loss, this erosion means that the bereaved often touch a nerve with the main characters. With occasional exceptions, such as Nate's distraction over Lisa's disappearance when dealing with the bereaved of Dorothy Kim Su (Momo Yashima) in 'Death Works Overtime' (3:11), they have a deeper sympathy for their clients, both deceased and living. Rico cares for the corpse, Nate comforts the bereaved and David attends to the funerary rites with his knowledge of appropriate rituals for the different faiths. This personal touch means that they can provide for a wide range of funeral services and respond to individual requests. As Kevin Lamb (Dennis Christopher) says to Nate and David in 'Nobody Sleeps' (3:4), 'I was told that you would be more open to accommodating certain requests'. Importantly, the depiction of the Fishers' accommodating attitude to the funerary process represents a change in funeral cultural within contemporary

Western society. In resisting the temptation to sell the business to Kroehner, they actively refuse to succumb to the impersonalised funerary ritual which characterises the 'big business' approach to modern, secular and industrialised funeral practice. It further marks an ongoing transition from modern approaches to death to a more postmodern one.

From the 'Traditional' to the Postmodern

As well as exploring ways that dead bodies are transformed and disposed of and how death pollution is managed, *Six Feet Under* explores changes in attitudes and practices towards death, dying and bereavement. Reasons for this relate to two other sociological and anthropological functions of the funerary ritual. As well as the disposal of the dead body, funerals mark a rite of passage for the bereaved, to mark the changing symbolic social status of the bereaved (from wife to widow, for example). Secondly, funerals celebrate the survival of the group. An individual may have died and their death precipitated an existential crisis for those left behind, but the funerary rites, predicated on tradition and anteriority, indicate that society (and its codes and conventions) can transcend the death of any individual.

In traditional societies ritual marks the rites of passage; it allows for the community to pause and commemorate/celebrate the different stages of a person's life – from birth and marriage to death. Ritual instils social and cultural values in its participants and gives life and experience, including bereavement, social meaning. In a secular world, however, the dwindling of traditional religious customs means that the life stages through which one passes are not given the same social significance. Without a cultural infrastructure to socialise mortality, the passage from life to death increasingly becomes an isolating and meaningless 'non-event' (Bauman 1992). This is reflected in death rituals becoming more austere and sterile. Even where people still believe in traditional forms of religion, such as Christianity, the commercialised and industrialised nature of the death ritual leaves funerary rites devoid of psychological or social value. These cere-monies instead reveal the ways in which death has increasingly become a taboo subject and separated from the everyday. Such distancing and turning the funeral away from 'an essentially existential experience into an essentially retail one' (Lynch 2000: 162) mean that bereavement and grief are increasingly shut away from the public gaze. As Phillippe Ariès has asserted in his classic book, *Western Attitudes Toward Death, from the Middle Ages to the Present*, '[s]orrow does not inspire pity but repugnance' (1976: 90).

As *Six Feet Under* suggests, contemporary funerals adhere to strict conventions concerning dignity and propriety, with public displays of extreme emotion strictly policed. The sociologist Jenny Hockey (1997) has observed that during funerals in Britain, for example, clergymen pay particular attention to bereaved women and move in quickly when necessary to prevent them from uncontrollably breaking down. Keeping watch over the grieving subject and monitoring the behavioural codes by the bereaved can be witnessed in the funerary rituals at the beginning of season one of *Six Feet Under*. In 'Pilot' (1:1), Ruth starts sobbing during the viewing of her dead husband's body, and is quickly ushered away by her younger son, the experienced funeral director. Nate is surprised and turns to his younger sister: 'She's so sad she has to be taken out of sight?' Claire replies: 'They always do that. The second someone starts to lose it they take them off into that room. Makes all the other people feel uncomfortable, I guess.'

David's sense of professional propriety – his dour reserve, controlled demeanour, respectful silence – can be read as speaking about commercialised and secular attitudes towards death. By contrast, Nate's description of a Sicilian funeral in the same episode, where village women openly weep and wail over the corpse, indicates for him the importance of catharsis to heal the community and help the bereaved to grieve the dead. Such public demonstrations of un-restrained grief and out-of-control hysteria appear to him as 'probably much more healthy' than the restrained American way. Later, at his father's graveside, Nate berates the 'clean' and 'antiseptic' funeral ceremony arranged by his brother. His outburst gives Ruth licence to express how she really feels, whereupon she collapses in grief onto the soil which will soon cover her dead husband's body. The programme's sympathy here is with Nate and Ruth, as the satirical faux television commercials for funerary products such as the 'New Millennium Edition Crown Royal Funeral Coach' and the 'Franklin Leak-proof Earth Dispenser' provide an explicit critique of the commercialisation of funerary culture. By depicting a transgression of normalised codes of behaviour during funerary rites, and by poking fun at mainstream funerary culture, it offers up transformative possibilities for the viewer. In this reading, Nate is the one who acts progressively to try and transform the emotional and social bankruptcy of the modern, secular funeral. This straightforward dichotomy between David (modern) and Nate (traditional) is, however, misleading.

Instead, they both reflect an engagement with changes in attitudes towards funerary culture. Partly this is because David knows the burial rituals of numerous religions, and that he himself is a Christian. He is familiar with the various contents in the 'ritual objects' room; and he is able to offer advice and make arrangements for a range of funerals throughout the series, including the Jewish funeral in 'Back to the Garden' (2:7) and the Thai Buddhist one in 'The Secret' (2:10). Yet while these different funerals represent a more multicultural society, made up of a rich blend of traditions and values, the representation of these funerals also suggests a diverse, reflexive, accommodating and responsive attitude towards the conduct of these rituals. The Jewish funeral is modified, for example, to reflect the family's distress that the deceased had apparently committed suicide, although the Fishers soon realise that the victim died accidentally from autoerotic asphyxiation. In 'Familia' (1:4) the wake is conducted along traditional lines, but later Paco's gang leader holds an impromptu prayer gathering, which includes the Fisher family.

This is complemented later in the series with other depictions of humanist approaches to death and dying. Increasingly today, funerals often include readings from favourite books or poems, as well as much-loved pieces of music or songs from popular culture. Examples of such personalised rituals include the biker funeral in 'It's the Most Wonderful Time of the Year' (2:8) and the constructed opera stage in 'Nobody Sleeps' (3:4). In the biker episode a middle-aged Hell's Angel, Jesse Ray Johnson (Frank Ross), is killed when his Harley-Davidson collides with a truck while on his way to work as a department store Father Christmas. His widow, Marilyn (Rusty Schwimmer), and friends want a customised, spray-painted coffin (the same as his Harley, in fact) and have specific requests for the Christmas Day funeral for which they are willing to pay. The subsequent wake, accompanied by kegs of 'Bud' and cases of Jack Daniels, is more an all-day party than a funerary rite. As Nate looks on, the assembled bikers hold up their cigarette lighters and salute Jesse with their drinks, accompanied by the Blue Oyster Cult's nihilistic anthem 'Don't Fear the Reaper'. Similarly, in 'Nobody Sleeps', a mourner performs 'Nessun Dorma' from Puccini's opera *Turandot* during the service for a gay theatre lighting designer amidst a specially constructed set in the slumber room. Combining the transformative potential of liminal space where difficult truths can be uttered, and a ritualised moment of community, the deceased man's partner celebrates the number of sexual partners they both shared. Both the biker funeral and the 'gay opera' serve to bring their respective social groups together, to celebrate the survival of these communities, to emotionally come to terms with the loss of a loved one and friend, and to signal the end of the period of liminality. In these ritually infused moments, where cultural meaning is instilled, the Fishers are transformed themselves; while Nate takes his newly acquired Harley-Davidson for a high-speed drive along the coastal road, inspired by Marilyn's advice to live life to the full (2:8), David attempts to come to terms with the difficulties involved in his relationship with Keith (3:4).

Six Feet Under articulates an ongoing shift in funerary culture. It shows that the evolution from 'traditional' forms of ritual to modern, secular ones has not been an entirely happy one. Instead, it offers a blend of the traditional *and* the modern, to reflect a more postmodern attitude – one that seeks a return to older values in conjunction with the new. These more postmodern values offer the possibility of better coming to terms with death and bereavement in the contemporary (Western) world.

Of Transformation and Endings...

In sociological studies of death in modernity there is a consensus that death has been sequestrated from everyday life. It has become institutionalised, with the dying secreted away in hospitals, old people's homes and hospices. Funerary practices have also become increasingly commercialised and managed by big business. This is handled in *Six Feet Under* with the Fishers' ongoing resistance to the Kroehner takeover, and by the explicit critique of commercialised funerary culture with the spoof television advertisements in the first episode.

Within modern society this secularised, institutionalised and economically rationalised approach to death and dying turns death into a taboo subject. Such silencing results in grief becoming repugnant, and bereavement a private act to be carried out away from the public gaze. If grief is not publicly acceptable, and with funerary rituals becoming increasingly sterilised and industrialised, what we find is that bereaved individuals no longer know how to deal with grief.

If grief is hidden from public view, then media representations of bereavement take on a new importance. As the sociologist Tony Walter (1999) suggests, it is through media representations of public mourning following major disasters (such as 9/11) and high-profile deaths (like Diana, Princess of Wales) that people learn about responding to death and strategies for mourning. *Six Feet Under* emerges as progressive precisely because it breaks the taboo of death and the silence surrounding bereavement, as it places dying, the dead body and intense sorrow at the heart of its drama. The series also provides a space of liminality which allows not only for the themes of death to be openly acknowledged and discussed, but also for the deceased, the bereaved and the central characters to speak what cannot be said elsewhere. As a progressive media representation of the business of death, it further makes known the transformative properties of what happens to the body after death as well as the changes taking place to those processes. But, as Tony Walter argues, the ongoing transition in attitudes towards death and bereavement is a slow and uneven process. The televisual representation of death, liminality and transformation in *Six Feet Under* thus extends these new, postmodern discourses into the private sphere of the domestic audience. In a sphere where the privatised and isolated experience of death might still be acutely felt, *Six Feet Under* can make a radical intervention and propose profound social change.

four

Sex, shocks and stiffs: *Six Feet Under* and the pornography of the morbid

Season one, episode five, 'An Open Book': ageing porn star Jean Louise McArthur, screen name Viveca St John (Veronica Hart), is killed by her own pussy. The segment is brief but rife with innuendo: panning the cosmetic paraphernalia scattered across Viveca's bathroom, the camera settles on Viveca, wooing her pet cat tub-side like a lover, preparing for an impending rendezvous by reclining into a bath. 'He's got a big fat dick. And he fucks like a jackhammer,' she confides of her date, swooning in a swirl of bubbles and sighing, 'Those never last.' Within seconds Viveca's pedicured toes are tensing convulsively in a visual allusion to orgasmic ecstasy. Her cat has nudged her hot rollers into the bathwater, electrocuting her.

In the parlance of porn, this image – Viveca's final, climactic shudder – constitutes a kind of 'money shot', a depiction of an irrepressible bodily spasm that, in this instance, ironically blurs *le petit mort* with the moment of death. Within the framework of hard-core porn, the money shot fulfils an essential function: testifying to the authenticity of the experience being filmed – and the limit of acting, or 'faking it' – by zeroing in on a moment of reflexive, involuntary physical expression, the paroxysm of male ejaculation. By highlighting a body that is quite literally unable to contain itself, the money shot provides a fleeting glimpse of 'genuine' affect, of the private self uninflected by the norms of public performance; porn scholar Linda

Williams calls it 'the ultimate and uncontrollable – ultimate *because* uncontrollable – confession of sexual pleasure in the climax of orgasm' (Williams 1999: 101). Resonating with the quality of unadulterated 'truth', therefore, the money shot represents the logical culmination of what philosopher Michel Foucault describes as the 'will to knowledge' regarding sex – the irremediable cultural compulsion to exact sexual confessions as a means of understanding one another and ourselves. As Foucault writes (1998:78):

> We must make no mistake here … the West has managed … to bring us almost entirely – our bodies, our minds, our individuality, our history – under the sway of the logic of concupiscence and desire. Whenever it is a question of knowing who we are, it is this logic that henceforth serves as our master key … Sex, the explanation for everything.

In the case of Viveca St John, the connection between sex and self is unusually overt; as a porn star, Viveca's persona – and, what's more, her livelihood – are inextricably bound up with her legibility as a sex symbol. For Viveca and her partners in porn, sex is not a secret but rather a source of pride and profits; at her funeral, her former colleagues shamelessly bring sexuality to the fore, tearfully eulogising her career break as a fledgling fluffer, her peerless flair for fellatio and her near-sacrosanct successes in the sack (as one mourner laments, 'fucking Viv is at the top of my list of things to thank God for'). Indeed, by the time a sobbing former co-star (Sandra Oh) bursts in on one of David's client meetings to exclaim, 'Her tits have never looked better!' the funeral proceedings have come to seem less a testament to truth than a burlesque of grieving; the sheer surfeit of sexuality imbues the proceedings with the spirit of ribald farce. The cardinal question of identity, in this sequence, hinges on performance – and specifically on whose self-presentation is less 'genuine': Viveca, the actor whose hypersexual affect is nakedly in evidence (David calls her surgically enhanced bosom 'beautiful, in a completely *artificial* way'), or David, the closeted gay man who's trying desperately to keep up appearances (Viveca's posthumous response to his remark: 'Men loved them! Well, real men.').

Beyond first blush, however, this very tenor of parody – the aesthetic of campy theatricality that prevails throughout the solemnities – can be seen to illuminate the key 'truths' at stake in the construction of social identities, and specifically in the presentation of a culturally viable self. As Foucault and others have argued, conventional codes of propriety serve a particular socio-economic purpose: to produce and perpetuate an industrious, efficient and essentially law-abiding workforce. In the culture at large, the control and care of the self are considered vital markers of citizenship, fundamental to the broad matrix of manners and mores that render the body 'more obedient as it becomes more useful and conversely' (Foucault 1977: 138). This explains, at least in part, why David chastens Nate for revelling in Viveca's sexual exploits; he perceives Nate's antic banter with Federico over Viveca's cadaver – the conversation kicks off with 'this chick fucked a snake!' – as at odds with commonly agreed-upon business ethos, reminding him, 'Nate. What we do here is serious.' The incursion of stark sexuality into the ceremony of the funeral therefore gives rise to what cultural critic Laura Kipnis, describing pornography, calls a 'festival of social infractions … confronting its audiences with exactly those contents that are exiled from sanctioned speech, from mainstream culture and political discourse' (Kipnis 1996: 164). In effect, the funeral goings-on become an instance of camp – by queer scholar Jose Munoz's definition, 'a mode of enacting the self against the dominant culture's identity-denying protocols' (Munoz 1999: 120) – bringing to light not simply the productive labour that self-control facilitates but the work that the act of controlling the self demands.

Returning to the notion of the money shot, then, a striking point of contrast emerges between the body that is incontrovertibly out of control – and that, by virtue of its disorderliness, smacks of authenticity and 'truth' – and the figure lying serenely in the slumber room, the quintessence of self-contained composure. In Viveca's instance, ironically, the boorish elegies for the base and bodily function as a foil for the impenetrably passive corpse; her former entourage may lampoon the norms of etiquette, but Viveca's mien is finally – if not by virtue of her décolletage seemly – at least sedate. Viveca's body – the intended focal point of the 'viewing' – is, paradoxically, lacking in the potential for 'real' fleshly inappropriateness; whereas the money shot derives its appeal from the revelation of 'truth', the funereal viewing hinges on the manufacture of a facsimile, a final, artfully assembled image of the coherent self. That Viveca's posthumously cockeyed bust has been propped up with canned goods – Federico gleefully admits to having wedged 'a can of cat food under each boob' – is irrelevant; what matters, in the words of Viveca's former lover, Larry Wadd (Terence Knox), is that 'she should look spectacular... that's the most important thing'. Rather than expand the scope of what is visible, therefore, the viewing serves conversely to reiterate the parameters of what should, culturally speaking, appear on display.

Examining the money shot and the slumber room viewing side by side, moreover, points towards key questions about the nature of spectatorship, and specifically about the capacity for these two categories of image to exert any kind of compelling, transformative impact on the viewing subject. Like 'the industry' in the Fisher's native Los Angeles – the entertainment business – the death care trade trucks in the production and sale of the spectacle, positioning the viewing as a catalyst for spiritual healing. The series riffs repeatedly on the parallels between LA's image-centric commercial focus and the funeral industry's imperative that the cadaver look not just 'real', but optimally attractive; as the voice-over for a mock mortuary product commercial intones, 'she looked her best every day of her life... don't let one disfiguring accident change that' ('Pilot', 1:1). The figure cut by the corpse, then, meticulously revamped, docile and at rest in an exorbitantly marked-up coffin – David pitches one such box as 'more than just a casket. It's a tribute, really' ('The Will', 1:2) – represents a startling accretion of capital, the extravagant finale on which the successful functioning of the entire funereal apparatus rests. Mesmerising in its claims to verisimilitude, the image of the corpse can prove unsettling in its relationship to 'truth', the pinnacle of the cultural emphasis on the body as semiotic surface. Yet, for the bereaved, the consumption of this spectacle remains primarily a passive enterprise; the Fishers hover at a respectful distance, poised to enforce standard behavioural protocols – to prevent 'casket climbing', for example, or usher those who succumb to excessive outbursts of misery to a heavily curtained private mourning area. In the end, the ritual of the viewing seems clearly in the service of perpetuating a docile citizenry, providing a publicly acceptable forum for controlled affective expression and diligently schooling subjects as to the norms for containing grief.

The money shot, by contrast (homing in on the moment of unfettered bodily expression), epitomises what is sometimes deemed transgressive in porn; as Kipnis contends, 'the out-of-control, unmannerly body is precisely what threatens the orderly operation of the status quo' (Kipnis 1996: 134). In the context of *Six Feet Under* as a series, Viveca's demise is only one of a proliferation of 'money shots', revealing an ongoing preoccupation with the trope of the body out of control. The opening act of each new episode, for example, depicts a death – ironically, the archetypal instantiation of closure. While usually less patently eroticised than Viveca's passing, these sequences provide a similarly voyeuristic glimpse of climactic physical expenditure, moments of departure that are at times peaceful but more frequently convulsive and grotesque. Although predictable in their adherence to a standard format (they invariably start off the narrative, providing a certain structural under-girding for the ongoing and more complex Fisher family storyline), these prefatory money shots actively subvert expectations, playfully misleading us to evoke surprise; we're never quite sure who's going to die or how. By angling for a collective gasp – trying to provoke moments of shock or horror – the images jar the audience into a state of active viewership, temporarily rupturing the seamless suturing process characteristic of the classic spectatorship paradigm. For a fleeting few seconds, therefore, these initial images 'pester and thwart the dominant' (Kipnis 1996: 165) by putting the coherence of the self in jeopardy; as film scholar Barbara Creed writes of the effects of horror on sci-fi spectators, 'the viewing subject is put into crisis…the "self" is threatened with disintegration' (Creed 1990: 137).

This 'crisis' of unexpurgated, surprise visibility, moreover, as juxtaposed with the carefully choreographed ritual of the viewing, establishes a fundamental tension that structures and informs the broader narrative arc of the Fishers' process of healing. The first episode of *Six Feet Under*, in which Nathaniel, the Fisher patriarch, is instantaneously crushed by a bus while leaning behind the dash of his brand new hearse to light a cigarette, immediately establishes the 'shock value' of the money shot: the potential for a climactic end to launch a new journey – in this case the family's – towards self-realisation and genuine mutual understanding. Over and over throughout the course of the series, the Fishers find themselves viewing or acting in money shots of their own; repeatedly occupying positions of voyeuristic spectatorship or unexpected exposure, they enact unwitting visual confessions that force the family members in question to perceive one another – and themselves – in new and potentially jarring ways. (Think of Ruth walking in on Nate giving

Brenda head, for example, or Nate nonchalantly popping in on his brother's VCR to discover – much to David's chagrin – gay porn.) These startling moments of unregulated bodily expression derive particularly potency when juxtaposed with the family's typically controlled conduct, throwing the 'truth' of their routine interactions into doubt. In effect, these interstitial money shots – much like their analogues at the opening of each show – foreground the spectacular quality of self-presentation, the proverbial cat food tins belying upstanding tits.

For the Fishers, further, the question of containment assumes a heightened degree of urgency; the fact that they live at work – and are in a literal sense at home with death – means that they inhabit a space where boundaries are contested as a matter of course. The notions of 'family' and 'business' are tangled into an impossibly complex knot, lashing the Fishers forcefully to cultural codes of bodily control and decorum. Their experiences of inadvertent sexual display and spectatorship incur an added charge in violating not simply the constraints on sex in the workplace – philosopher Georges Bataille writes that the taboo on sexual freedom exists 'to make work possible…work is productive' (Bataille 1986: 68) – but the interdiction against inappropriate (i.e. non-conjugal) sexual expression in the family as well. As Foucault observes, the family occupies an instrumental role in governmentality, serving to contain sexuality – Foucault calls the family 'a hotbed of constant sexual incitement' (Foucault 1998: 109) – while assiduously denying its intra-household existence to the culture at large. The sudden surfacing of sexuality in the Fishers' money shots, then, stands out sharply against the family's embattled efforts to erect and police proper boundaries; consider Ruth admonishing her soon-to-be employer-cum-lover, Nikolai (Ed O'Ross), 'this is a place of business – there are grieving people here. I can't have you skulking around with that look in your eye – that sex look' ('The Room', 1:6), or Claire testily reminding her mother 'there's a thing called *knocking*' after Ruth bursts into her daughter's bedroom to find Claire cursing a video game nemesis: 'Suck on this, you little fuck' ('Familia', 1:4).

Among the most material examples of the Fishers' beleaguered attempts to regulate boundaries and behaviour, of course, are those involving their handling of the cadavers, which – even in death – fail to assume a reliably orderly posture. Throughout the series, the

Fishers struggle to contain the renegade oozing, stinking, farting and shitting that occurs prior to the embalming process; as David snaps to Nate, 'talk to me when you've had to stuff formaldehyde-soaked cotton up your father's ass so he doesn't leak' ('Pilot', 1:1). Like the hard-core money shot, in which the image of fluid spilling over the bodily borders is the sine qua non and explicit focal point, these references to uncontrollable corporeal eruptions suggest a kind of transgressive unruliness; only when the corpse has been laid out as spectacle is the promise of fail-safe coherence fulfilled. The permeability of bodily margins – staunched only as an effect of capital, in the conflation of 'self' and 'sign' at the slumber room viewing – materialises the notion of the body in excess of itself, pointing positively towards the potential for growth and change, towards an ongoing state of 'becoming'.

In the end, this sense of expansive possibility – this struggle to realise a 'true' identity, an alternative, as Claire articulates, to the citizenship mandate that 'you go to college, get a job so you can be a good consumer' ('Brotherhood', 1:7) – cannot be fully visualised; in itself, the money shot is an effect of the capitalist emphasis on image and spectacle. The depiction of the out-of-control body, a response to culturally dictated norms of self-presentation, is also contingent on these norms, serving as a temporary, fetishistic stand-in for the cultivation of self-knowledge and genuine affective intensity. Even in porn, as Williams notes, training the spotlight on ejaculation requires the male performer to temporarily disengage from the communion at hand, 'perfectly embod[ying] the profound alienation of contemporary consumer society' (Williams 1999: 107). What is key to the Fishers' progress towards 'healing', however, is their active response to these visual confessions: their attempts to incorporate the newly gleaned information to fortify their emotional bonds. Edging away from relationships mediated by the spectacular or constrained by convention, they begin more successfully to explore and exteriorise deep-seated, nebulous feelings; as Claire describes, 'I just feel like there's something inside me. I'd just like to find out what it is' ('The Will', 1:2). Paradoxically, then, in laying bare the 'truth' of the out-of-control body, *Six Feet Under*'s money shots impel the Fishers forward on their journey towards deeper and more gratifying mutual connection and understanding, simultaneously exposing the gap between what can be rendered visible and what can be known.

Part 2

Mourning and melancholia: American cultural crisis and recovery

five

American Gothic:
undermining the
uncanny

'America, land of the happy ending, famously has an aversion to
matters of mortality... When it comes to death and dying, the average
American recoils. Hollywood aids and abets, as well as reflects this:
death in films or on TV is mostly dealt with in one of two ways – either
with spectacular, impersonal violence, or with intense, simple-
minded sentimentality.' Thus a British critic hailed the 'surprising'
success of an 'off-kilter "dramedy"... set in and around [a] family
business, an independent funeral home in Los Angeles – ironically
the world's capital of death denial' (Whittle 2002). Such observations
are commonplace in discussions of *Six Feet Under*, including those by
the series' head writer, Alan Ball, who has declared that 'one reason
our culture is so shallow is that we ignore death – we pretend it
doesn't exist. The death care industry in America has become all
about hiring professionals to take care of it all and sanitize it' (Clinton
2001).

But, if *Six Feet Under*'s success surprised the reviewers, its critical
premise should not have. The claim that mortality has replaced sex
as America's most censored subject is itself geriatric, dating back to
Evelyn Waugh's 1948 novel *The Loved One*, Geoffrey Gorer's 1955
Encounter essay on 'The Pornography of Death' and Jessica Mitford's
best-selling 1963 exposé of the US funeral industry, *The American
Way of Death*. In 1968 the historian Arnold Toynbee summarised

these views in the proclamation that 'death is un-American, an affront to every citizen's inalienable right to life, liberty and the pursuit of happiness' (131). Meanwhile, far from denying the 'death care industry', Hollywood exploited its comic potential. Waugh's satire of Whispering Glades Memorial Park (LA's real-life Forest Lawn) was filmed by MGM in 1965, in a comedy featuring a mad cosmetologist, two fraudulent morticians, a suicidal injection of embalming fluid and a plot to redevelop a cemetery into a luxury spa by firing its corpses into space. Less spectacularly, the funeral home figured as the location for the coming-of-age comedy *My Girl* (1991) and its sequel *My Girl 2* (1994). So, neither *Six Feet Under*'s setting nor its apparent social critique are new. Indeed, this historical provenance informs the multigeneric character of its 'dramedy': a family saga wrapped round an already established satire of a Gothic theme – the disposal of dead bodies.

The connection between the funeral and the familial is also long established in America, originating in the Protestant traditions that dominated the country's early culture. Prior to the Civil War (1861–1865), death would ideally occur at home in the company of family, friends, a local physician and – sometimes – a member of the clergy. The deceased's body was then prepared for burial by female relatives, 'laid out' after being washed, shaved if necessary, dressed in a shroud and placed in a wooden coffin. For between one and three days it would remain in the home, often in a front room or parlour, watched over by family members, friends, volunteers and sometimes hired minders. The primary purpose of this vigil was to ensure that the deceased really was dead, as well as to permit the neighbourly visits and social eating and drinking which 'helped to counteract the fissure created by the death of a community member' (Laderman 1996: 31).

Often a service involving prayers or speeches took place in the home prior to the procession to a church or directly to the burial site. There the deceased was interred in a grave frequently depicted as a home, a place of repose with family and friends. This was in fact increasingly the case, as family plots were a frequent feature of the new 'garden' cemeteries of the mid-nineteenth century. And with the liberalisation of American Protestantism across the period, the popular image of the afterlife was transformed from the Puritan spectre of hell and damnation to one of spiritual homecoming. 'Death,' declared the Congregationalist minister Henry Ward Beecher, 'is only God's call, "Come home"' (1866: 232–233).

The transfer of death's ritual observance from the home of the deceased to commercial undertakers like *Six Feet Under*'s Fisher and Sons was largely a consequence of the American Civil War. Its terrible fatalities (more than 600,000 dead of wounds and disease – one-third more than the US dead in World War Two) necessitated new methods to transport bodies long distances for burial. Demand for the metallic 'caskets' developed before the conflict could not be met near rural battlefields. Where embalming had previously been reserved for cadavers used for dissection in medical schools, the wealthier families of the war's victims turned the practice into a profession. By 1863 four embalming/undertaking firms were advertising their services in Washington, DC, and many others operated near army hospitals and camps, or followed troops into the field. And, when President Lincoln was assassinated at the war's end, the techniques of his body's chemical treatment were reported at length in the press and made visible in the public display of his open coffin.

In the years following the Civil War, this commodified management of death developed into the modern funeral industry, supported by a renovated Protestantism that stressed the continuity of the spirit rather than the corruptibility of the flesh. The preference for embalming over cremation also reflected a Victorian fascination with *preservation* – of flowers, earlier building styles and bodies fortified against decay. In the 1880s undertakers renamed themselves 'funeral directors', with a newfound professional ethos ('the keeping of the body to [the] completeness and certainty of an exact science' (Farrell 1980: 151)) and trade journals hawking a range of expensive and ultimately futile products for staving off the inevitable. By the 1920s the funeral 'homes' or 'parlours' of these professional undertakers – complete with preparation laboratories and funeral chapels – had replaced the actual home as the main site for the American care of the corpse.

Only 20 years later, according to Alan Ball and Alan Poul's companion volume to the HBO series, the fictional Fisher and Sons Funeral Home is opened in a large house on 2302 West Twenty-fifth Street in Los Angeles (2003: 10–11). The multi-gabled building, with its mullioned windows, pointed arches and stained glass around the doorway, is patently Victorian Gothic. (In real life, it houses the

Philippine Historical Society.) Its ground-floor interior, as designed by Art Director Marcia Hinds, maintains the late Victorian style, with dark panelling, floral wallpaper, sconce lighting, pelmeted curtains, mahogany furniture and potted ferns. In homage to another Gothic setting, the Bates Motel in *Psycho* (1960), porcelain birds provide a major decorative motif (Trockle 2004: 58). Throughout the first season of the series, the precise layout of this building is deliberately obscured. In Ball's description, the house's family quarters feature 'layers...windows looking in on windows...because the family is so insulated from each other and so sort of repressed, I wanted there to be almost like there's a room and there's a room surrounding the room' (season one DVD commentary).

What is clear from the outset is another patently Gothic motif: the location of death underground, where corpses are embalmed, reconstructed and cosmetically enhanced. In the floor above are the sombre public rooms, in which mourners are received and services conducted. And above this live the Fisher family, in a house that is truly a funeral *home*. Thus the historicised topography traditional to the Gothic novels of the eighteenth and nineteenth centuries and the horror films of the twentieth – the quotidian present over the buried or 'encrypted' past – is revived for a twenty-first-century family firm in its third generation. And that which is repressed is discovered at the deepest level of this structure, in the subterranean morgue where the sons must go about their father's business.

Read like this, *Six Feet Under* becomes 'dollar-book Freud', in Orson Welles's famous description of the manifest psychodrama of *Citizen Kane*. But the film this TV series most recalls is not the 1941 *Kane* but the 1986 *Blue Velvet*, and its hugely conspicuous citations of Freud's essay 'The Uncanny' (1985). Not only is David Lynch's drama of evil in small-town America rife with Freudian symbols, but the primal scene, the threat of castration, sadomasochism, infantile sexuality and male homosexuality are also written directly into its narrative. In one scene a cross-dressed male character lip-syncs to Roy Orbison's 'In Dreams', with its line referring to 'the candy-coloured clown they call the Sandman' – the title character of the E.T.A Hoffman story of Oedipal conflict, castration anxiety and gender ambivalence whose interpretation is the centrepiece of 'The Uncanny'. Not surprisingly, *Blue Velvet*'s knowing anticipation of its psychoanalytic readings gave pause to critics inclined to produce them. One complained of its threat 'to make interpretation redundant' (Creed 1988: 97); another diagnosed the film's 'eliciting of, and desire to gag, interpretation' as a particularly postmodern perversion (Stern 1992: 81); and a third described the film's eminently 'readable' reflexivity as a representation of the uncannily cinematic President of the eighties, Ronald Reagan: 'made-up, artificial and amnesiac' (Mulvey 1996: 56).

Two decades later, with Reagan finally dead and *Blue Velvet* consigned to critical history, *Six Feet Under*'s narratives of 'death and dead bodies... the return of the dead, and... spirits and ghosts' invokes the thematics of the uncanny in what Freud described as 'the highest degree' (1985: 364). In particular, the father's subterranean occupation recalls the experiments conducted by the father in 'The Sandman'. In Hoffman's 1816 story, a curious young boy steals into his father's room one night to find him clad in a long smock using 'strange implements' to fashion human bodies: 'I seemed to see human faces appearing all around, but without eyes – instead of eyes there were hideous black cavities' (Hoffman 1982: 91). In the series' pilot episode, a flashback reveals a frightened boy discovering his gloved and aproned father embalming a corpse. Like the patriarch in 'The

© the authors

Sandman', the father in *Six Feet Under* will himself die, and he too will be 'laid in his coffin...his features...again mild and gentle' (94). Both sons become disturbed young men and both fall in love with beautiful, but rather strange, women. Both are named Nathaniel.

Freud uses the family relationships in Hoffman's story to illustrate his theory that horror begins at home. Tracing the etymology of the German word for 'comfortable' or 'cosy' (*heimlich*), he discovers a strange convergence with its opposite. *Heimlich* can mean 'intimate' or 'familiar', but it may also mean 'hidden', 'concealed' or even 'secretive'. Thus *unheimlich* – 'weird', 'gruesome', the equivalent of the English 'uncanny' – reveals the literally 'homely' root of horror: the secrets of domestic life. The strange familiarity of the uncanny is produced by the revelation of that which is both known and concealed, the repressed emotions of intimate existence. In the case of Hoffman's Nathaniel, Freud identifies a repressed fear of an Oedipal father who threatens his son with a feminising wound – the blinding equivalent in unconscious fantasy to castration.

If death is America's best-kept secret, the funeral *heim* would seem the ideal setting for such repressions and revelations. For Nate Fisher, the repressed fear is that of death – his father's, his wife Lisa's and that threatened by a potentially lethal malformation in his own brain. The fate of an undertaker unable to face mortality seems dark enough for any Gothic tale. Yet, as more than one critic has observed, '*Six Feet Under* offsets the morbidity of its themes with a certain sentimentality' (Lawson 2004: 10; Trockle 2004: 57). In apparent acknowledgement, the HBO Website entry for the series' third season announces it as 'the quirky, sometimes disturbing – but ultimately life-affirming – story of a resilient American family'. Drama or comedy, *Six Feet Under*'s ruling genre is the family saga, affirming the centrality and continuity of kinship itself. Episode by episode, the Fishers' resilience as family and firm endorses the very optimism that its setting threatens. By the end of season one, the family has not only survived the death of its patriarch but also reconciled huge divisions in age, sexuality, ethnicity and lifestyle. In an age of global economic power and a city torn by racial conflict, Fisher and Sons has fought off Kroehner International's takeover and rehired Federico Diaz, the talented Latino mortician Kroehner had lured away. By season three the funeral home has expanded to include Rico as business partner and three generations of Fishers under its roof.

Although the generally upbeat tenor of this narrative is complicated by episodes of a more melancholy tone, these also advance the series' family values. Thus one of the bleakest deaths in the series' second season, that of a solitary middle-aged woman who chokes while dining alone and is not discovered until the smell of her decomposing body alerts neighbours a week later, is softened by the unusual care taken by Ruth and Nate to carry out her funeral wishes ('The Invisible Woman', 2:5). In doing so they not only dignify the death of Emily Previn (Christine Estabrook) but also re-establish the kinship that seems to have failed her. Fearfully contemplating Emily's fate as a warning against her own future isolation, Ruth assembles her reluctant family to become the mourners at the lonely woman's funeral. There, Father Jack (Tim Maculan), the Fishers' own vicar, preaches to Nate, David, Claire, Ruth and Rico that 'every life is a contribution. We just may not see how.'

This oscillation between isolation and community parallels that between repression and revelation in the series' psychodramas. If the individual Fishers' characteristic secrecy seems over-determined by personal circumstances (sexual guilt, adolescent distrust, fear of homophobia) it is also mandated by the narrative deferral required by serial melodrama. The misunderstandings (Neale 1986) that drive its plots and evince its pathos (if only Ruth and Claire / David and Keith / Nate and Brenda knew how much each loved the other!) depend upon an exaggerated reticence that periodically gives way to an equally exaggerated disclosure (often under the influence of drink or drugs). The former frequently supplies the (melo)drama and the latter the comedy in HBO's 'dramedy', with the two often alternating at dizzying speed within single episodes.

An outstanding example of this rapid succession of moods and genres is in 'Life's Too Short' (1:9). The opening death is a particularly poignant scene, in which a small boy's fatal discovery of the gun beneath his mother's bed is intercut with the chat of his neglectful teenage brother Gabe (Eric Balfour) and a classmate smoking marijuana in a room down the hall. When the gun, predictably, goes off, Gabe and his friend Andy (Timm Sharp) can only exclaim stoned curses at the consequences and get the dope out of the house. As always, the ensuing inter-title identifies the victim in the graphic style of a headstone inscription – Anthony Christopher Finelli,

5 November 1994–18 April 2001. The usual fade to white inaugurates the story proper, which interweaves the sorrowful preparations for Anthony's funeral with David's attraction to Kurt (Steven Pasquale), a handsome young dance instructor. Meanwhile, Ruth's lover Hiram (Ed Begley, Jr.) attempts to revive their relationship with an invitation to an overnight camping trip, for which she must seek time off from her job at the flower shop. When the weary Nate, who has just discovered his failure in the funeral director's exam, tells Billy and Brenda about his sense of inadequacy in dealing with Anthony's distraught mother, Vickie Dimas (Wendy Schaal), Brenda points out that there is no word for a parent who loses a child. With the four main storylines of the episode (Anthony's death, David's affair, Ruth's camping trip with Hiram and Nate's anxiety about his competence as a funeral director) established, the pace picks up in a series of short scenes intercut between each strand.

— At a gay club Kurt introduces David to Ecstasy, and an evening of frenetic dancing and sex.
— The next morning David attempts to arrange a funeral with a tremendous hangover.
— Andy tells Gabe's high school friends about Anthony's death.
— David contemplates taking more 'E' to fight his hangover. But when his mother interrupts him, he hastily drops the tablets in an aspirin bottle.
— Parker McKenna (Marina Black) warns Claire against renewing her disastrous relationship with the grieving Gabe.
— To bolster Nate's confidence, Brenda invites him to compare the professional procedures of other funeral firms.
— Claire looks for Gabe at his home and speaks briefly to his wretchedly withdrawn mother.
— In the preparation room, the still hung-over David scrubs the blood from Anthony's fingers.
— Pretending to be the grief-crazed daughter of parents killed in a helicopter crash, Brenda tests the counselling abilities of an amazed funeral director (David Wells), who can only recommend matching caskets.
— As Ruth packs extensively for her one-night camping trip, Claire enters the kitchen with a headache and takes a tablet from the aspirin bottle.

— A second funeral director (Matt McCoy) attempts to take advantage of Brenda's apparent grief by recommending a series of overpriced products.

— When Claire encounters Gabe bringing his little brother's soccer clothes for his burial, he confesses that the fatal accident was his fault.

— Ruth unpacks extensively at the campsite.

— At a third funeral home, a coughing Brenda impersonates a terminal cancer patient arranging her own funeral with the pseudo-therapeutic encouragement of its director, Rosemary (Dale Raoul), while an appalled Nate looks on.

— David fits a soccer boot on Anthony's foot and then telephones Kurt.

— Claire discovers David, clad in a tight black T-shirt, looking for the aspirin bottle prior to his date with Kurt.

— After drinking champagne with Hiram around the campfire, Ruth takes a tablet from the aspirin bottle for her headache.

— David and Kurt meet Keith, David's ex, and his current boyfriend, Eddie (Terrell Clayton) at the club.

— As Hiram snores, a thirsty Ruth gulps water.

— Keith disapprovingly watches David snort drugs on the dance floor.

— Dressed in her nightgown, a dreaming Ruth wanders through a Disney woodland, kissing the trees.

— David discovers Kurt kissing another man at the club and declines a threesome.

— In bed with Brenda, Nate confesses that her impersonation of a dying woman frightened him. 'I will die someday,' she replies; 'we all die.'

These short scenes are followed by two summary sequences. In a continuation of Ruth's dream she and her dead husband tenderly reunite to discuss the joys and failings of their marriage. She then wakes to Hiram's congratulations on her spectacular lovemaking the night before. At Anthony's funeral the boy's estranged father (Gabe's stepfather, Sam Finelli, played by Ted Marcoux) arrives late and physically attacks the youth for his neglect of his son. After Nate evicts him from the chapel, the father confesses that the gun was his, left behind for his wife's protection while he was away. Nate sternly informs him that his chances of being with his son have expired and that his own life is a ticking clock. In a brief coda Ruth returns home happily, to be greeted by Claire and David. She then returns the aspirin bottle to its place. In her bedroom, Claire comforts the weeping Gabe.

Here the combination of the Gothic narrative (the untimely death and violent funeral of a small boy) with its satire (Brenda's increasingly histrionic performances of grief and the funeral directors' variously unthinking, exploitative and smoothly consoling responses) and the life-affirming family saga works to undermine the uncanny. In the domestic setting of Anthony's death, the Oedipal conflict of Gabe and his stepfather, and the uncanny revelation at the episode's conclusion that the 'fateful and inescapable' (Freud 1985: 360) pistol had been left in the house – beneath the mother's bed! – by the violent father, the Finelli tragedy is *unheimlich*. But Anthony's family is carefully distinguished from the *heimlich* Fishers in class terms (Gabe's inarticulate, chain-smoking mother, the deadbeat dad who's been out of touch for years), as well as in their very different relation to drugs (disaster for Gabe throughout the series, sexual release for David and Ruth). Where Anthony's estranged father is expelled from his son's funeral, Nathaniel Fisher, Sr, is reconciled with Ruth in her Ecstatic dream. And his ghostly visitation is not in the least uncanny. As Freud warns, 'Even a "real" ghost…loses all power of at least arousing gruesome feelings in us as soon as the author begins to amuse himself by being ironical about it and allows liberties to be taken with it. Thus we see how independent emotional effects can be of the actual subject-matter in the world of fiction' (1985: 376).

Although 'dramedy' might intensify the horror of death by combining genres to achieve a genuinely disturbing humour, the tragic impact of Anthony's accident is increasingly mitigated by Brenda's comic narrations of the same experience. Similarly, her demonstration that the funeral business – with its smooth condolences and overpriced caskets and plots – is, as Nate concludes, a 'racket' is contrasted with the Fishers' genuine response to Anthony's death. Here the series retains its satirical portrait of the commercialised 'death industry' while directing it away from its family firm, whose reluctance to cash in on Gabe and his mother's grief is underlined by David's insistence that they should not recommend an expensive open casket reconstruction. Yet, in doing so, *Six Feet Under* exculpates not only the Fishers but also their trade, in precisely the way Jessica Mitford warned against in her Foreword to *The American Way of Death* (1963:9):

> This would normally be the place to say (as critics of the American funeral trade invariably do), 'I am not, of course, speaking of the vast majority of ethical undertakers.' But the vast majority of ethical undertakers is precisely the subject of this book. To be 'ethical' merely means to adhere to a prevailing code of morality, in this case one devised over the years by the undertakers themselves for their own purposes.

From beyond the grave, so to speak, Mitford's 1963 indictment of 'ethical' undertaking implicates *Six Feet Under*'s family business in the exploitation it purports to oppose, its profits dependant upon 'that intangible quality, sincerity' (17). *The American Way of Death* also anticipates the series' resistance to the uncanny in its discussion of the then new practice of 'grief therapy', whereby the funeral industry begins to claim a psychiatric imperative for its 'floral tributes' and 'memory pictures'. If *Blue Velvet* pre-exempts psychoanalytic interpretation by narrativising a casebook of psychopathologies, *Six Feet Under* goes one better by narrativising their treatment. Not only are its scripts salted with Freudian references, like those to 'The Uncanny', but it teems with characters who actually are psychiatrists, couple therapists or counsellors, or psychologically minded clerics like Rabbi Ari (Molly Parker), as well as psychiatric patients (Billy) or subjects of psychological study (Brenda). Self-improvement courses like 'The Plan' and Brenda's sex addicts support group (both in season two) swell the psychobabble, which commences in the series' very first episode with her question about Nate's anger with David: 'Are you mad at him, or the fact that we're all going to die?'

Most importantly, as Mitford warned of the US death care industry, *Six Feet Under* represents undertaking itself as a psycho-therapeutic vocation. Thus, in 'Life's Too Short' (1:9), Nate's crisis of confidence is provoked by the catatonic withdrawal of Anthony's mother and his anger by the emotional illiteracy of his competitors. Throughout the series, good grieving, like good living, requires the release of repressed feeling. So the high camp funeral of 'Nobody Sleeps' (3:4) concludes with the bereaved lover, Kevin Lamb (Dennis Christopher), operatically declaring to the other mourners, 'I never thought I would be in a relationship at all...no one could possibly love me enough to stick around. But Bob stuck around' – sentiments that send David sobbing to Keith about their own relationship. Such revelations are not the hidden secrets of the uncanny, the very disclosure of which arouses horror. Instead, these longings (for love, loyalty, a future that's 'worth it') can, and – in the ethos of the series – must be brought to light.

Far from acknowledging death, this grief therapy accords with what Jacques Lacan has called 'American psychoanalysis', the post-war ego psychology 'offered to Americans to guide them towards happiness' (1977: 231). This is achieved by cheerfully denying the insatiability of desire, desire that he describes – citing Freud – as 'borne by death' (1977: 277). Quirky, disturbing, but ultimately life-affirming, *Six Feet Under* both satirises and performs this function. Indeed, the series assumes the very 'dramaturgic role' that Mitford observed in the funeral business, 'in which the undertaker becomes a stage manager to create an appropriate atmosphere and to move the funeral party through a drama in which social relationships are stressed and an emotional catharsis or release is provided through ceremony' (1963: 18). The irony of so exact and unintended a repetition would not have been lost on the author of 'The Uncanny'.

I am indebted to Stephan Trockle for research support on this article.

six

Buried lives: gothic democracy in *Six Feet Under*

DANA HELLER

I wanted to show that these characters are kind of buried... They're sort of living Six Feet Under...

Alan Ball (creator of *Six Feet Under*)
(Magid 2002)

In the pilot for the HBO series *Six Feet Under*, Nathaniel Fisher – husband, father and director of Fisher and Sons Funeral Home – is killed in his own hearse, in a violent collision with a Los Angeles city bus, while driving to the airport on Christmas Eve to meet his son ('Pilot', 1:1). By becoming a corpse and by entering the realm of myth, Nathaniel is reduced to a shadow presence that capriciously haunts the *mise en scène* of the series. His abrupt removal from the domestic scene kills off the figurative authority of patriarchal law and order, thus abandoning the surviving Fisher family, and all questions of memory and identity, to incoherence and disruption. But one of the central ideas of *Six Feet Under* is that such ruptures in genealogies – familial and national – are critical moments in the process of realising and remembering the plenitude and progressive aspirations of the American social body.

Such processes are not easy to set into motion, especially in a nation largely founded on the idea that it is not only possible to elide the ghosts of the past, both distant and recent, but beneficial to do so. It is therefore not surprising that nineteenth- and twentieth-century American cultural production demonstrates a high degree of ambivalence with respect to paternal figures and figurations, their legacies and the stability of the national body in the face of the many disruptive historical contradictions – slavery, Native American genocide and xenophobia, to name a few – that persistently threaten social and political agitation. As heir to this tense and conflicted history, *Six Feet Under* engages a Gothic critique of American family romance. This critique reveals Oedipal stability, and by metaphorical association a seamless and inviolable version of the national narrative, to have always been a myth. For example, at Nathaniel's funeral, his son, Nate, criticises his younger brother, David (who, like their father, is a mortician) for overly sanitising the burial process. David responds angrily: 'You sanctimonious prick. Talk to me when you've had to stuff formaldehyde-soaked cotton up your father's ass so he doesn't leak' ('Pilot', 1:1). By organising viewers' introduction to the series' main characters around the traumatic loss and burial of the father's body, the creator of *Six Feet Under*, Alan Ball, situates the pilot within a long-standing American tradition of 'parricidal textuality', to borrow Russ Castronovo's term (1995: 31), and at the same time sets into motion a critical re-examination of that tradition. The result is a trenchant commentary on the repressed yet 'leaky' dimensions of American society and selfhood.

Such observations will come as little surprise to anyone familiar with Ball's previous work, most notably his Oscar-winning screenplay for the film *American Beauty* (Sam Mendes, 1999). This film rehearses many of the themes that resurface in *Six Feet Under*, including voices from beyond the grave (the film is narrated by a dead man), the hypocrisy of a middle-class marriage and the ineluctable forces of sexual yearning, paranoia and violence that lurk beneath the rose-tinted surface of affluent suburbia. Pronounced elements of Gothic cultural production (including a young heroine who lies about having lost her virginity, and a psychotic villain) give shape to a narrative which, although not a horror film per se, has been described as 'scarier than *The Blair Witch Project*' (Daniel Myrick and Eduardo Sánchez 1999) (Baughman: www.popmatters.com). Many critics have interpreted the climactic murder of the disillusioned, middle-aged hero, Lester Burnham (Kevin Spacey), by a homophobic neighbour as a critique of white heterosexual masculinity. But, more than this, *American Beauty* provides a sustained meditation on all that the national narrative conceals beneath its well-trimmed uniformity: a denial of the messy truth of American history.

This chapter argues that *Six Feet Under*, although not a Gothic text in the strict sense, employs distinctly Gothic conventions in its study of psychic and cultural dislocation, or the 'turns and tendencies in the dismantling of the national subject' (Martin and Savoy 1998: vii). Of course, given the protean and diffusive nature of the genre in American cultural production, the question of what 'Gothic' in the strict sense might mean has remained open to debate. In *Love and Death in the American Novel*, Leslie Fiedler argues that American literature is fundamentally Gothic in character, 'a literature of darkness and the grotesque in a land of light and affirmation' (1982: 10). In contrast to the British Gothic's preoccupation with class conflict, Fiedler reads the American Gothic impulse principally as an expression of Freudian neurotic states, a tradition defined by a pathological obsession with death and a fear of adult sexuality.

More recent critics have treated the Gothic as an ambivalent mode of 'narrating the nation' (Bhabha 1990), or as a means of interrogating the past and of reasserting those histories and figures that have been repressed in American culture. Gothic narrative confronts the contradictions that challenge national ideals of innocence, purity and equality, thus summoning up in Teresa Goddu's estimation, 'the historical horrors that make national identity possible yet must be repressed in order to sustain it' (1997: 10). 'Like the abject,' writes Goddu, 'the gothic serves as the ghost that both helps to run the machine of national identity and disrupt it' (10). Indeed, for a new generation of critics the national machinery is haunted above all by the historical brutalities of racism. Gothic form thus becomes instrumental insofar as it refuses to allow that element of 'darkness' long associated with American romance to function in a purely symbolic register (Morrison 1993). On the contrary, American Gothic reclaims that darkness as the racial 'other', and in doing so reminds us that its meanings are inescapably historical, the mark of a collective social contradiction that is not easily reducible to individual psychological conflict. Rather, the Gothic demands to be understood as a record of the ghostly, repressed and silenced body of the nation.

Moreover, the national narrative represses death itself, or the ever-present 'ticking clock'. The mass culture of the United States is a culture that trembles in the face of the inevitable decay of the body, marketing all manner of youth and pleasure-extending commodities and shunning all contact with cigarettes, fat, disease or other reminders of the body's inevitable demise. American capitalism mobilises vast resources in an effort to defer, deny and disguise death. But death, the ultimate abject, is a central character in *Six Feet Under*. The raw truth of it confronts the Fishers at every turn, both publicly and privately. A new employee, who is fired for being too forthcoming about her private life, complains of the Fisher family 'everyone is so fragile. And can't bear to hear anything. I've never worked in a funeral home that was this depressing' ('The New Person', 1:10). The Fishers tend to deny their more intimate relation with sorrow. And yet, as members of the family are visited by the ghost of Nathaniel, and by other 'dead' characters that appear from time to time to converse with, observe and advise them, they are prompted to question the truth of what they know about themselves and about the past. Viewers are thus invited to view the Fisher family as a site of relentless interpretive struggle. In episode after episode, these struggles play out across the boundaries of public and private, juxtaposing the public performance of obligation to the commercial 'death care' industry with the private performance of obligations to love, intimacy, sexuality and domesticity.

In this way, the 'home' of 'Fisher and Sons Funeral Home' suggests multiple, contradictory meanings. It refers, on the one hand, to a collapse of the illusory social boundaries that ostensibly defend the private family against the brute forces of history and social change. 'This is what you've been running away from your whole life, buddy boy,' Nathaniel tells his son, Nate, when he arrives at the morgue to identify his father's corpse. 'And you thought you'd escape. Well, guess what? Nobody escapes' ('Pilot', 1:1). History inevitably reclaims us all, forcing us to confront not only our own mortality but also the irreparable death of an innocent fantasy of nationhood. Our liberation from this fantasy suggests the transformative possibilities of 'Gothic democracy', a progressive social vision in which abject 'others' direct future narratives of national identity and belonging.

We see this vision unfold as the random strangers whose deaths trumpet the beginning of each new episode collectively suggest a portrait of the nation that is at first aberrant and anonymous: a tedious, talkative husband is bludgeoned to death by his wife ('The New Person', 1:10); a young gay man is murdered in a hate crime ('A Private Life', 1:12); a bakery janitor is chopped to pieces while cleaning an industrial dough-kneading device ('The Foot', 1:3); a Korean woman is shot during a hold-up in a convenience store ('Death Works Overtime', 3:11). As David and Nate come into intimate contact with them through their vocational engagements with restorative cosmetology, their professional interactions with surviving friends, lovers and relatives, and their commercial investments in the 'grief industry', the dead of *Six Feet Under* provide a gloss on the moral shortcomings and mortal frailties of the living. In a flashback, viewers discover that Federico 'Rico' Diaz is drawn to the study of mortuary science following his father's death from a fall, the impact of which crushes his face. Nathaniel Fisher miraculously restores his father's appearance to the way that young Rico wishes to remember him. The power of the mortician's art is that it rehabilitates the surface of social relations. The power of the dead is distinguished, however, by the fact that they – unlike the living – are unburdened of their surfaces, utterly free to speak their minds and acknowledge the deeper truth.

In contrast, the Fishers contain dark secrets that they have difficulty fully acknowledging. David, the responsible 'good son' of the family, struggles to accept his homosexuality and rise above his fears of rejection by family and Church. This conflict is often the contentious focus of his off-and-on-again relationship with Keith Charles, an openly gay African-American policeman for whom being 'out' is a mark of honour. The family matriarch, Ruth Fisher, has been having an adulterous affair with a hairstylist whom she met at church. Nate is obsessed with his health and on the run from adulthood, commitment and family. Claire, the youngest Fisher, is an outcast at high school, ambivalent about attending college and routinely appalled by the artificiality and hypocrisy of the world around her. As the series opens with the shock of Nathaniel's death, the Fishers' secrets begin coming to light and their characters gradually emerge as oddly out of sync with the social values and norms that they would, on the surface, appear to represent.

However, surfaces – and surface narratives – can be deceptive, and this is a point that *Six Feet Under* reiterates not only through its characters but also through its location. The series is set in California, a primary locus of American myth and one of the more prominent sites for the discovery and interrogation of national identity in American literature. While Gothic writers, from Nathaniel Hawthorne to Stephen King, have tended to set their narratives in New England, and while an equally strong Gothic tradition, represented by writers such as Flannery O'Connor, has roots in the American South, the mythical landscape of the American West – and California in particular as a receptacle for all that gravitates toward the farthest western boundaries of the nation and the national imaginary – features prominently in American Gothic texts. This is especially true in cinema and television texts. Los Angeles, which – not insignificantly – means 'the angels', provides a fitting location for Fisher and Sons Funeral Home, itself a border station between the world of the living and the dead. As the origin of Hollywood legend and lore, and as an infamous gateway to hope, youth, success and prosperity, Los Angeles would seem to contradict Gothic decay and terror. However, Los Angeles's culture of the hyper-real and its glorification of celebrity narcissism provide a sinister and mysterious setting for interrogations of the American Dream. The chartreuse hearse that Claire drives to and from school undercuts the very idea of style and enacts a morbid inversion of the automobile as an American symbol of youthful energy, mobility and glamour. When Claire and Gabe (Eric Balfour) have sex in the roomy tail end, *Six Feet Under* challenges the American idealisation of young love by depicting it literally as a frolic in the back seat of a hearse ('The Will', 1:2). And when Claire steals the severed foot of a corpse and hides it in Gabe's locker to avenge a betrayal, the narrative admits to the splintering of romantic illusions by referencing the Gothic trope of body snatching ('The Foot', 1:3).

Alan Ball describes *Six Feet Under* as '*Knots Landing* set in a funeral home' (Peyser 2002: 54). This allusion to the series (1979–1993) that focused on the intersecting lives of five California families locates *Six Feet Under* within the popular genre of family melodrama. However, the constant presence of death eschews the superficiality and relentless camera motion, the soap opera formalism and tight close-ups, that drive most commercial network hour-long dramas. In sharp contrast, the mystery of human mortality casts a constant sidelong glance over the lives of the Fishers. The action is played in wide shots, a visual element that emphasises the human insignificance and existential isolation of characters. In this way, *Six Feet Under* rigorously defies classification according to the standard rules of television aesthetics, playfully remixing elements of popular literary and visual formats in addition to Gothic, including soap opera, family melodrama, satire, comedy and romance. These elements are combined with a realist dedication to the details of mortuary science so exacting that it has won praise from real-life funeral directors (Peyser 2002: 58). Much of the pleasure of watching the series derives, in fact, from this confusion and collusion of the disturbingly real and unremarkably surreal, as when Nate encounters a corpse with an erection ('angel lust', Rico informs him) ('The Will', 1:2) or when David casually exchanges sarcastic quips with a dead porn star while at the same time embalming her discoloured remains ('An Open Book', 1:5). But, once again, to overlook the importance of such dislocating moments would be to miss the point of *Six Feet Under*, as the opening epigraph to this chapter highlights. Indeed, the very title of the show, while referencing the Gothic trope of living entombment, admits to the absence of boundaries between the living and the dead, the desiring body and the decaying body, while also suggesting ambivalence as to the question of whose desires remain hidden beneath the surface of national narrative.

Like the heartland couple in Grant Wood's classic painting, 'American Gothic' (1930), the Fishers appear to be a buttoned-up, dour lot. 'Oh, Jesus! No accident you guys are undertakers,' says Brenda Chenowith, Nate's girlfriend. 'You take every fucking feeling you have and put it in a box and bury it' ('Familia', 1:4). However, viewers quickly learn that wild yearnings lurk beneath this staid image. These yearnings find expression through fantasy sequences. The morning after Claire's first sexual encounter with Gabe, she giddily enters the kitchen and removes her robe to reveal a sequence gown before breaking into song. 'Oooh, what a little moonlight can do-oo-oo,' she croons, with her mother and David providing spontaneous back-up vocals ('The Foot', 1:3). While vacuuming the funeral parlour carpets, David's determination to fully embrace his sexuality inspires a fantasy musical rendition of 'Got a Lot of Livin' to Do', with him at the centre surrounded by male dancers in Bob-Fossestyle costumes ('The New Person', 1:10). The Fishers at such moments appear less on the run from life than eager to embrace it, creatively and passionately. As the biblical dimensions of their name suggests, they are searching for an authentic way to live among others, according to their own inner rhythms, in defiance of a social imaginary in which no female body and no homosexual body is ever appropriate.

And, along these lines, it is worth noting that the dead who populate the basement mortuary of the Fishers' home more often than not die from unnatural causes. After three seasons, or 39 episodes, of *Six Feet Under*, eight of the deaths depicted were the result of murder, two were the result of suicide and six occurred from vehicular accidents. Three of the victims suffocated (two while eating and one while practicing autoerotic asphyxiation), two were electrocuted, six died from trauma to the head, eight were shot, two unintentionally killed themselves and one died from lethal injection. Only 14 have died of illness or some other natural cause, such as old age (Television Without Pity, 2003). The world generated by the opening deaths of *Six Feet Under* is a world of random violence and chaotic mishap, a world in which gruesome tragedy waits, potentially, around every corner. Frequently these tragic overtures are overlaid with black humour and irony. A sleazy con artist dives into his luxurious backyard swimming pool while persuading a mark to invest in a pyramid scheme, and cracks his head open ('The Will', 1:2). A department store Santa riding to work on his motorcycle turns to wave to a group of children on the roadside and is crushed by a truck, as the kids look on in blank astonishment ('It's the Most Wonderful Time of the Year', 2:8). In *Six Feet Under*, death is the ultimate contrivance that lies in wait to reveal the uselessness and fraudulence of middle-class aspirations, morals and cultural practices. In death, we are all fated to become the punch line to a sick joke that was on us all along.

In the midst of so much counterfeit moralising and mayhem, as they strive to embrace their own fleeting and contradictory embodiment, the Fishers often turn to ethnic and racial others who appear to embody (or to have formerly embodied in life) modes of being and desire that are genuine and courageous. Thus Ruth's ambivalence about her new-age hairdresser boyfriend, Hiram (Ed Begley, Jr), leads her into the arms of a Russian immigrant and florist, Nikolai (Ed O'Ross), whose uncomplicated sensuality and unrestrained appetites recall her to carnal pleasures that she otherwise methodically denies, meagrely and neatly portioning out her existence as she meagrely and neatly portions out her food: one pork chop, three Brussels sprouts, two potatoes ('Back to the Garden', 2:7). Nate's repressed misgivings about his marriage to Lisa are brought to the surface by the corpse of William Aaron Jaffe (Josh Radnor), a young Jewish husband and father who in 1975 told his wife that he was going out for a newspaper and drove his VW Beetle off a forest road, where hikers discover his remains 25 years later. 'You are so fucking trapped,' he sneers at Nate, appearing beside him during his funeral. 'You look me in the eye and tell me that sometimes you don't want to get in your car and just start driving and never look back. Come on, I dare you' ('The Trap', 3:5).

Keith is enlisted in the service of providing David's moral/historical conscience, as David battles against his internalised homophobia and his closeted existence. With Keith's admonishments to live honestly and defend himself, viewers begin to see David move towards greater self-acceptance. For example in one episode Keith convinces David to go away with him for a weekend to 'Los Lomos', a romantic resort ('The Eye Inside', 3:3). When they arrive, David is intimidated on seeing that all the other guests are hetero-sexual. In a hilarious fantasy sequence, a man vomits and a mother

© the authors

79

clutches her son in alarm, shouting 'you can't have him', as David and Keith enter the pool area. In reality however, nobody seems to care that they are a gay couple. Keith affirms this when he wraps his arms affectionately around David and asks a poolside waiter to take their photograph. Still David cannot stop worrying that he makes others around him uncomfortable. 'Sometime I just get exhausted by the running commentary in my head all day long about how to be,' he admits to Keith. 'Is this shirt too tight? Is that gesture too flamboyant?' Here David expresses a queer cultural awareness not unlike W.E.B. Dubois's (1994) famous 'double consciousness' of the African-American, or the 'sense of always looking at oneself through the eyes of the other, and measuring one's soul by the tape of a world that looks on in amused contempt and pity' (2). In this way, the series assumes commensurability between the dread effects of racism and homophobia in fracturing and alienating those identities that are positioned outside the national narrative. As an African-American gay man, and, moreover, as a man whose work as a police officer/ security guard carries associations with masculine authority, Keith carries the cultural and social capital necessary to lift David out of his self-entombment. Fittingly, then, in the afterglow of drunken, raucous sex, David bangs on the wall of their hotel room and shouts, 'We're gay in here,' thus signalling not only his evolving critical stance in relation to compulsory 'heteronormativity', to use Michael Warner's term (1993: xxi), but his refusal to be boxed in, confined and silenced within a coffin-like space of his own consignment.

Appropriately, then, Fisher and Sons Funeral Home (or 'Fisher and Diaz', as it is renamed when Rico buys in as a third partner and surrogate 'brother') is an open, public site of intimate cross-racial, cross-ethnic, multicultural encounter and negotiation, an archive of different bodies and rituals that do not easily coalesce within any singular image of the national family. We see this as the Fishers reluctantly comfort an elderly black man (Bill Cobbs) who indignantly refuses to leave the side of his dead wife until he too dies from grief ('The Room', 1:6), and when a Thai family interrogates a puzzled Nate as to his familiarity with the guidelines for organising a traditional Buddhist funeral ('The Secret', 2:10), and again when the Fishers receive the corpse of a Mexican-American gang-banger, Manuel Pedro 'Paco' Antonio Bolin (Jacob Vargas), and are forced to confront their own racist presumptions as they are faced with the task of arranging a traditional Mexican funeral for the young man's family and gang associates ('Familia', 1:4). Nate senses the mutual distrust that threatens to undermine their business with the Bolins. Fearing that they may turn to another funeral home, Nate and David ask Rico, who is Puerto Rican, to work with the family – a request that suddenly racialises relations among the three men and spurs Rico's resentment. 'Why? Because I'm Latino, I know about gangs?' he snaps. Only after David explains that they may lose the funeral otherwise does Rico agree to help. Nate cautions David to keep out of the way. 'We are so white,' he says. 'If we step in we will fuck everything up.'

However, the cultural barriers and racial tensions that prohibit communication among the living are bridged in death, when David receives coaching in self-respect and dignity from Paco's corpse ('Familia', 1:4). During his embalming process, Paco opens his eyes and begins berating David for doing nothing to defend himself after earlier being called 'faggot' in a grocery store parking lot. Paco's encouragements lead to David's confrontation with Matthew Gilardi (Garrison Hershberger), a bullying corporate representative from a funeral home franchise that is seeking to buy out Fisher and Sons. When Gilardi threatens to 'bury' Fisher and Sons within a month, David leans forward and looks him straight in the eye: 'Someday, when your mind isn't on Fisher & Sons, I will find you or someone you love. I'm not saying anyone is going to die. There are tragedies far worse than death. Things you couldn't even dream of, you spineless, candy-ass corporate fuck.' Stunned, Gilardi backs off, as once again the disenfranchised spirits that haunt the can-do platitudes of American corporate capitalism disrupt its historical narratives of self-determination. In the episode's final scene, the Bolins invite the Fishers to gather with them in a prayer circle in the main room, where Paco's funeral is being held. Grief, loss and the refusal to fall prey to humiliation are the forces that apparently unite the Fishers and the Bolins, despite differences of race, ethnicity, class and sexuality. Paco, who is also part of the prayer circle, holds hands with David. His final advice to David, as his coffin is carried away, is 'don't be a bitch'.

This parting piece of advice is important, as it shifts the focus of the closing scene away from the sentimental politics of shared feeling back to the nagging and unresolved question of power.

Indeed, the dead of *Six Feet Under* do not ask for our sympathy; they are presented as objects of ethical enquiry, not as objects of feeling. And, despite its strategic use of the Gothic convention of necromancy, or communication with the dead, viewers of *Six Feet Under* can be certain that the corpses who commune with the Fishers do not truly walk the earth. The rules of the game are made clear: the dead appear only to the living, as manifestations of their inner questions and darker truths. 'They're not really ghosts,' Ball explains. 'They're a literary device to articulate what's going on in the living characters' minds, so I didn't want them to seem supernatural. I didn't want to do any spooky lighting or otherworldly stuff. When our characters are talking to the dead, it's not much different than staring at the wall. When death has touched your life in such a frighteningly intimate way, your entire world becomes surreal' (Magid 2002).

However, as these identifications with the dead who occupy the Fishers' heads begin to mirror the lived identifications that cross boundaries of race, ethnicity, class, gender and sexuality, it becomes possible to argue that *Six Feet Under* constitutes a surreal requiem for a Utopian fantasy of the nation. The logic of this argument stems in part from the assumption that a particular image of white, middle-class patriarchal family life has long served as an extension of a particular political fantasy of the nation, with its unshakeable economic growth and ideological coherence. Anxieties and insecurities about proper gendering and sexual behaviour – particularly in relation to other markers of identity, such as race, ethnicity and class – have remained central to twentieth-century debates over the health of American society and the nation. The truth of one's sex and the symbolic manifestations of one's relationship to that truth are measures of a mythical, much-longed-for coherence that helps hold the nation (and its others) in place. This coherence has been manufactured through what Lauren Berlant (1997) calls a 'nationalist politics of intimacy', a conservative ideological agenda that has personalised the space of citizenship and national culture by making the private heterosexual family the foundation of national survival (7).

Gothic democracy critiques this agenda by rejecting social fictions of naturalness and affirmative normalcy that are rooted in myths of gender. For example, concerned that she and Claire lack intimacy in their relationship, Ruth determines to foster closeness by visiting a recently divorced cousin who has a teenage daughter Claire's age ('An Open Book', 1:5). When they arrive, however, Claire and Ruth find they have nothing whatsoever in common with this insipid, incessantly cheerful mother-daughter pair, who advocate spinning classes and dieting, and whose intellectual acumen is revealed over a game of Scrabble to be negligible. In the end, Ruth and Claire do experience the moment of mother-daughter bonding that Ruth had hoped for, occurring as they secretly escape from their cousin's house at dawn before they can be forced to attend an early morning spinning class.

At the same time, Gothic democracy critiques the ideology of national symbiosis by championing what Rosi Braidotti (2001) has termed the 'teratological imaginary', an imaginary that revels in difference – zombies, mutants and monstrous bodies positioned on the outskirts of normalcy and convention (383). Within this imaginative framework, bodies undergoing transformation by processes of ageing and disease take on a special importance as ontological rebels that express the traumatic yet dynamic instability of the Western subject unmoored from consumerist ideals of perpetual youth, health and glamour. 'It's frightening how much we change,' says Ruth when confronted with an old photo of herself, nude, that was taken in a hotel room the night before Nathaniel, Sr, left for Vietnam ('The Room', 1:6). Yet Ruth's erotic longings are not diminished by the culture's taboo against acknowledging the sexuality of post-menopausal women – a taboo that writers explore in the third season episodes tracing Ruth's unrequited crush on Arthur, the creepy, twenty-something mortician who interns with the Fishers. 'Within the teratological paradigm, ageing and death signify "an embodied difference that has historically been coined negatively – by the metaphysical cannibalism" of a consumer capitalism that feeds upon the desires of its citizenry' (Braidotti: 388). The commercials for funereal products that are woven into the series pilot in this way constitute a satirical commentary on capitalism's marketing of the dead for its own ahistorical reproduction. The 'New Millennium Edition Crown Royal Funeral Coach', is described as 'sleek, sophisticated, seductive', and pitched with the slogan 'Because your loved one deserves the very best in style and comfort' ('Pilot', 1:1). In contrast, the dead of Six Feet Under have no use for the comforting pieties of capitalism, pieties that suggest a culture locked in a perpetual present, in denial of history and mortality. As funeral home directors and as sons newly 'un-fathered', the Fisher brothers find themselves dislocated from the very pieties that they are daily compelled to peddle.

Gothic forms tend to come to the cultural forefront at times of social and economic upheaval. *Six Feet Under* premiered just three months before 11 September 2001, a day that thrust the nation violently into a history that it had too long remained blind to, causing the voices of the dead to resound with a force that continues to traumatise the national imaginary. *Six Feet Under*'s exploration of the everyday consequences of Gothic democracy demonstrates the contradictory powers of the dead to decentre our master narratives and at the same time grant us the kind of singularity that enables the coalescence of diverse national stories, a manner of affirmative dislocation that constitutes a passionately political force of belonging. Alan Ball is rightly ambivalent about our great white fathers' legitimacy as sources of coherent identity, an ambivalence made evident in the opening sequence of *Six Feet Under*, which depicts a cemetery tombstone with Ball's own name inscribed on it. Authorship may be a fiction that grounds us in an illusion of immortality and narrative coherence, but *Six Feet Under* invites us to question the artifices and institutions that sustain an illusory sense of being safe and anchored in the shadowy (his)tory of our progenitors.

seven

Politics, tragedy and *Six Feet Under*: camp aesthetics and strategies of gay mourning in post-AIDS America

Responding to AIDS, gay artists in the eighties were torn between political art that demanded changes and a more personal style of art imbued with a sense of tragedy that allowed a space for mourning. Douglas Crimp gives a sense of the conflict in his aptly titled essay 'Mourning and Militancy', first published in 1989. Tony Kushner's Pulitzer-Prize-winning 1992 drama, *Angels in America*, helped resolve this dialectic between the actively political and the tragically personal. Like two other Pulitzer-Prize-winning works of literature emerging from the subcultures affected by AIDS, Jonathan Larsen's musical play *Rent* (1996) and Michael Cunningham's novel *The Hours* (1998), *Six Feet Under*, which was conceived by the openly gay Alan Ball and first appeared on HBO in 2001, follows in the tradition of *Angels in America*. In contrast to works such as Jonathan Demme's 1993 blockbuster *Philadelphia*, which tried to explain AIDS from a straight perspective, *Six Feet Under* attempts, in the wake of AIDS, to apply the lessons of gay mourning to the human condition by uniting the tragic and the political.

Few of the deaths featured in the series are actually caused by AIDS. Nonetheless, the representation of death in *Six Feet Under* frequently echoes the tropes of the rhetoric of AIDS. Answering the charge, for instance, that meaningless promiscuity caused her death, Jean Louise McArthur (Veronica Hart), the deceased porn star who worked under the name Viveca St John, declares that she loved every man with whom she ever had sex ('An Open Book', 1:5). Alluding to the humiliating loss of bodily control that sometimes accompanies AIDS, Alfred Jones (Bill Cobbs) defines love as the ability to clean up after one's partner has soiled his/her pants in a movie theatre ('The Room', 1:6). This is comparable to the turning point in Kushner's *Angels in America: Part I, Millennium Approaches*, when Louis breaks down because his HIV-positive partner, Pryor, has had bloody diarrhoea in the hall (1992: 48). When baby Dillion Cooper dies of sudden infant death syndrome (SIDS), his mother (Veronica Lauren) asks an extreme form of the question often asked at the funeral of young gay men who died of AIDS: 'How can the beginning and the end be so close together?' ('The Trip', 1:11). When Victor Wayne Kovitch (Brian Kimmet) dies of Gulf War syndrome (GWS), his obituary merely notes that he died 'after a long illness', like many an AIDS obituary. At the viewing, his brother Paul (Wade Andrew Williams) asks one of Victor's former comrades, 'You sick?' ('Brotherhood', 1:7). Private Bailey (David Henry) responds, 'No. Never got sick. I don't know why.' This too is a typical discussion from the world of AIDS, as survivors try to understand why they were spared. In 'The Last Time' (2:13), Nate spends time visiting Aaron Buchbinder (Glenn Fitzgerald), another character whose obituary merely states that he 'died of an unbearably long illness'; although he, in fact, does not have AIDS but pancreatic cancer, his death mirrors the long painful death caused by HIV. In the opening episode of the fourth season, Claire looks at Nan Golden's photographs of people with AIDS as she attempts to develop her own authentic artistic vision, suggesting the importance of the AIDS crisis for modern art ('Falling Into Place', 4:1). Again and again, *Six Feet Under* explodes the rhetoric of gay responses to AIDS and re-uses the fragments of that discourse in a general discussion of death.

The response of *Six Feet Under* to AIDS mirrors the efforts by many artists and writers to break the links between death and same-sex desire that have existed at least since the late nineteenth century emergence of the modern concept of homosexuality. Jeff Nunokawa finds in Oscar Wilde's *Portrait of Dorian Gray* evidence for 'a deep cultural idea about the lethal character of male homosexuality' (1991: 311). Mortality looms in the very title of Thomas Mann's *Death in Venice* (1912), a canonical early representation of male-male desire. The rhetoric surrounding the AIDS epidemic reinforced all these linkages with frightening intensity. In 2004 the Traditional Values Coalition, a conservative religious lobbying group in Washington, DC, still bluntly published on its Website that 'homosexuality = Death'. Crimp has provided a thorough analysis of a number of authors from within the gay community, including Randy Shilts, Michelangelo Signorelli, Andrew Sullivan and Larry Kramer, who have implied that something about the modern homosexual lifestyle is itself responsible for the spread of AIDS and thus linked to a culture of death (2002: 1–26). Given the omnipresence of this connection between homosexuality and death, many artists working with AIDS struggled first and foremost to tear apart the equation of 'homosexuality = sickness = death' (Poirier 1993: 2).

In film, the artistic medium most directly related to *Six Feet Under*, thoughtful directors have also attempted to disentangle the web that connected desire and death. Establishing a pattern that *Six Feet Under* also follows, Bill Sherwood's 1986 film *Parting Glances*, for instance, critically rejects one character's idea to understand AIDS as a modern *Liebestod* or love-death. Politically, gay responses to AIDS could not afford any romanticisation of sexuality and death, thanatos and eros. A 1987 video piece by John Grayson, called the 'ADS-Epidemic' (for 'acquired dread of sex'), directly takes on the literary historical tradition with the line 'this is not a *Death in Venice*' (Crimp 2002: 79). If artists were to avoid suggesting that homosexuality caused AIDS, they would have to disavow the strong linkage between death and same-sex desire that was part of the West's cultural heritage.

Six Feet Under scrupulously avoids the pitfalls of linking same-sex desire and death. In no way is the gay community seen as excessively sexual or particularly kinky. If anything, the gay David is the most uptight sexually. In contrast, Nate Fisher has had lots of girls in his life, including Brenda Chenowith, with whom he has sex in a closet before he even knows her name. Brenda, in fact, becomes a full-fledged sex addict. Claire Fisher is the one experimenting with crystal meth because her boyfriend, Gabe Dimas (Eric Balfour), says it makes sex more exciting. Even Ruth Fisher overcomes her inhibitions to have an active sex life. There is not a sense in *Six Feet Under* that sexuality per se is a danger needing suppression, or that homosexuals in particular are introducing some kind of virus into an otherwise healthy community. Indeed, that community – white, bourgeois America – is shown as deeply unhealthy and in need of reform. In general, the series rejects sentimental portrayals of the traditional family. Flashbacks to home movies merely underline the wounds of childhood – the way, for instance, that both David and Claire feel, for different reasons, that their father neglected them. Although the first season ends with a redemptive family festivity ('Knock, Knock', 1:13), it is Federico Diaz's family, and thus distinct in terms of culture and class from the Fishers.

Rejecting the imposed linkage between homosexuality and death, many in the gay community relied on the camp tradition to confront the horrors of AIDS. Rosa von Praunheim's 1985 film *A Virus Knows No Morals*, for instance, brings a dark sense of humour to something deadly serious. In this early German response to AIDS, biting laughter accompanies the critique of almost every major societal institution: medical scientists, represented by 'Dr Blood', who works at the 'Institute for Pestilence, Plague and Death', candidly admit that as many people will live off AIDS (through government research grants, for example) as die of the disease; nurses bet on which patients will die first; and religious characters masturbate to images of Boris Becker in their closets. Through it all, a drag queen chorus encourages safe sex as they sing songs such as 'You've Got Your Future in Your Hands' (sung to the tune of 'You've Got the Whole World in Your Hands'). Similarly, John Grayson's 1993 musical *Zero Patience* confronts the censorious myth of 'Patient Zero' (whom Randy Shilts and others blamed for spreading AIDS) with humorous over-the-top musical numbers.

Six Feet Under carries on this campy tradition with its fake ads, its interpolated musical numbers and its outrageous fantasy scenes. When Claire sings 'What a Little Moonlight Can Do' after a successful erotic adventure ('The Foot', 1:3), her musical fantasy underlines the limits of realism as much as any drag queen. In an article by Virginia Heffernan in *The New York Times*, Lauren Ambrose, the actress who plays Claire, remarks on the particular ability of what she calls the 'Alan Ball world' to balance 'incredible over-the-top moments and then these very truthful moments' (2004: 1). The same article discusses the willingness of the show to tackle 'grand and even garish emotion' without 'ever lapsing into pathos'. Heffernan attributes this aspect of the show to the performances of the actresses. It would, perhaps, be more precise to say that the actresses' performance of gender and femininity allow the series to make major statements without seeming melodramatic – and a camp aesthetic heavily colours their performance of gender (2004: 18).

The camp style has been particularly fond of melodrama, both loving and sending up the outsized emotions and 'sappy happy' endings of melodramatic fiction. Eva Cherniavsky argues that AIDS dramas in particular have made use of the genre of melodrama (1998). *Six Feet Under* takes advantage of this tradition of campy melodrama as it tries to put forth a vision of the meaning of life. Tracy Montrose Blair (Dina Waters), who is almost a caricature of femininity, introduces one of the most moving scenes in the first season. In 'Knock, Knock' (1:13), lamenting the death of her aunt, Lilian Grace Montrose, Tracy cries, 'I've never felt this alone in the world. And I'm used to being alone. I know what it's like. Now I find out that there's this whole new level. Why do people have to die?' When Nate answers her that people die in order to make life important, and urges her to make the most of each day the way her aunt had, he is able to articulate what Ball himself calls the message of the show without seeming excessively didactic because that message is embedded in lightness and humour. In Ball's commentary about the scene on the DVD edition of the first season, he refers specifically to the ability of Tracy's comedic character to move the audience to 'a different place'. Part of the uniqueness of her character is her talent at playing a variety of roles in rapid succession – bright and perky on the phone, then dismissive and businesslike as soon as she hangs up, for instance. The efforts of *Six Feet Under* to answer big questions about mortality work best within the framework of a campy appropriation of melodrama.

In her famous 1964 essay 'Notes on Camp', Susan Sontag describes the phenomenon as lovingly ambivalent and essentially apolitical, which does describe the stance of *Six Feet Under* to melo-drama. The camp humour of gay artists such as Rosa von Praunheim or John Grayson, however, tends to be more overtly political. *Six Feet Under* also has clear moments of social critique. In the first season at least, the bogus commercials for death care products are alienating in a Brechtian sense ('Pilot', 1:1). As Ball states in his DVD commentary on the first season, the ads emphasise both the commercialisation of death as well as the use of advertisements to fund television and art in general. The critical assessment of the commercialisation of death runs throughout the show; Nate, for instance, periodically gives voice to twinges of conscience about the obscene mark-ups in the industry, and he actually acts on the principles behind his qualms when he buries Lisa in the wilderness without embalming her or putting her in a casket ('Falling Into Place', 4:1). Of course, the real enemy in the show is not the small funeral home but Kroehner, a large chain company that uses rationalisation and all the tools of modern capitalism to drive small businessmen out of business. Kroehner, whose representative is repeatedly called a 'Nazi fuck' and whose company bears a Germanic-sounding name, seems to unite fascism and capitalism in a way that conforms to analysis by the Frankfurt School.

The series also takes a clear stand on homosexuality. Homophobia, in the family and in organised religion, receives significant attention as David tortuously and wrenchingly comes out of the closet. When a young gay graduate student named Marcus Foster (Brian Poth) is brutally beaten, the series reveals how deep homophobia runs in American society ('A Private Life', 1:12). Marcus's own father (Arthur Taxier) seems to blame the death on his son's sexuality. When his mother, Patsy (Joan McMurtrey), says that she had worried so much about AIDS that she never thought about the danger her son faced by simply being on the street, she implies that homophobia is an even more entrenched problem than AIDS itself – that AIDS is, in fact, a symptom of homophobia

At times, however, *Six Feet Under* straddles the boundary between exposing social ills and acquiescing to the tragedy of their existence. Its portrayal of social stratification in the United States is unrelentingly grim and offers little hope for change. The wealthy Chenowiths live a life seemingly unencumbered by bills or the need for regular employment. The Fisher sons pursue the family business as if they were members of an undertaker caste. In the first season, Claire's boyfriend Gabe Dimas (Eric Balfour) represents an underclass that seems to have no hope of social mobility. Even Rico's ability to become a partner in the firm Fisher and Sons is the result of an inheritance, not of pulling himself up by his own bootstraps. Because *Six Feet Under* makes no calls for any change in these structures, it is hard to know whether the depiction of this socially frozen society is a political critique or merely a melancholy observation.

Nor does the series make specific political calls for change on other social issues either. While much art and literature concerned with AIDS made direct attacks on political figures important in their own era, such as President Ronald Reagan or Senator Jesse Helms, the characters in *Six Feet Under* rarely address contemporary politics. Unlike much cultural work on AIDS, *Six Feet Under* has few concrete proposals for policy change on any issues that could affect death in the United States, let alone AIDS. There is no discussion of the country's inadequate health insurance system, the poorly staffed drug rehabilitation programmes, or other health care crises afflicting the poor, the young, the old or the immigrant population. This absence of calls for specific political action raises the possibility that the show is not primarily about political action but more a working through of the tragedies of human mortality.

To a certain extent, the political mission of *Six Feet Under* is different from many other works of art devoted to AIDS, because the show is also about the rehabilitation of masculinity in a post-patriarchal society. This rehabilitation is particularly tricky because of the campy melodramatic form of the series. In her analysis of the possibilities and dangers of relying on melodrama to represent AIDS, Cherniavsky argues that melodramatic representations of AIDS position the gay male in a role typically filled by women (1998: 377). Ball must therefore be particularly overt in his focus on masculinity in order to overcome the feminine implications of melodrama. The absence of lesbian characters is symptomatic of the show's concentration on masculinity. The biggest overt anxiety surrounding David's sexual development is not the threat of AIDS but, rather, his endangered masculinity. When he and Keith watch *Oz*, another HBO series devoted to masculinity, the scene that they see involves two characters talking about whether life in the prison has made one of them into a 'bitch' ('An Open Book', 1:5). When the gang member known as Paco – born Manuel Bolin (Jacob Vargas) – dies, his apparition admonishes David not to be a 'bitch' ('Familia', 1:4). When David comes out to Rico, he ends the discussion with the exclamation 'I am a man'. The series' concern about masculinity becomes especially apparent in the episode about Gulf War syndrome ('Brotherhood', 1:7). While the episode brings out parallels between GWS and AIDS, it also seemingly endorses the masculinist and nationalist discourse of the military. The title of the episode,

'Brotherhood', refers both to the male bonding that takes place among the men in the first Iraq war as well as to the bonding that takes place between Nate and David to the exclusion of their sister Claire. In mourning patriarchy and attempting to remake masculinity, the show has a political agenda that is at times quite different from that of most work on AIDS.

In considering the role of mourning in gay cultural responses to AIDS, Michael Moon has argued that because of homophobia gays and lesbians are unable ever to achieve the normalcy that the Freudian *Trauerarbeit* (work of mourning) promises (1995: 235). This is worth mentioning because *Six Feet Under* relies explicitly on Freudian vocabulary, particularly through the Chenowiths. Margaret and Bernard Chenowith are both psychiatrists, while Billy and Brenda have both been extensively analysed. To take one example of the significance of psychoanalysis for *Six Feet Under*, dream sequences function in a Freudian manner in numerous episodes. Although an analysis of the use of Freudian thought in *Six Feet Under* would go beyond the scope of this chapter, it is suggestive that the institution of psychiatry incorporated in Dr Gareth Feinberg (author of *Charlotte Light and Dark*) and the Chenowiths is held up for considerable sceptical scrutiny. The series indicates by its distance from institutional psychiatry that its allegiance is not to normalisation and medicalisation but, rather, to a Freudian discourse that offers the potential for a more radical critique. Ultimately, then, though *Six Feet Under* does not always share the same agenda as other AIDS works, it does promote a political project as it simultaneously attempts to offer a work of mourning.

The importance of at least a theoretical possibility for the co-existence of mourning and political action became increasingly clear for many AIDS activists throughout the nineties. Kushner's 1992 *Angels in America* pointed the way for the possibility of bringing together a camp sensibility, Brechtian alienation, bitingly corrosive political satire, a highly specific and self-conscious political agenda and tenderly elegiac representations of private sorrows and personal loss that allow for the work of mourning to go on. Significantly, it was HBO that produced a critically acclaimed and widely publicised television adaptation of *Angels in America* in 2003, suggesting that the company was particularly open to efforts of artists such as Kushner and Ball. Like *Angels In America*, *Six Feet Under* unifies mourning and politics by relying on a tradition of thought developed in the gay community in response to AIDS. Eschewing conventional linkages of homosexuality with illness and heterosexuality with health, gay artists utilise a camp sensibility both to rejuvenate humanist messages and to call for pointed political action. While comedic alienating effects might have pre-empted any efforts to help readers or audiences mourn their losses, authors such as Kushner are able to reintroduce a sense of mourning and the tragic into their works without losing their political edge. Alan Ball's *Six Feet Under* applies the lessons that the gay community has drawn from its battle with AIDS to universal questions of mortality.

Robert Deam Tobin would like to acknowledge his current sabbatical as a Rockefeller Fellow in Columbia University's Program for the Study of Sexuality, Gender, Health and Human Rights.

eight

Americanitis: self-help and the American dream in *Six Feet Under*

I realized that I knew nothing... In the next instant – after I realized that I knew nothing – I realized that I knew everything... It was so stupidly, blindly simple that I could not believe it. I saw that there were no hidden meanings, that everything was just the way it is, and that I was already all right. All that knowledge that I had amassed just obscured the simplicity, the truth, the suchness, the thusness of it all.

Werner Erhard, who founded the self-actualisation group, est, after having this 'epiphany' on a California freeway (quoted in Kaminer 1993: 63)

'Jesus, just pull your dicks out and measure them – let's get this over with,' begs Claire Fisher of her brothers Nate and David in the pilot episode of *Six Feet Under* (1:1). The problem, she suggests, could not be more obvious. David is bitter that Nate abandoned his family for a life in Seattle, leaving him to run the family business; while Nate – rightly so – says his brother is just jealous. He's also repressing his own guilty feelings, of course. Claire is hardly the only one so psychologically proficient. Nate and Brenda compare their families' neuroses shortly after meeting. Hers is certifiably demented, making his – with his 'control freak' mother and 'wild like me' sister – relatively normal (1:1). Thematically, the show's writers mirror the Fishers by simply laying it out there: a father dies, leaving his sons both resentful and slightly relieved. It is hardly the most original of themes, for either the characters or the viewers. This is, after all, a culture infused with recycled psycho-babble, where widows really do cry out 'we didn't die' (1:1), and everyone – from disaffected teenagers to National Book Award recipients – idolise, even identify with, the heroine of *Charlotte Light and Dark*, the charming story of a barking eight-year-old girl and her therapist.

Way past Oedipus's crossroads, when wanting to kill your father and sleep with your mother did the trick, the characters on *Six Feet Under* battle with a hotchpotch of pseudo-psychological and pseudo-spiritual jargon that is more akin to self-help than straight psychology – and far more uniquely American for it. One can only imagine what Freud might have thought of Ruth's imaginary tome, 'How to Insist Your Daughter Has an Eating Disorder', or the series' mass-market television show *Dr Dave*, the talk show host whose viewers believe 'only makes love when you want to' ('Making Love Work', 3:6). As on Main Street, USA, self-help – of this 'clichéd', 'mass-market' sort – is omnipresent in *Six Feet Under*. Not even minor characters evade its grasp. Kroehner's Mitzi Dalton Huntley (Julie White) has made lambasting 'victim mentalities' a career strategy, and Ben Cooper (Adam Scott), David's short-lived boyfriend, takes beta blockers to relax. And, just when you think you've seen it all (Ruth's 'blueprint', for instance), you meet 'crunchy-granola backpacky' Lisa, who worships garlic as a 'miracle herb' and shuns movies because 'film is processed with gelatine. Gelatine comes from horses' hooves. Hence the global slavery of animals' ('Driving Mr Mossback', 2:4).

While it may poke fun, however, *Six Feet Under* does not, like its HBO cousin *The Sopranos*, stage the psycho-babble only to dismiss it in an orgy of bloody 'self-actualisation'. Rather, it views the culture's obsession with self-help as an almost irrepressible by-product of middle-class American anxieties surrounding success, fear and narcissism. From its beginnings in Puritan New England, self-help has fed America's notorious sense of optimism by suggesting that a desire for success is completely natural and attainable – if you only work for it. The early Puritans published tracts like Samuel Hardy's *Guide to Heaven* (1673), which argued that heaven's gates were open to those who abided by certain values, namely 'work, diligence, and thrift' (Starker 1989: 13–14). And one of the country's founding fathers, Benjamin Franklin, was the Dr Phil McGraw of his time, earning a place in history for his practical guides on how to boost one's social standing and pocketbook. Always a middle-class phenomenon, self-help in the centuries to come gave way to countless functional guides on how to achieve concrete success (be it earning $10 million or losing 10 lbs), as well as to theories of self-actualisation and wish fulfilment that encouraged people to cloak such crass materialism in a vague spiritual power (think The Plan or its real-life equivalents, est and The Forum) (Starker 1989). This unbridled optimism informs the old adage that America is a country not of 'haves and have nots,' but of 'haves and will haves' (Glassner 1999: xviii). Whether through hard work, ruthless stock deals, herbal supplements, chants or what you will, you are the architect of your life.

Given that Dr Spock's classic book *Baby and Child Care* (1946) is 'ranked second only to the Bible in its popularity with Americans', self-help today is still far more than a pastime, and much more like an American religion (Starker 1989: 4). Indeed, six months before *Six Feet Under* premiered, *Newsweek* magazine dubbed this 'the Age of Oprah'. With her 'gratitude journals', 'finding your spirit' segments, and 22 million weekly viewers, Oprah (complete with a television show, magazine and book club) exemplifies the enormity and power of this national addiction (Clemetson 2001). Whether you are struggling with those last 15 lbs, or a presidential hopeful out for the precious female vote, she's your 'girlfrin', as she might put it.

That is not to say that Americans, like the characters on the series, are never sceptical of self-help. Part business creed, part sex manual, part psychotherapy, part diet plan, part ticket to spiritual enlightenment, self-help is America's high school prom queen, equally adored and reviled. Like Ruth, who writes a letter to her dead mother forgiving her 'for all the terrible things she did to me', ('The Plan', 2:3) but then responds to Claire's assertion that growing up in a funeral home made her family freaks by saying 'oh, boohoo' ('An

Open Book', 1:5), Americans are often suspicious that their best friends might really be big frauds. Consequently, while the Atkins low-carb diet is the latest fad (again), Mr Atkins himself is being posthumously scrutinised for being overweight on his deathbed (*People* 2004). And the three daytime divas of self-improvement – Martha Stewart, Rosie O'Donnell and even Oprah – have all been in high-profile trials responding to charges that they are loud-mouthed, controlling liars, if not worse.

Six Feet Under puts this national love-hate relationship on the couch – mimicking it and, at its best, diagnosing it with severe (to say the least) success hang-ups and anxiety problems. In doing so, it attempts to analyse the ironies inherent in self-help, and, consequently, American views of success, individualism and power. If I am really in control of my life, why so many experts? Must I confess to being powerless before I can gain that control? Is my life living up to the American Dream? Is that a valid question, or a narcissistic one? And, if my main objective is to help myself, what do I do with others? In asking these questions, the series performs the logic of self-help, both its silly and seductive sides. The Plan, after all, is to self-help what Kroehner is to the funeral business. Repairing her shingles often leaves Ruth in shackles. But, on the other hand, hearing her hammer away at her family – 'fuck my lousy parents... my selfish bohemian sister and her fucking bliss... my legless grandmother... my dead husband and my lousy children and their nasty little secrets' – is cathartic for Ruth and her viewers ('The Plan', 2:3). So, what do we make of our times when all this supposed nonsense actually works?

'I suffer from that American thing, big-time – always looking around for someone better,' Aaron Buchbinder (Glenn Fitzgerald) tells Nate shortly before he dies at 26 of pancreatic cancer ('I'll Take You', 2:12). While Nate assures him it is not too late to connect with someone, Aaron brushes him off. A drive for success, a diagnosis of it as a problem, and yet an inability to escape the desire for someone, *something*, better, is both the primary force driving self-help America and the central plot of *Six Feet Under*. Nearly all the characters suffer from this 'American thing' – from David's vision of sending out 'Ben and David' Christmas cards, to Keith's frustration with his meaningless security job, to Claire's art school, to Rico's insecurity about providing his family a good, middle-class life. Nate, however, breaks the mould. He spends most of the third season second-guessing his decision to marry Lisa. In 'The Trap' (3:5) – and in classic self-help fashion – he envisages himself in his better life, speeding around in his car, completely carefree, smoking, even listening to – no joke – a song about being 'not dead yet'. When he awakes he is outside, sneaking a smoke.

As these examples suggest, the meaning of 'success' is not always easy to define. 'I came out of the closet...I'm in a committed relationship,' David tells Father Jack. 'So, I don't know, shouldn't my life be better?' ('Twilight', 3:12). The fear of having missed opportunities, or let other lives pass you by, often contributes to the show's melancholy tone. 'I got pregnant the first time I'd ever had sex. It changed my life for ever,' Ruth tells Claire, confessing also that she 'used to' wonder how life would have been different ('Everyone Leaves', 3:10). Most revealing, this perpetual longing only gets worse as things seem to get better – as if American optimism is propped up only by a fear of falling. It is after Vanessa and Rico become solidly middle class, with a house, an inheritance and a partnership with Fisher and Sons, that Vanessa becomes clinically depressed. And during Lisa's cringe-inducing massage session with Brenda, she breaks down into tears, saying that her 'life has never been so good' ('Tears, Bones and Desire', 3:8).

Interestingly, it was this sort of unqualified, general anxiety that contributed to the rise of the self-help market in America. Much of the 'success literature' of the late nineteenth century, Steven Starker in his book *Oracle at the Supermarket: The American Preoccupation with Self-Help Books* (1989) suggests, was in response to a growing sense that 'America had become too civilized, too complicated, too loud and too fast; it challenged and exceeded the nervous capabilities of many of its citizens...[indeed] increased democracy and liberty in America burdened citizens with too many difficult choices' (33). The result was an array of 'lesser nervous afflictions', many of which we see on the series like 'anxiety, tension, headache, insomnia...alcohol abuse, and simple unhappiness' (32). Living the American Dream – whatever it may be – is stressful; so much so that a German physician visiting the country at the time called the 'new' disease 'Americanitis' (34).

Anxiety still plagues Americans today. According to Barry Glassner, author of *The Culture of Fear* (1999), Americans are more uptight than ever – particularly about the idea that their life may end before they really had a chance to live it. Citing a study that calculated the number of supposed illnesses affecting Americans – from heart disease (59 million) to migraines (53 million) – Glassner concludes that it was 'determined that 543 million Americans are seriously sick – a shocking number in a nation of 266 million inhabitants' (Glassner 1999: xii). One of the more ironic elements of self-help is that, while it professes to free you from anxiety (with titles such as *How to Achieve Security, Confidence and Peace; How to Avoid Stress Before it Kills You*; and *How to Beat Death*), it often induces it (Starker 1989: 2). In the pilot, Ruth worries about 'death traps' like smoking and reminds Nathaniel, seconds before his fatal crash, to take his blood pressure medicine (1:1). And even Keith's partner (Eric Bruskotter) in the police force spouts new age jargon when he warns Keith that 'you keep everything bottled up inside you. That's not good. That creates cancer' ('The Invisible Woman', 2:5). Similarly, characters frequently substitute 'security' for 'happiness'. 'I loved that you were a cop,' David tells Keith ('I'm Sorry, I'm Lost', 3:13). 'The thought of being with you made me feel safe. Though I can't imagine what I thought I needed protection from.'

Though the characters frequently spout self-help jargon, like many Americans, they still remain highly suspicious of the genre. Nate is grateful that with Lisa, unlike his previous girlfriends, he doesn't have to walk through a 'minefield of her childhood', dotted with signs reading 'Caution: unexplored daddy issues everywhere' ('Making Love Work', 3:6). And Claire's scepticism is forever jammed in high gear. 'I wish that, just once, people wouldn't act like the clichés that they are' ('The Foot', 1:3). But Brenda, who regularly calls self-help on its narcissistic and herd-like tendencies, is the most cynical. She has an allergic reaction to Nate's assumption that she's writing a memoir, 'the story of your fucked-up childhood, but from your point of view' ('The Invisible Woman', 2:5); and, while writing her novel, the words 'All you do is observe yourself' appear on the screen. Later, she envisages her therapist Dr Michaelson (Kim Myers), recommended by Melissa (Kellie Waymire) to help her overcome her 'sex addiction', saying: 'You don't need any help. You've clearly evolved beyond the need for therapy. I'm actually in awe of you. Because I'd be fucking strangers like a truck-store whore on crack if I wasn't so inhibited by my pathetic Judeo-Christian upbringing' ('The Secret', 2:10). Among other things, Brenda confronts here a central paradox of self-help. If having sex with multiple men makes her happy, why should she be anxious about it? Nate is in a similar situation. Although his marriage is stifling, he feels obligated to enjoy the sense of safe success that it is supposed to provide. So, he wonders rightly, is happiness in America simply complacency masquerading as achievement?

Despite these concerns, self-help still manages to seduce. Hence Olivier, the self-help maestro extraordinaire, who encourages his captive audience of art students to listen to themselves and their hearts above all, but to do so while hanging on his every word and running his errands. Claire eventually calls Olivier on his contradictions, but not before he woos her and her boyfriend. Even disbelieving Brenda joins a 12-step programme and *almost* confesses to being powerless and living life as if it were just 'one long hot fuck with God' ('The Last Time', 2:13). And in the fourth season, she decides to become a therapist, in a 'if you can't beat 'em, join 'em' move. At other times, the ability to choose or not choose to live a life without maxims is in doubt. 'I always thought by being gay I'd avoid fucking my mother,' Keith tells couples counsellor Frank Muehler (Arye Gross). 'But I guess that's not the case' ('You Never Know', 3:2). You can critique it but you cannot escape it. Self-help is who we are.

A more complex – and important – question than whether the characters succumb to self-help is whether the show's creators do. To a certain extent, all the psycho-babble seems to make the writers more nauseous than Claire at a high school pep rally. For one thing, they often portray self-help as purely market-driven. 'People'll want to read that!' Nate says of Brenda's tell-all non-memoir ('The Invisible Woman', 2:5). In the next episode, Sarah, Ruth's bohemian sister, treats tarragon that she buys from the high-end coffee shop Dean and DeLuca as though it were a herbal supplement from the gods. '[They] have these fantastic spices in test tubes – very mad scientist!' she boasts to Ruth ('In Place of Anger', 2:6). The writers are also not above taking easy shots at self-help in all its silly, self-righteous glory. Lisa's boss Carol (Catherine O'Hara) swims naked to feel like a 'warrior' ('Perfect Circles', 3:1), and must eat cake in a 'safe white place' ('The Eye Inside', 3:3). In couples therapy, Keith and David learn to share their feelings about *everything*. 'Okay, I [felt] shamed,' David tells Keith while making dinner, 'when you said I already added pepper' ('Perfect Circles', 3:1). Finally, the show's creators frequently suggest that self-help is simply a cliché, even a cliché of a cliché. 'The death of romance in a regimented artificial world – lovely,' says Sarah of what she thinks is art created by Claire (but is, instead, something Claire rescued from the rubbish), because it takes a new age drama queen to know one ('In Place of Anger', 2:6).

Yet the characters are not the only walking, talking, self-hating clichés around. For all their jabs, the show's creators have given *Six Feet Under* a rather derivative form as well, particularly in its adoption of soap opera tropes. Alan Ball, the show's creator, has called it '*Knot's Landing* in a funeral home' (quoted in Gamson 2001). And the insular, incestuous world of the series more closely resembles a soap opera than any other show on HBO, such as *The Sopranos*, *Sex and the City* and *The Wire*, which emphasise how work and friends can either supplement or replace traditional families. This is not so on *Six Feet Under*, where brothers plant wet kisses on sisters and sons picture their mothers in their beds. This unremitting focus on the family is in line with the ethic of self-help, which, Wendy Kaminer claims in her scathing critique of it, *I'm Dysfunctional, You're Dysfunctional* (1993), supports the idea that 'unhappiness begins at home…No soap-opera is more compelling than our own' (12). Soap operas and self-help also seem philosophically linked in the series, given that the fragments of soap operas that the *characters themselves* watch in the show contain moments that mimic self-help mantras. Accurately differentiating sentences like 'we always end up in a universe in which we exist' ('Perfect Circles', 3:1) from ones like 'you must open the door. Put out the flames…invite your father to come visit you' ('The Plan', 2:3) is an impossible task.

But nothing resembles the soap opera more than the outlandish and unlikely plots in *Six Feet Under*. Laura Miller of *Salon* names a few: in addition to 'perilous brain surgery…we've had such other classic soap devices as the sudden appearance of a baby…a surprise inheritance…and the startling return of the dangerous Billy, the crazy but now medicated brother of Nate's girlfriend Brenda, from the institution where he'd been socked away' (Miller 2002). To this we could add missing persons, dental records and run-ins with the Russian mob. These plot devices are more complicated than they may initially seem, particularly as they relate to our discussions of self-help. While much of the show suggests the need to disarm or at least debunk clichés, these storylines do the opposite. They make the series into a sort of performance piece. Instead of countering the anxieties and fears the self-help market feeds off, this aspect of *Six Feet Under* materialises them. Here anger does cause cancer, or at least costs you your job. Here you can really get a headache and have a life-threatening disease. Here smoking does lead to death, if only indirectly – remember that Nathaniel misses the fatal red light while bending down to light a cigarette. The series enacts self-help themes in other ways as well. If mind really trumps matter, as many psycho-gurus have suggested, did Nate actually will Lisa's death? And, while Ruth sounds like Oprah in the pilot when she snaps: 'We didn't die,' when she says the same thing to justify her quick marriage to George in the third season it makes sense ('I'm Sorry, I'm Lost', 3:13).

This affinity for formulaic plots is made even stranger when we consider the political and cultural context the series came of age in. While the first season ended approximately three weeks before 9/11, the last two seasons aired when language about American exceptionalism and vulnerability were rampant. We lived in a 'new normal' but would prevail. All others were either 'for us or against us', because 'we would not let the terrorists win'. As awful as the attacks were, the rhetoric that followed from politicians and the larger culture was deeply invested in the self-help tropes about success and anxiety that I have explored. Americans, it was said, had never been more anxious, but also never more determined to succeed. According to Starker, self-help literature is particularly adept at speaking to Americans in times of need or social struggle. He quotes a book entitled *Success!* from the turbulent seventies (1989: 142):

> Cities are crumbling and going into bankruptcy, the world's survival seems to hang on the whims of the Arabs, taxes are higher than ever, and poverty seemingly ineradicable – all this is true. But you can still succeed.

This and other works from this period, Starker suggests, emphasised the need for self-sufficiency, to protect oneself against a vague, growing threat. 'Store enough food for one year. Survival starts here!' (143). This sort of 'self-ism' was prevalent after the 9/11 attacks as well – in high sales for duct tape, and hyped-up stories about child abductions (i.e. strangers invading our houses, taking our innocence). National security was of the utmost importance. No matter how simplified the clichés, they were ultimately taken to be true and had to be defended. As David tells Keith in the second season, '[security's] the national obsession. It's the new freedom' ('The Last Time', 2:13).

In comments like this one the series seems aware of the dangerous role of such banalities in post-9/11 America. Nevertheless, in the second and third seasons, the show also seems to re-enact the central 'truisms' of the period – particularly in its actualisation of fears that I discuss above. In the first episode of the second season, which premiered in March 2002, David is treated for gonorrhoea with Cipro, a drug that is also used against certain anthrax exposures and which many Americans were said to have stockpiled after the anthrax attacks that followed 9/11. There are also references in these seasons to the need to prepare for the worst. When Brenda tells Nate that she does not believe in a life after death, 'just survival', he wonders how she can live like that. 'I've been prepared to die tomorrow since I was six years old... [since I] read a report on the effect of nuclear war. I wake up every day pretty much surprised that, uh, everything is still here' ('The Plan', 2:3). Facing a life-threatening force of his own, arterial venous malformation, Nate vacillates from a position of anxiety to determination – riding his motorcycle, running against doctors' orders. His insistence on persevering, on living life in this 'new normal', is highly reminiscent of that post-9/11 trope that begged Americans to go out, shop, fly, do anything so that the terrorists would not win. And, AVM-free in the third season, Nate seems to have beaten his enemy through the grace of God, blind luck – or just through sheer American determination to succeed.

The need for security, or, more specifically, to protect yourself from others, is also a theme *Six Feet Under* explores in the second and third seasons. Countless characters – Brenda and Billy; Claire and Gabe, then Russell; Rico and Vanessa; Lisa and Carol; and, especially, Nate and Lisa – must choose between caring for themselves and caring for others. As Claire says to Russell, 'I'm not some nurse who's here to take care of the misfits... You're going to have to figure it out on your own' ('Everyone Leaves', 3:10). These are self-help clichés one can relate to. We even agree with Brenda's mother (a scary thing normally) when she tells her daughter 'you've spent 32 years being your little brother's nursemaid to avoid having any emotional life of your own' ('Driving Mr Mossback', 2:4). Further, for all the fun the series has at Ruth's expense, The Plan's 'You are the architect of your life' motto is never completely dismantled. These characters who so often dream of different lives actually attain them quite frequently. Ruth had a long-term affair with Hiram (Ed Begley, Jr) outside her marriage. Her husband also had a secret life – with a secret room, secret records and a secret pot stash ('The Room', 1:6). Even Lisa drinks Dr Pepper (and, we learn in season four, does a whole lot more) when Nate is not looking. It seems that, if you could only suspend your responsibility to others, you might realise your full potential, your power. In both post-9/11 America and in the series, this has a gendered aspect to it as well. To justify the use of military might after the attacks, politicians often evoked masculine images to explain the need to cast off others in order to protect oneself. Borrowing from the highly successful self-help book, one commentator quipped before the Iraq War, 'Americans are from Mars and Europeans are from Venus.' At times the men in *Six Feet Under* seem equally – and sympathetically so – tied to the apron strings of the women around them. Lisa harps on at Nate for everything, from smoking to even (very energetically) killing a snake that came too close to their daughter. Even David confesses that he liked to sleep with women, but couldn't handle their emotional side – the 'Honey' and the 'children's names' ('Making Love Work', 3:6).

Of course, to enact situations or feelings is not necessarily to endorse them. There are numerous counter-examples that would suggest that intimacy and attention to others are a vital part of life. The few moments when Claire and Ruth actually connect are some of the most moving of the entire series. And it is Brenda that Nate turns to at the conclusion of season three, because, despite all the twisted stuff, they need each other. That self-help clichés are at once contradictory, simplified but also often true – as the show ultimately seems to suggest – is cogent. Embracing life today because we could die tomorrow, while not exactly original, is good advice. And, at its best, the series makes viewers realise how much they have invested in self-help jargon, particularly about success. While we sympathise with Nate's frustration at being born into the funeral business, we wonder if being a manager at a Seattle food co-op was really all one could hope for either. Likewise with Brenda, who was accepted by Yale but is nevertheless 'just' a massage therapist – and often an unemployed one at that.

But sometimes perpetual contradiction and incessant irony can defuse the hope of ever saying anything meaningful. As Claire tells Olivier: 'You constantly contradict yourself. So nothing you say ever means anything' ('Death Works Overtime', 3:11). While the show thematises this problem, it occasionally seems resigned to it. At one moment repression is a killer and we are happy to see David defeat it by coming out. In the next moment, however, repression seems the better option, as when Keith tries to confront his violent father, who is only abusive in return. The potential problem with the series is not that it refuses to provide clear-cut answers. There is no art without contradiction. And pointing out the slippery and seductive nature of self-help jargon is a vital gesture, particularly given the politics of the day. Its ability to do just this – and with such elusive themes as success, anxiety and fear – is what makes *Six Feet Under* a great show. But accepting clichés without any possibility of judging them, simply because they may contain a morsel of truth or because they provoke emotional reactions, is a different – and, as we have seen, a politically suspect – matter. 'I think an artist has a responsibility to do more than just give in to every emotional impulse,' Claire tells Olivier ('Death Works Overtime', 3:11). It remains to be seen whether the series will succeed in this truly daunting task, and become not just a great show – but the best.

Part 3

Post-patriarchal
dilemmas (I):
making visible
the female
subject

Emily Previn, 1954–2001

I choked on the life God gave me   /
when Death made a catch in my throat.
There was no one around who could save me,
so I choked on the life God gave me.
There was no one I knew to engrave me,
so a less estranged stranger took note:
I choked on the life God gave me
when Death made a catch in my throat.

She picked out the clothes for my dressing
in the casket I wished open wide,
while her son hated being left guessing.
She picked out the clothes for my dressing,
while her son called me names for expressing
my life as one long solitude.
She picked out the clothes for my dressing
in the casket I wished open wide.

That same woman stood in the chamber
wondering if she would end up like me:
there was no one to call, to remember.
That same woman stood in the chamber,
seeing Death was a solitary number
(and her children all there to agree).
That same woman stood in the chamber
wondering if she would end up like me.

    Peter Wilson

nine

Mother knows best:
Ruth and representations
of mothering in *Six Feet
Under*

Wendy Lesser of *The New York Times* dismisses *Six Feet Under*'s matriarch Ruth Fisher (now Sibley) as being a mere 'doormat for the show's producers to step on' (2001: 28). Comparing Ruth unfavourably to Tony Soprano's harridan of a mother, Livia (Nancy Marchand), from *The Sopranos*, Lesser maintains that Ruth is 'an infinitely less compelling' character whose biggest problem is that 'she embarrasses her kids'. Other critics are less than complimentary about Ruth, including Phil Rosenthal, who describes her as 'the increasingly cartoonish matriarch whose misguided search for direction in her life will become a running gag' (2002). Linda Stasi has no better opinion of her when she says 'Ruth is so wooden, she makes Mary Tyler Moore in *Ordinary People* look like an emoting machine', adding that 'she is a ready-to-explode mess in ankle socks and housedresses' (2001). But is this a fair assessment? Is it not true to say that there is more to Ruth than these critics give her credit for, and that she is far more complex than these initial responses would suggest? Surely to dismiss Ruth in this way is missing the point.

If the narrative of *Six Feet Under* can be defined as liminal, with each episode beginning with a death and ending with a burial, could it not be argued that Ruth's positioning within this narrative represents another kind of liminality: that of the middle-aged, post-menopausal mother with adult children? While orthodox psychoanalytical theorists Other the mother in the symbolic (Freud 1995; Lacan 1977), feminists attempt to revise such thinking by bringing her into discourse (Klein 1930; Horney 1967; Cixous and Clement 1986; Chodorow 1978; Kristeva 1980; Irigaray 1991). Despite such attempts there is still a tendency to reduce the mother to her parental role, focusing on the nurturing, breastfeeding pre-Oedipal mother who has meaning only in relation to her children and nothing else. There is little attempt here to clarify what happens to the relationship once the child becomes independent and moves away. In this instance motherhood is repressed and silenced, invisible to society and reduced to a metaphor (Boulous Walker 1998: 135).

This chapter will examine the complex representation of the mother and the maternal in *Six Feet Under*, arguing that Ruth's narrative positioning reveals an aspect of mothering that is routinely repressed and silenced within patriarchy. If, as Robert Tobin asserts, Ruth is a good example of 'a generation of women who had spent their lives entirely under the thumb of patriarchy' (2002: 87), I will argue that Ruth's narrative finds her negotiating her way through uncharted territory while offering us an innovative subject position which allows the 'unrepresentable to emerge from the patriarchal restrictions of representation' (Boulous Walker 1998: 135).

Just Another Smother Mother?

Superficially at least, Ruth seems to conform to the type of mother traditionally found in melodramatic texts ('Pilot', 1:1). Framed in her kitchen she is surrounded by the men in her life; her son David who assumes the role of the patriarch by sitting at the table, criticising his mother and her husband at the end of the telephone. Flushed and busily preparing a Christmas Eve dinner, Ruth's conversation with Nathaniel is practical and yet critical as she fires off a list of chores for him to do. The tone of this conversation makes it easy to forget that Ruth is Nathaniel's wife and not his mother, as she talks to him like a recalcitrant child, one that must be cajoled, cared for and criticised to enable Ruth to maintain her role as the ideal nurturing mother. It is not long before this representation is rendered strange and our expectations shattered. Arguably, it is Nathaniel's rebellion against Ruth's critical mother's voice that causes his untimely death. Not the long-drawn-out death caused by smoking, but a quick, final totalling of his life, brought about by a momentary lapse in concentration while lighting a crafty cigarette. Ruth's reaction to the news of Nathaniel's death is both violent and indicative of how this maternal representation is going to be much more complex than that of her melodramatic predecessors. Domestic devastation ensues and David is met with the sight of his mother collapsed on the kitchen floor, surrounded by the wreckage of her morning's labour and the words 'your father is dead and the pot roast is ruined'.

If patriarchal discourse works so hard to silence the mother, then Ruth's tone here exemplifies a double register breaking through that repression. Nurturing and yet critical, her questioning and rebuking is reminiscent of the role of the mother's voice in early childhood. On the way to the mortuary to identify Nathaniel's body Ruth asks her daughter: 'Are you having sex? Are you doing drugs?' ('Pilot', 1:1). That Claire is momentarily freaked by her mother's questioning is not only because she *is* high on drugs *and* considering having sex with Gabe but because Ruth picks this exact moment to question her daughter. Freud may assert that the formation of the superego 'retains the character of the father' (Freud 1995: 642) but here we can clearly see how the mother's voice functions in this formation. If the superego retains dominance over the ego 'in the form of conscience or perhaps of an unconscious sense of guilt' (ibid.), it is the mother that gives voice to this authority as the primary caretaker of children. The death of Nathaniel relieves Ruth of this burden. As he appears to family members, Nathaniel articulates their guilty consciences and innermost fears; not only does this allow us access to their interior lives but it releases Ruth from the onerous role of giving voice to the 'law of the father'.

The binary nature of the family home and funeral home further complicates Ruth's positioning within the Fisher family. If the sex/gender divide in modern society is due to 'natural and biological' functions which assume that 'women's primary social location is domestic' (Chodorow 1978: 9), then Ruth's liminal status is reinforced by this uncanny fusion of work and home. Ruth may have been associated with the abject due to her role in the 'primal mapping of the body' where the child learns about its body through its mother's role in sphincteral training (Kristeva 1982: 72) but the corpse is the ultimate in abjection as it is literally 'the place where meaning collapses' (2). In the Fisher home, then, it is arguably Nathaniel and the men that are most associated with abjection, dealing daily with corpses and bodily fluids. As David tells Nate, 'Talk to me when you've had to stuff formaldehyde-soaked cotton wool up your father's ass so he doesn't leak' ('Pilot', 1:1). It is Nate's memory of his father inviting him to touch a corpse that causes him to flee the family business, not the shame associated with maternal authority and toilet training. This notion is reinforced by Nate and David's argument about the defecation of a corpse ('The Will', 1:2). Scolding her two sons for bickering, Ruth ignores the nature of their argument, and neither son shows any of the embarrassment or shame traditionally associated with the abject once the child enters into 'the order of the phallus' (Kristeva 1982: 74). Kristeva may argue that there is a split between the worlds of maternal and paternal authority, but this is arguably not the case in the Fisher family home.

If the 'law of the father' and maternal authority in the Fisher household are confused, then the uncanny grouping around the dinner table reveals a further confusion. Planning a special family dinner, Ruth reveals that she is having a sexual relationship with her new employer and florist, Nikolai (Ed O'Ross), telling her children: 'We're all adults – we're all sexual beings – we should acknowledge that' ('In the Game', 2:1). Asserting her role as sexual woman with the right to speak about such matters finds Ruth's adult children sniggering and behaving like – well – children. Even if 'by 1986, the mother/sexual woman split was healed' (Kaplan 2002:183), there is no such healing for the middle-aged mother/ sexual woman, as '[h]er sexuality simply does not exist beyond her reproductive potential' (Boulous Walker 1998: 136). Safely en- sconced in the family home, their mother taking care of them and with their own sexual lives, the Fisher children reveal their reluctance to accord their mother the same privileges. The first time Claire meets Hiram (Ed Begley, Jr) she envisages her mother having energetic sex with him on the kitchen counter; later David imagines his mother reaching under the table and informing the assembled company that she 'can't get enough of [Hiram's] cock' ('Brotherhood', 1:7). While the Fishers can tolerate Ruth's eccentricities, it is her sexuality that causes them the most consternation and is a good example of how 'In patriarchal terms the feminine should be either woman or mother, never both' (Boulous Walker 1998: 136).

If Ruth's children are reluctant to accept their mother's sexuality it is, arguably, because they want to keep their family intact and unchanging. This dilemma is focused on the *mise en scène* of the kitchen, which, according to Alan Ball, 'is the heart of the home, the source of nourishment and sustenance, the congregating place, the hearth' (Magid 2002: 76). Despite the fact that the kitchen holds a central place in the lives of the Fisher family, and especially Ruth, Ball adds that 'it's not a completely warm and rosy place, because the Fishers live in the constant presence of death' (ibid.). Developing this point further, I would suggest that the kitchen is also symbolic of Ruth's inner journey as, locked in domestication, she gradually becomes lost in her attempt to find a place in the world. Although she is initially positioned as swathed in the warmth of her kitchen, busily preparing the Christmas dinner and anticipating her family reunion, she soon becomes trapped and the kitchen threatens to overwhelm her. 'The Room' (1:6) finds Ruth standing statue-like, gripping a saucepan, with her children bustling about her. 'The Invisible Woman' (2:5) sees Ruth dreaming of her bare house, stripped of furniture and devoid of life; the domestic space here is cold and unforgiving. Low camera angles, wide lenses and sinister lighting turn the hitherto cosy kitchen into an uncanny prison, emphasising the emptiness of Ruth's life.

The double register of Ruth's speech is further evidence that the domestic is a key part of her existence and makes strange her role as a mother. It is not simply that Ruth conflates two registers in her speech but that the clash of tones makes strange her efforts to connect with people. Looking at a nude Polaroid of her younger self, Ruth tells Nate the history of the photo (taken by Nathaniel before he went to Vietnam in 1965), saying: 'It's frightening how much we change. Are you staying for dinner, dear?' ('The Room', 1:6). Ruth does not merely sublimate her emotional state to practical issues but allows the inner conflict between domesticity and personal develop- ment its full expression. David finally admits to his mother that he is gay, and an emotional discussion ensues. Admitting that it was so much easier when they were small, as they 'used to tell her everything', Ruth composes herself to ask if he is staying for dinner. Through tears she adds the non sequitur 'We're having veal' ('A Private Life', 1:12). This equation of food with comfort is not restricted to her children. Hiram takes her out for dinner to tell her, guilt-stricken, that he has met somebody else. Ruth takes the news calmly and tells him: 'Let's order dessert. That'll cheer you up' ('Knock, Knock', 1:13). Refusing the toast that Ruth has prepared for breakfast results in Claire being accused of having an eating disorder ('Pilot', 1:1), and it is ultimately a solitary dinner in a cavernous kitchen that signals the end of domestic bliss for Ruth ('Back to the Garden', 2:7).

If You Go Down to the Woods Today...

If the Fisher family are happy to keep their mother in her domestic role, devoid of sexuality, it is Ruth who forces her children to grow up while exposing the fiction that it is the mother who keeps her children down with her in the Imaginary to fulfil her needs. Realising that her children do not need her any more is a shock for Ruth, but it also illustrates how the sexuality of the mother has to be expelled from the home ('Life's Too Short', 1:9). If it is the *woman-mother* that represents the greatest threat' to patriarchy and 'is exiled to the margins of society' (Boulous Walker 1998: 136), then Ruth here demonstrates the limits of this exile by telling Hiram that women should not go camping while menstruating as bears are attracted to the smell of blood. There is, obviously, a whole discourse here that Hiram is completely unaware of, which reveals the limitations behind the way 'Christianity balances its ambivalence toward woman, its contempt and idealisation in the figures of Mary and Eve' (ibid.). If Eve's 'aggressive sexuality' (ibid.) is to be contained in nature then it is only when she is not demonstrating her ability to reproduce that she is safe in doing so. Ruth's ecstatic midnight wandering reveals the rampant sexuality hidden beneath her prim, repressed façade. Hallucinating her dead husband, she tells him that she misses what they had, to which he replies, 'Well, go find it again.' The next morning Hiram tells a flushed Ruth that she had never before been so passionate with him. Ruth's laugh here is reminiscent of the 'Laugh of the Medusa' outlined by Hélène Cixous (1980), and while it is clearly a source of discomfort for Hiram it is also a warning of what lies hidden beneath Ruth's repressed exterior.

If Ruth's sexuality is initially positioned as akin to nature and outside the domestic environment, what of the other side of the binary, the 'domesticated image of the Virgin Mary, the mother devoid of sexual desire' (Boulous Walker 1998: 136)? We first see this side of Ruth in the pilot episode the day after her hysterical confession of a long-standing affair at Nathaniel's funeral. Now composed, with hair loose, she asks Nate to stay for a few more days. Evoking the memory of the idealised mother of Nate's childhood, Ruth gets her own way. Waiting for the outcome of Nate's surgery ('The Last Time', 2:13), Ruth, hair flowing, is clearly situated as the ideal mother surrounded by her children, and is reminiscent of Michelangelo's 'Pieta', the iconic sculpture of maternal suffering. Discovering that she is grandmother to Nate's daughter Maya, ('I'll Take You', 2:12) gives Ruth a chance to relive a part of her life that she had so reluctantly left behind. Happily falling back into the role of nurturing mother, cradling her granddaughter, hair loose and tousled, Ruth is positioned as the Madonna, the ultimate icon of idealised maternity. This positioning may initially seem unproblematic and in keeping with the binary of Virgin Mary / Eve that I have argued is traditionally sanctioned by patriarchy, but Ruth's assertion that 'a woman's hair is the gateway to her sensuality' ('The Eye Inside', 3:3) retrospectively problematises this assumption and hints at Ruth's grasp of her positioning, along with her ability to manipulate it.

Speaking Fiercely From the 'I'

Ruth may be aware of how she is positioned but it is clearly not going to be an easy escape for her. Having tried many strategies to fill the void left by the death of Nathaniel, Ruth finds herself at a meeting of 'The Plan' ('Out, Out, Brief Candle', 2:2) and is clearly attracted to the idea that she can achieve self-fulfilment regardless of her own unhappy past. Moved by the graduation speeches, especially from a 41-year-old woman who speaks 'fiercely from the "I"', Ruth seizes her chance to achieve similar subjectivity, and later that day confronts Nate and David about the whereabouts of the $93,000 she invested in the business. Seeing the new casket wall recently purchased by her sons, she indignantly demands to know how they paid for it and asks to see receipts and accounts. To the bemusement of her sons she tells them, 'I am speaking *fiercely* from the "I"', and fierce she is: body shaking, clenched fists and an angry expression on her face.

Unaccustomed to this kind of power she asks, 'Do you mind?' before leaving the room with a flourish.

'The Plan' (2:3) proves to be cathartic for Ruth, and her angry outburst at the seminar the following day sees her again speaking fiercely from the 'I'. Clearly exhilarated by her success, Ruth seizes on this discourse and spends the next episode forgiving old enemies and speaking to her family in building metaphors. It is not until she discusses Keith's niece, Taylor (Aysia Polk), with David that he is moved to tell her: 'Mom, I'm happy for you if this whole Plan thing of yours has enabled you to draft your own blueprint or patch up some of the cracks in your foundation but...just between you and me you're starting to sound like a crazy person and I think it's time you kept that shit to yourself and minded your own fucking business' ('Driving Mr Mossback', 2:4). While her children are tolerant of Ruth's eccentricities and accept her as an adult with the right to have her own life, here she goes too far; the combination of the mother's critical voice and the subjectivity accorded it by the Plan makes this a voice too powerful to be accepted by her family. The Plan may promise happiness but it does not offer an unproblematic solution to Ruth's dilemmas, and, further, it does not offer a solution to her repressed and silenced positioning within society and her family. As if to emphasise this, 'The Invisible Woman' (2:5) shows Ruth, alone, contemplating old photos of her young family. It is a moment of pure despair as it becomes clear to Ruth that her role as a 'stay at home' mother has become redundant. Obviously, this is the downside to an occupation so lauded by society, and, with the repression of mothering in culture, is something that rarely finds representation. Left alone, Ruth faces the reality of her situation and loses hope of ever finding her subjectivity again.

The arrival of her granddaughter seems to offer Ruth an opportunity to relive the part of her life that she so obviously mourns. However comfortable Ruth may feel, Maya is not *her* child, and it is not long before the cracks begin to appear in her relationship with her new daughter-in-law, Lisa. Unaware of how mothering has changed in the past 30 years, Ruth feeds her granddaughter peanut butter ('Perfect Circles', 3:1). Lisa phones her and agitatedly informs her mother-in-law the error of her ways. Apologising, Ruth explains that peanut butter was never a problem when her children were young. This simple defence of her actions shows the intransigent position occupied by Ruth. Having been a mother in the late sixties and seventies does not prepare her for being a grandmother now, and Ruth is clearly made redundant by her ignorance of the mothering skills expected in the twenty-first century. Dr Spock may have been good enough to dispense wisdom to mothers of Ruth's generation, but here Lisa reveals how the ideology of mothering has completely changed. In order to continue her role as childminder to Maya, Ruth will have to educate herself into what is expected from modern mothers and carers. This brutal fact shocks her into realising that, not only is she finding it impossible to re-insert herself into society, but also that she can no longer rely on the now outdated mothering skills that have carried her through her key role in life.

'The Eye Inside'

It is Bettina (Kathy Bates) who temporarily rescues Ruth from this untenable position – a straight-talking, irreverently mischievous woman who embodies the transgressive possibilities of the unruly woman. Kathleen Rowe suggests that the unruly woman's power comes not from the fact that she signifies castration but rather that she threatens patriarchal belief systems. 'What most threatens that set of beliefs is not (or is not *only*) the vagina, but the female mouth and its dangerous emanations – laughter and speech' (1995: 43). Ruth is appalled when Bettina steals a scarf on their shopping trip ('The Eye Inside', 3:3). Confidently confiding in Ruth that 'fortunately women our age are invisible, so we can really get away with murder', it is clear that Bettina is aware of the fact that in society's eyes both she and Ruth not only are invisible but occupy a liminal space. The shopping trip proves instructive, as the banter between the two women shows us a side of Ruth that has been hidden up until now. Shoplifting a lipstick, Ruth begins to embrace her liminal status, while tentatively, with Bettina's guidance, she begins to uncover the woman that has been submerged under her all-encompassing role as mother.

'Nobody Sleeps' (3:4) sees the complete transformation of Ruth under the tutelage of Bettina. If motherhood is to be the focus this week, then Lisa's problematic path towards her 'nurturing mother' role is contrasted with Ruth's trajectory out of it. Waking in his marital bed, Nate attempts to rouse Lisa. To his horror it is Ruth purring sexually at his side, and not his wife. Of course, the classic Freudian interpretation of such a dream is of the son's Oedipal desire for the mother – and we soon discover that Nate's nightmare is becoming a reality when Ruth and Lisa are framed together in the kitchen, looking uncannily alike. It would seem that Nate's dream is not simply about his desire for his own mother but shows a tentative understanding of just how his Oedipal journey has led him to repeat his father's life. The sins of the father are not only revisited on Nate, however, as it becomes clear how this repetition impacts upon women. Being cared for by Lisa and befriended by Bettina, Ruth is shown a way out of the rigidity of her roles. From the 'Pilot' episode onwards Ruth has struggled with split subjectivity – mother to her family and sexual woman to her lover and hairdresser, Hiram. While she has, in some ways, managed to merge these subjectivities, the introduction of Bettina's unruliness and Lisa's nurturing unleashes a merging of all her past selves and underlines Rowe's assertion that the unruly woman's 'rebellion against her proper place not only inverts the hierarchical relation between the sexes but unsettles one of the most fundamental of social distinctions – that between male and female' (1995: 43). Laughingly revealing uncomfortable truths about herself and her sons, Ruth crosses a line and forces them to reveal *their* repression. Not only does she cross the line of family secrets laid bare but she also tipsily crosses the line between funeral and family home and death and life. Languishing on the set of the following day's funeral, Bettina and Ruth enact their own deaths, and later, accompanied by a now awake Maya and a merry Lisa, dance to the words 'I'm an ordinary girl. Burning down the house. Wait till the party's over.' It should be clear enough that Ruth's Medusan laugh in 'Life's Too Short' (1:9) has come full circle, found its joyful expression and signals the death of the old Ruth.

*   *   *

It is clear that Ruth still has many mistakes to make despite her liberation by Bettina. Her friend's departure in 'The Trap' (3:5) leaves Ruth alone again. Impulsively hugging Bettina on the stairs the women observe Arthur Martin, the new apprentice who will provide Ruth with an alternative focus for her newly unleashed self. It should be no surprise that Ruth becomes a voyeur over the course of season three; after all, she has attained a new symbolic status and '*her* desire sets things in motion' (Kaplan 1993: 204). Stalking Arthur, she actively pursues her desire, kissing him unexpectedly on the lips and then doing it again despite his protestations ('Tears, Bones and Desire', 3:8). Regardless of his six previous marriages, Ruth impulsively proposes to George Sibley out of loneliness, and shows us that Ruth may have completed a journey but, in many ways, she is still repeating old patterns ('Twilight', 3:12). Marriage may not be made in heaven but it does fulfil Ruth in many ways; and it is one way of ensuring adult company and a fulfilled sexuality. Lisa's death at the end of season three also returns Ruth to a mothering role, albeit that of surrogate mother to the now motherless Maya. The patriarchal family may be reconfigured but it again promises to test the limits of Ruth's liminal positioning.

Kaplan suggested as long ago as 1983 that 'the Mother offers a possible way to break through patriarchal discourses since she has not been totally appropriated by dominant culture' (1993: 11). It is clear that the death of the patriarch in *Six Feet Under* allows representations of mothering, and especially the middle-aged mother, to become, for better or worse, reconfigured. Emerging from the death of her husband, Ruth's journey towards a new symbolic role clearly problematises many assumptions about the maternal role along the way. Ruth's narrative may not be particularly revolutionary (after all, she does marry a man who receives faeces in the post ('In Case of Rapture', 4:2) rather than enduring a life of loneliness), but the fact that Ruth has a narrative at all is due to the fact that *Six Feet Under* lifts the lid on repression and exposes numerous liminal spaces for us to see. It seems to me that steeping each narrative in the omnipresent threat of death allows traditionally taboo and dangerous areas safe expression. Ruth's narrative may not tell us if mother knows best, but it does give us a rare and honest glimpse into her world.

ten

'Like, whatever': Claire, female identity and growing up dysfunctional

Let's face it: Claire Fisher is a mess. She takes crystal meth, is in the habit of falling for unsuitable and often highly unstable young men, pinches a severed cadaver foot to place in a classmate's locker for lovelorn reasons, is suspected of being an arsonist and has had an abortion. Critics agree she is acting out – a teenage rebellion put down to the sudden death of the father she had yet to know (Leonard 2001: 93; O'Hehir 2002). But are her 'mistakes' the blunders of a grieving daughter dealing with the loss of her father, or a symptom of a confused young woman groping for an identity in a post-feminist, post-patriarchal world?

Being a series that takes the demise of the paterfamilias as its starting point, *Six Feet Under* offers, superficially at least, a unique opportunity for producing a female subject who is beyond patriarchal constraints. But, and as I shall argue, this is no easy task. This chapter traces the complex narrative territory negotiated by Claire Fisher as she seeks to understand who she is – an uneasy journey from perceived invisibility to troubled teenager and struggling artist. An unexpected addition to the Fisher clan, born some 14 years after David, Claire feels that she has missed out. No one noticed her growing up: her elder brother had left home, her other sibling was closed down and closeted, her father too busy with dead bodies in the basement, her mother preoccupied with keeping house, and her family home full of grieving strangers. All this changes when a city bus ploughs into her father's new hearse, instantly killing him. Suddenly everyone is taking a keen interest in her. Bitterly she objects to the attention paid to what she does with the rest of her life, when she was basically invisible beforehand. But how does this surveillance police the teenager as she struggles to become her own woman? Complicating the process further is her interaction with the other female characters, from whom she learns about female identities and social roles. But it is precisely through this interaction that we find out just how complicated, conflicted and confusing the process of acquiring female identity proves to be.

Underlying my argument here is the thought that contradictions producing female subjectivities – between endorsing traditional notions of femaleness and introducing insurgent ones – are embedded right into the dramatic structure of *Six Feet Under*. The series appropriates other television confessional formats – daytime talk shows, serial melodramas and soap operas – as well as the American rewriting of Freud's 'talking cure' (Starker 1989) – self-help, self-actualisation, ego psychology, 12-step revisions and counselling – which privileges individual self-knowledge over patriarchal dependence. Just as the series confronts us 'with the departure of the father who seems to bear the phallus' (Tobin 2002: 87), *Six Feet Under* draws on the individual-oriented therapies made popular during the anti-authoritarian period after World War II (Shattuc 1997: 114) – therapies that transferred agency from expert to patient (Adler 1959; Horney 1939, 1964; Fromm 1956; Miller 1969). Such discourses continued to increase because post-war American society busied itself challenging patriarchal power – the Vietnam War, the possibilities provided by emancipatory movements like second-wave feminism, gay and civil rights, and a counter-culture defined by popular music, new age philosophies and experimentation in the arts. But, moreover, *Six Feet Under* is saturated in these anti-authoritarian social rules and cultural values. Put simply, Claire remains enclosed in the power relationships produced by this contested social world.

Troubling the Oedipal Text

Just as Sigmund Freud seemed 'unable to solve the riddle of femininity' (1986: 415), the Fishers find Claire's female growing pains hard to handle. Nothing is known of her movements; and nobody really knows what she thinks or what to say to her. Noticeable in the first few episodes is how the family talk about rather than to her. Suspicious that she might be responsible for setting fire to the house across the road, her family assume the worst ('Familia', 1:4). While Ruth refuses to believe Claire would do such a terrible thing, her brothers are not too sure: 'She hates us,' opines David. Later, while watching a rerun of that other TV show about a fatherless brood, *The Partridge Family* ('the family who sings together stays together' rings out from the television), Nate tries to reach out to his younger sister to find out if anything is wrong. Claire plays along: no, things aren't okay – her pimp is threatening to beat her up for not turning enough tricks and take away her smack. Responding to Nate's maddened reaction, she retorts: 'Why do you naturally have to assume I'm in trouble?' Such a moment, coming in the fourth episode, puts into operation an entire range of formal, thematic and narrative conventions used over the series to position her as a conundrum and compel her to speak about why she is a problem. Her family, educators, school guidance counsellor – and, of course, the *Six Feet Under* serial structure – demand that she endlessly talk about her sexuality, justify her behaviour and communicate her most intimate feelings.

Seasons one and two find Claire seeing the school guidance counsellor, Gary Deitman (David Norona). She is initially sent to him to explain why she put a corpse's foot in a classmate's locker ('The Foot', 1:3). Her justification of 'protesting Footlocker's inability to sell a decent-priced sneaker' placates no one. But Claire's presence in this therapeutic space reveals how female behaviour bears the taint of abnormality and is labelled as dysfunctional precisely because the clinical (male) space of the counsellor's office defines it as such. Julia Sherman detailed back in 1975 the ways in which psychoanalysis proved detrimental to female patients: from promoting 'dependency and mystification [and] locating the problem and the blame within women' to 'providing a negative view of women [and] handy rationales for the oppression of women'

(Sturdivant 1980: 52). Is it any wonder that the series' other female patient, 'Charlotte', resorted to barking at her therapist and why Claire is often reduced to sulky silence?

Just as the televisual dramatic form provides a space for inciting a discourse of female subjectivity – presenting it for an audience, staging dilemmas, allowing the viewer to observe and read a performance – the clinical space also functions as an incitement to discourse. Yet, as Foucault describes, such presentations of self unfold within a power relationship, in which 'the authority who requires the confession, prescribes and appreciates it and intervenes in order to judge, punish, forgive, console, and reconcile' (1998: 61–62). If Foucault is to be believed, then Gary is there to infer meaning, solve dilemmas and heal familial rifts. Under his watchful gaze, and removed from her close kin, Claire's revelations become defined as an emotional display, as about a disclosure of a dysfunctional family, of a female self laid bare. Immediately Gary asserts his dominance by inviting Ruth to join them ('An Open Book', 1:5), making known that interpretative power resides not with the one who speaks but with 'the one who listens and says nothing' (Foucault 1998: 62). Claire has no say in the matter: 'I told her it wasn't my idea.' Gary deciphers Claire's unhappiness – that she missed out – for Ruth. Claire stops him: 'No, you said that. I told you I don't think there was a time when this family was ever happy.' Ruth and Claire start bickering, while Gary sits back to listen (a virtual position shared by us). Letting the women exhaustively rehearse their complaints produces humour while revealing certain truths about this mother-daughter alliance. But Ruth and Claire emerge as exhibiting 'signs of distress and mild clinical depression' (Ball and Poul 2003: 144) precisely because what they say is read as troubling by the secular interlocutor who desires to bring about an emotional adjustment and modify female behaviour. That Gary offers only platitudes ('I think you should have more of a dialogue. Make time for it. Schedule it. Remember, any relationship is work.') is not the point. Instead, it is his hermeneutic function to incite a discourse about an indifferent mother and depressed daughter over which he keeps watch that is key here.

Nowhere are attempts to police female behaviour more sharply brought into focus than when Claire is required to talk about sex and desire. Of course, the reason she is seeing Gary in the first place is because of her sexual relationship with Gabriel Dimas (Eric Balfour). Foucault draws our attention to how medical and psychiatric institutions 'analysed' the female body as 'saturated with sexuality' (1998: 104) and inherently pathological. Claire is often required to talk about her feelings for Gabe despite her wish to discuss something else ('A Private Life', 1:12; 'The Plan', 2:3; 'Driving Mr Mossback', 2:4). The more she tries to comprehend how *she* feels, the more Gary interrupts and pathologises her narrative in ways she often cannot anticipate. It is a repeated pattern whereby he gives her permission to speak frankly but when she does he imposes meaning on what she says. In the aptly titled episode 'The Invisible Woman' (2:5), Gary mentions the 'sexual tension between them'. It is a strangely inappropriate moment, coming after Claire's violent outburst towards Parker McKenna (Maria Black) for cheating on the Standard Assessment Tasks (SATs). Despite Gary telling her that she is displacing, he introduces a new topic. 'And now is probably a good as time as any to talk about the sexual tension between us.' Claire lets out an incredulous 'What?' He continues: 'It exists. It is a normal part of transference and counter-transference.' Claire is stunned – and silenced. Seen from her uneasy position, the process of probing for any traces of sexuality and desire, of wrenching out the most stubborn confessions, and of opening the female subject to unremitting scrutiny is made uncomfortably visible here. Never let us forget how the *mise en scène* of that office, with its closed venetian blinds and counsellor peering out from behind the desk, hems her in and often leaves her prowling like a trapped animal around the room.

Although Gary aims to build up her self-esteem and sense of self (he is, after all, responsible for getting her onto the Sierra Crossroads programme and passing on details of LAC-Arts), is not the therapeutic process circumscribed? Only certain things can be uttered – despite Gary telling Claire she can say anything. Articulating disappointment and annoyance over what she sees around her, while interpretable within the male confessional space, often fails to give adequate voice to her frustrations. She is often lost for words, silenced by thwarted rage or says things she does not quite mean. Rigor mortis is not only the preserve of the cadaver here. It also speaks of stultifying discourses available to the female subject when attempting to utter 'I'. Claire's irritation seems to me less about her rejection of normative female social roles – daughter, sister (of which I will come to later) – than about the limits of discourse to adequately express and describe her experiences, her desires, her identity. But try she must. Just as a death structures each episode to offer a liminal space for suspending rules and challenging taboo, Claire represents within the narrative logic of *Six Feet Under* another kind of liminal space: a gendered

© the authors

liminality in which the possibilities for representing female identity differently are, for better or worse, negotiated.

Desiring (Female) Identity

There is something suspect about the way Claire spits out her indignant rage. Despite railing against the world and its hypocrisies, one wonders if she does not protest a little too much. Fantasising about the future lives of her classmates – one a rich lawyer blissfully wed with two kids ('you must be unbelievably happy'), another with a Masters in French who gives up living in Paris and becomes a successful television development executive with an obsession for the body perfect and a slight substance abuse problem ('but you look great') and another who runs a successful interior lighting design firm until succumbing to ovarian cancer before reaching 30 ('that totally sucks') – reveals a paradoxical Claire ('Brotherhood', 1:7). Hovering on the edge of this 'in' group finds her caught between desperately wanting to fit in yet not belonging, between resisting but not immune to long-held normative messages about the svelte body and female achievement. Playing with these narratives in her head reveals how she has imbibed dominant cultural models of female accomplishment, whereby marriage and children equal happiness while singledom results in nothing but loneliness or death – despite what feminism tells her. Her subsequent friendship with Parker is riddled with similar contradictions; for, while Claire hates how Parker masquerades as the bright, perky straight-A student to play the system, she enjoys her company. Possibly it is because she takes pleasure in the ways in which Parker 'acts out her own hidden wishes' (Modleski 1997: 42). Ensnared in an endless struggle for self-definition, Claire is obsessed with understanding identities, definitions of self and lifestyle labels. Yet looking on at other women to help her make sense of who she is and what she wants proves to be a profoundly contradictory and ambivalent process.

Raging against glib stereotypes does not prevent Claire from using them to make sense of others. Taking part in the Sierra Crossroads programme – an outward bound course recommended by Gary that encourages participants to test their physical endurance and find spiritual enlightenment by traipsing in the mountains (or, seen another way, a course which polices behaviours and turns out responsible and emotionally balanced citizens) – proves a miserable experience for Claire, made worse by the discovery that Parker is also participating ('Crossroads', 1:8). Confiding in another seeming misfit, Topher (Jordan Brower), she hides her discomfort by posing the question of who would play Parker in the movie of her 'perfect life': Julia Roberts or Sandra Bullock? Topher does not think she rates that high, at best 'one of those *Buffy*, *Dawson's Creek* chicks'. Such a self-reflexive interchange, pitching a cause and effect Hollywood movie subjectivity where a protagonist achieves self-knowledge in 90-minutes against an open-ended televisual one that focuses on the endlessly solipsistic struggle of becoming (one need only think of Buffy Summers, Willow Rosenberg and Joan Girardi for other examples), reveals how different narrative forms and mass media images come to know the female subject.

Claire might think she knows who Parker McKenna really is, courtesy of culturally produced clichés to help her unlock meaning, but the joke is ultimately on her. Less virtuous and hard-working movie heroine than scheming nymphomaniac stalking men and power and populating television soaps (Modleski 1997: 41), Parker belongs firmly to a televisual narrative world (once Parker becomes identified as a TV villainess she becomes friends with Claire). But, more importantly, Claire is not immune from such a narrativisation process. Driving around in her lime-green hearse, living over a funeral home and moping around school appearing tortured leads Parker to conclude that Claire is 'like this Goth, arty freak girl, who is – like – tragic and suicidal'. Claire may dismiss such labelling – 'That is so not who I am' – but she belongs nonetheless to the newer televisual phenomenon of the hypersensitive young woman out to debunk clichés defining normative feminine roles while changing the script in the process (like *Buffy the Vampire Slayer*, *Joan of Arcadia* and *Charmed*). No easy task. Revealed in the ways in which Claire makes sense of herself and self-obsessively talks about her social world is an indication of how trapped she is by cultural definitions and social norms not of her making. Nowhere are the contradictory processes involved in producing female identities made more apparent than when Claire interacts with the women around her. Such contested encounters – hearing different voices, playing with a media lexicon of cultural identities, exposing clichés, challenging gendered expectations – reveal how Claire learns to be dysfunctional while acquiring subjectivity.

Claire is awed at meeting 'Charlotte' from *Charlotte Light and Dark* – the child protégé with the 185 IQ who is 'like way smarter than the people who [were] analysing her, and so [was] constantly fucking with them' ('In Place of Anger', 2:6). 'It's like meeting Gandhi. Or Jesus,' gushes Claire ('The Room', 1:6). Brenda is having none of it. 'Don't tell me. The book spoke to you. Like it was written specifically for you…' But Brenda misses the point. That her story reaches out to 'lonely' teen girls like Claire, and that 'Charlotte' is the poster-girl for disaffected adolescent females, says much about how the female becomes labelled dysfunctional for dissent and annexed to mental illness (Foucault 1998). This book is not read by the likes of Claire as a psychological study of a child with borderline personality disorder, but is to her about exposing techniques that identify the female as a problem and offering strategies for resistance. Uncovering the nature of Brenda's precocious behaviour and putting it into discourse (*Charlotte Light and Dark*) makes her knowable and subject to constant surveillance. Only Brenda knows the price paid for her defiance. But her performing psychological disorders and disrupting her treatment – for building up narratives and tearing them down – reveals to Claire, able to read against the patriarchal grain, the pleasures involved in refuting labels, interrupting those with the power to define and resisting cliché definitions.

Such a relationship may offer a unique opportunity to explore ways of critiquing schemas of knowledge that subjugate the female subject. But heck no. Instead, Brenda and Claire bond, normally accompanied by alcohol and a spliff, over complicated and high-maintenance boyfriends – and one man in particular ('The Room', 1:6). Brenda's younger brother, Billy, immediately captivates Claire. Her intense connection with the mentally unstable but artistically gifted Billy lasts for two seasons (and resumes in season four), in which Claire comes to replace Brenda as Billy's confidante after the brother-sister relationship disintegrates ('It's the Most Wonderful Time of the Year', 2:8; 'Someone Else's Eyes', 2:9). Exhilarating but inappropriate relationships with sexually dangerous and emotionally tortured young men prove a pattern for Claire. Soon after meeting her heroine, Claire starts replicating the codependent relationship Brenda has with Billy with Gabe ('The New Person', 1:10; 'The

Trip', 1:11). She becomes his emotional nursemaid as he deals with the death of his stepbrother, Anthony Finelli (Jake Gridley), who accidentally blew his head off with a gun while in his older brother's care ('Life's Too Short', 1:9). Bonding over intense loss and a pointless tragedy translates, in Claire's mind at least, into a fiction about misunderstood young lovers against the world. She easily slips into the selfless role of a Mills and Boon heroine seeking to bring back the brooding hero, damaged by tragedies not of his making, from the brink, armed with nothing more than an egg Mac-Muffin and a true heart.

But is this protective behaviour just learnt from Brenda? It seems to me that Claire may not be so different from her mother after all. Despite rebuffing her mother's attempts at intimacy, and endlessly harping on about how Ruth sacrifices her own needs for the sake of her family, Claire proves to be just as smothering as Ruth in her dealings with men. Gabe soon feels trapped by Claire constantly questioning his every move and suffocating him with kindness. While she protests that she has good reason to be concerned, her performance of ideal soap-opera mother – 'who has no demands or claims of her own' (Modleski 1987: 39) – makes visible how she is learning to sublimate herself and assume a nurturing role. Talking about her doomed relationship in therapy with Gary (paralleled by Brenda attempting to write her own narrative following Billy's rejection) leads to Claire bringing forth a discourse about a female identity predicated on losing selfhood and eclipsed by the all-consuming needs of her man. Superficially at least, it confirms a Lacanian schema whereby the female exists nowhere in the (male) symbolic. But incessantly talking about it, grappling to understand what is happening, does make strange.

Heeding no warning from television archetypes like Parker or her mother, Claire learns instead about the pitfalls of doomed love and the dangers of misreading tormented young men from a movie script. The realisation that Gabe has let her down (again) – lying to her, pilfering embalming fluid from her brothers' prep room to make 'fry' (dope soaked in the liquid), revealing that he was involved in an armed robbery – finds Claire slumped in front of the telly watching *Badlands* (1974). The story about Kit (Martin Sheen) lashing out against a society that writes him off and his misguided teen companion (Sissy Spacek) hits a nerve. The desolation of this intense yet ill-fated romance, and story of murders committed by a frustrated anti-hero because he knows he will never belong, gives a narrative order to what happens later to Claire ('The Plan', 2:3). Playing out the story of doomed lovers in the badlands of an LA suburb at night rewrites the movie ending, with Claire coming to her senses and Gabe taking flight after shooting at another driver for poking fun at Claire's hearse. Making the script turn out right defines Claire's future attempts to find love. But, time and again, fairy-tale movie endings give way to messy television break ups – from would-be indie rock musician Phil (J.P. Pitoc), who does not want to be exclusive ('The Eye Inside', 3:3), to fellow art student Russell Corwin, with whom she enjoys an intense affair before she gets knocked up ('Death Works Overtime', 3:11) and he confesses to fooling around with their teacher, Olivier Castro-Staal ('Everyone Leaves', 3:10).

Can Claire escape these fairy tales, which convince women their only happiness can be found in romantic love and caring for a man? The unexpected arrival of Aunt Sarah (Patricia Clarkson), Ruth's younger sister, presents Claire with a possible alternative ('In Place of Anger', 2:6). Immediately entranced, she takes her aunt to see her artwork. Sarah's critique turns into an analysis of her niece: her work, like Claire, is marked by 'anger, urgency, passion. Resentment of the status quo. And some jealously of it as well…' Mistaking an arrangement that Claire rescued from the rubbish as being about 'the death of romance in a regimented, artificial world' risks exposing Sarah as a fraud. She may stray into pretension, but she is the first to recognise Claire's creative talents: 'You see through the veil.' No one has spoken to Claire like this before; in fact, no one has talked about her like this before.

Aunt Sarah may only be around for two episodes but she leaves her mark on Claire. Steeped in the counter-culture of alternative lifestyles and pop art (a muse for sixties Factory artists like Andy Warhol) and politicised by conscious-raising movements like women's rights, she presents Claire with a different way of being from her dutiful mother (although the visit does bring mother and daughter closer). The excesses of Sarah's bohemian lifestyle – with half-naked middle-aged hippies cavorting around a bonfire howling ('Back to the Garden', 2:7) – hold little interest for Claire. She is, nonetheless, introduced to new opportunities and a new language with which to speak. Hidden from Claire, however, is the price

Sarah paid for her choices. Using televisual conventions of self-disclosure, Sarah and Ruth air grievances ('In Place of Anger', 2:6). At the bottom of Ruth's burning resentment is her sense that Sarah had more fun than she did. Sarah divulges her buried narrative of disappointment and loss with the only man she ever loved dying when she was 21 and the longed-for children an impossibility because her ovaries are as 'dried as stone'. Sarah may speak the empowering language of feminism – of building women's self-esteem, self-image and identity – but the melodramatic tone reveals a concealed narrative of enduring infertility and the silence surrounding the sterile female body.

Yet the narrative of a young woman striving to find a unique voice structuring Claire's narrative arc represents a crisis of discourse. Encouraged by Aunt Sarah, and inadvertently helped by Billy, who asks her to take photographs of his naked and scarred body ('Someone Else's Eyes', 2:9), Claire is persuaded of her vocation as an artist. Applying to LAC-Arts coincides with the termination of her therapy. Her epiphany comes not in her final session with Gary but at her college entrance interview, where she re-imagines the audition from *Flashdance* (1983) with her legs coming off as she contorts her body to impress ('The Last Time', 2:13). It is the moment when she realises that creating art helped her cope with the un-sayability of bereavement and the pulsating ache of lost love. Crying inappropriately may have got her in, but season three finds her struggling to give actual representational form to her silent despair; she confesses she is an artist because she has 'a lot of pain' ('Nobody Sleeps', 3:4). Olivier, her form and space tutor, immediately identifies her as a promising student – but, of course, not as good as Russell. He reads her work depicting graveyards and death as good because it 'instantly makes me want to throw up' ('The Eye Inside', 3:3). Experiencing Claire's artwork as nausea is similar to how the body functions for the French feminists (Kristeva 1980, 1981) in 'shattering the logical coherence of symbolic thought and language' (Boulous Walker 1998: 111). (It is ironic that Ruth confesses to her daughter that she wanted to read the French feminists at college ['I'll Take You', 2:12].) But, pretensions aside, Claire's proximity to death and the corpse, living over the liminal space where the corporeal body lies between death and burial, places her in a unique position when developing representational forms that understand subjectivity as about process rather than identity. Producing new revelatory truths in her work reveals her uneasy attempt to intervene and put into discourse another kind of subjectivity.

Desiring to move beyond the social roles that confine other female characters, and aspiring to think differently, ends abruptly for Claire. No sooner has she started to find her voice then she falls pregnant ('Death Works Overtime', 3:11). She is the exact same age as her mother when she had Nate. Is history repeating itself? It does, in fact, seem that the melodramatic conventions of the *Six Feet Under* discourse have reclaimed Claire for dutiful motherhood. But, whereas Ruth married Nathaniel Fisher and moved into the family home, her daughter makes a very different choice. Deciding to have an abortion, she turns not to the discourse of motherhood (Ruth) but the one of female resistance (Brenda) for help. Knowing what is best for her, she remains haunted by her decision. Despite her visit to the afterlife with her father, and meeting those she has lost, including her aborted child and Lisa (where those learnt skills of mourning the departed and moving on come in very handy), Claire is still left holding the baby at her mother's wedding to George ('I'm Sorry, I'm Lost', 3:13). Tears start to flow. Is she crying because her mother is getting remarried, or at the thought of her own unborn child as she holds Maya? Or is she just learning to speak the melodramatic language of the adult female?

Being subject to intense scrutinisation means that Claire Fisher is required to talk endlessly about herself. But what she has to say is often unsettling. Speaking frankly about the hypocrisies she sees around her, challenging assumptions made about her, revealing inconsistencies between actual behaviour and what people say, or making known strategies of (female) resistance, Claire anticipates what Foucault has said about the task of truth being 'linked to the challenging of taboos' (1998: 130). But her thwarted attempts at making known these revelations and frustrated silences reveal how challenging discourse producing identities for women is a precarious process. When the dead patriarch heckles from beyond the grave that 'nobody escapes', it reminds us that there is an inevitability about returning to the Symbolic as the site of paternal signification that Freud and Jacques Lacan first imagined when gendered identities are assigned. But, more importantly, *Six Feet Under*'s compliance with and departure from television conventions reveals to me how female subjectivity emerges as fluid, unstable and contingent precisely because it is represented in aesthetic and narrative forms that say it is. In the liminal spaces of the series – its themes of death, its playing with conventions, introducing a character like Claire in the process of becoming – might we see the television discourse preparing for another kind of subjectivity, another discourse?

eleven

Desperately seeking
Brenda: writing the self
in *Six Feet Under*

'There's so much I don't know about you,' Nate Fisher tells his
girlfriend, Brenda Chenowith ('An Open Book', 1:5). Responding
to him, Brenda replies that she is 'an open book'. But is her
narrative so easy to read? Both feminism and postmodernism, argues
Lidia Curti (1998), share the need to search for new storytelling
methods – to constantly challenge accepted narratives that shape
men and women's lives. *Six Feet Under*'s Brenda Chenowith also
desires narrative forms to tell her tales. Having had a book written
about her as a child protégé with an IQ of 185 – *Charlotte Light and
Dark,* authored by Gareth Feinberg Ph.D. – she attempts to counter
the static, printed version of her 'self' with the creation of additional
narratives. From her childhood immersion in the fictional world of
another book – *Nathaniel and Isabel* – to seemingly endless self-
(re)creation and the writing of her *own* novel, Brenda moves from
telling one story to the next, from one version of her 'self' to another.

Brenda, as both storyteller and subject of a story, occupies a
multifaceted position. Giving her account is not a simple project,
negotiating her role and her subject position is no easy task. In order
to understand Brenda, or for that matter, any other woman's process
when putting pen to paper, the very act of writing demands re-
evaluation and reworking. If, as Sandra Gilbert notes in the aptly
titled 'Literary Paternity' (1979), the writer 'fathers' a text, what are

women doing when they tell their stories? Since Brenda has been narrativised in a psychological study, she reacts against patriarchal description as well as the male ownership of her story. Brenda consistently identifies and then violates borders, she disturbs boundaries; she struggles, as this chapter will argue, to develop specific frameworks for challenging patriarchal borders and gendered boundaries. Her project to contest grand (often patriarchal) narratives is, at the same time, both postmodernist and feminist.

Charlotte and Dora

It is not difficult to understand why Brenda does not jump at telling people about her starring role in the cult bestseller *Charlotte Light and Dark*. In her attempt to justify to Nate why she has never mentioned the book, Brenda explains that 'people always change towards me after they read [*Charlotte*] ... And now you're gonna read that book and think that you know me. Well, you know what? You don't' ('An Open Book', 1:5). Frustrated with the fact that those who read *Charlotte* see it as a complete account of who she is, Brenda rejects the validity of this grand narrative. Recognising Jean-François Lyotard's assertion that 'people are only that which actualizes the narratives ... by recounting them ... listening to them ... and recounting themselves through them' (1997: 23), I argue that Brenda develops strategies to resist an easy definition of herself. She insists instead on separation from *Charlotte*, asserting that the book fixes a sense of who she is that belonged first to the doctor and now the reading public – but never her.

Claire Fisher, Nate's younger sister, on seeing the book in Brenda's home, launches into how much she loves it. She is completely bowled over when Brenda's brother, Billy, reveals that Brenda '[is] Charlotte' ('An Open Book', 1:5) (and echoes this enthusiasm in season two at Brenda and Nate's engagement dinner). Brenda sarcastically interrupts Claire's reverie: 'Don't tell me. The book spoke to you. Like it was written specifically for you ... lonely little girls desperate for something to emulate. Because, apparently, they're not original enough to come up with anything on their own' ('The Room', 1:6). Despite her snarkiness and her desire to think of herself as an 'original', she misunderstands Claire's interest. Later

Claire describes *Charlotte* as 'this book about this girl who's being analysed, and she's, like, way smarter than the people who are analysing her, and so she's constantly fucking with them' ('In Place of Anger', 2:6). It is no small coincidence that Claire, another girl involved in the act of testing, retesting, forming and reforming her own identity, can understand what the young Brenda is doing here. Claire's insightful comment belies the fact that Brenda knows only too well the consequence of resisting. While Claire may understand the process, Brenda must live with the consequences – namely, that the reading of her identity from the published account is entirely beyond her control.

Much like Sigmund Freud's famous hysteric, Dora, the young Brenda resists the treatment which is eventually turned into *Charlotte Light and Dark*. Unlike Dora though, Brenda was unable to halt the analysis. Handed over at the age of six to 'strangers, experts, a bunch of academic fucks who scrutinise[d] everything' ('An Open Book', 1:5) (not to mention her psychiatrist parents, Margaret and Bernard Chenowith), we learn through flashbacks of her resistance: she refused to speak, and often resorted to barking and growling. Rather than a period of exploration and possibility, Brenda's childhood became a time of endless analysis, infinite prescription and constant surveillance.

Just as Freud promotes analysis as key to identifying Dora's 'problem', regardless of her objections, the title *Charlotte Light and Dark* demonstrates a similar self-confidence in making known hidden 'truths' about the abnormally precocious young Brenda. Of course *Charlotte Light and Dark* cannot hope to paint a complete picture of its very reluctant subject: even Freud admitted that Dora's premature end to therapy 'obliged' him 'to resort to framing conjectures and filling in deficiencies' (1997: 76) as he worked towards narrating an 'intelligible, consistent, and unbroken case history' (11). But the title of Feinberg's study purports to present Brenda from light to dark, black and white, beginning to end. Both texts dealing with Dora and 'Charlotte' respectively close down female interpretation of events and subjectivity. No matter how much she barked at the doctor and made her resistance known, *Charlotte Light and Dark* is still proclaimed by her psychiatrist to provide a full account, a complete insight into her personality and identity. Even Margaret explains to Nate that he should look no further if he wants to understand Brenda: 'It's all in the book,' she coos ('An Open Book', 1:5).

Despite Brenda's resistance to the *Charlotte* narrative, she still desires to identify an alternative one – a counter-narrative to the one written without her consent. She is somehow convinced that other people *know* who they are – people like her ex-boyfriend, Trevor (Tuc Watkins), and his wife, Dawn (Judith Hoag): 'I was watching Trevor and Dawn tonight, thinking they're just so, so, so complete,' she laments to Nate after the couple have left ('Out, Out, Brief Candle', 2:2). 'Like they have something that I will never have. Ever. Either I wasn't born with it, or it was beaten out of me. Or maybe, maybe, I made myself into a self-fulfilling prophecy…I don't know. I spent my childhood performing for clinicians, the rest of my life taking care of my train wreck of a brother, and I have no idea who I am.' Her diatribe leads her to conclude that if circumstances had been different – no *Charlotte*, no train wreck of a brother – she might have had a chance to figure out who she is.

Her revelation further suggests that, to her mind, completeness relates to normative social roles along with an intimate connectedness to a male other. It is as if she requires someone else to make her whole. Brenda imagines that Trevor and Dawn are complete as a result of their relationship (something she does not feel with Nate, as she confesses her frustration to him). Brenda's self-fulfilling prophecy relies on believing not only that the 'self' can be defined as having a beginning and an end, but also that identity is shaped by socio-culturally constructed roles: wife, mother and lover. Despite her disaffection with traditional feminine roles, and her rejection of a coherent master narrative written for her, she cannot quite escape the promise of completeness that traditional models offer women. Ironically, even though she refuses to accept such ideals, she nonetheless remains drawn to the notion that they may provide a sense of coherence for her. Tailoring versions of the social feminine self to suit – she asks Nate to marry her, for example – allows her to explore possible alternatives. But ultimately her search for new identities is confused by her desire to find her total 'self', not only as an individual but also in relation to someone else.

'My whole life seems like a dream,' Brenda says. 'It's like somebody else's life. If my life were a movie, I'd either get up or walk out.' ('In the Game', 2:1). Here Brenda expresses a disconnection from her own life, a sense that she is watching rather than participating. Using movies as a counterpoint allows her to indicate how she needs her life to be exciting, something with a story that keeps her interested but also provides a coherent cause and effect narrative. Unfortunately her life does not have a comfortable beginning, middle and end. Additionally, as a character on a television series, she quite literally must deal with an open-ended narrative. What better way to keep things interesting than to affect constant change while attempting to retain control? Resisting the analysis that gave birth to *Charlotte* now manifests itself as a desire to continuously take on new and different identities. Her wish to push the doctors away and prevent them from being able to diagnose her life transforms into a compulsive need to recreate herself in order to thwart others from doing the same to her. Appropriating identities and constructing alternative life stories for herself reveals how adept the adult Brenda is at masquerade. Let us not forget that when we first meet Brenda she is having anonymous sex with Nate in a broom closet at the airport. 'Are you ever going to tell me your name? asks Nate. 'Probably not,' responds Brenda ('Pilot', 1:1). If not for the fateful demise of Nathaniel Fisher, Sr, Brenda would never have had to move beyond the role of alluring siren who enjoys sexually pleasuring strangers. When forced to give her name to Nate's mother she without hesitation adds that she met Nate in a cooking class – creating identity comes naturally. In a later episode she assumes the guise of speech therapist Candice Bavard while waiting for Nate at a restaurant ('The Plan', 2:3); in Las Vegas she becomes Jasmine Brecker ('The Trip', 1:11). Her concocted plan that she and Nate go shopping for a funeral to help him recognise his talents as a funeral director turns into a frightening experience for him ('Life's Too Short', 1:9). Emerging from the washroom transformed into a woman dying of cancer proves more than a little unnerving for Nate, and he storms out. 'That's like that shit you pulled on those doctors,' he later exclaims. Nate is in part shocked by Brenda's ability to transform herself so convincingly and completely into someone else. He may not understand who she really is ('there's so much I don't know about you') but then neither does Brenda really know who she is behind the masquerades she performs so well. What is the 'shit' she pulled on the doctors? Playing roles proved a desperate and eventually failed attempt to thwart classification and pathologisation. But performing 'Charlotte' also meant Brenda somehow lost herself along the way. Playing with identities further results in a failure for her to be honest, especially with those she supposedly loves. Nate wants her to trust him with her 'self' – 'We obviously have an intense sexual connection,' he says. 'And, yes, I would like for there to be something more than that. But that can't ever happen until you trust me, which, apparently, you don't' ('An Open Book,' 1:5). He wants to get to know Brenda, but she is too preoccupied with watching how she creates herself – a behaviour learnt through years of psychotherapy, which in turn makes it difficult for her to let go of the control she has over self-representation and self-reinvention.

Brenda is simply too aware of the mechanisms involved in creating a persona. When Dawn explains that she read *Charlotte* in grad school as an example of a 'classic borderline personality', Brenda confesses that she 'actually went to the library, looked up the symptoms and started behaving just like that to fuck with them' ('Out, Out, Brief Candle', 2:2). Her constant testing, altering and transforming is her way of dealing with the aftermath of therapy and its diagnosing of an identity for her. Dawn, a writer and feminist, sees this as 'just a misogynistic attempt to pathologise women who refuse to toe the patriarchal line' (Out, Out, Brief Candle,' 2:2), but Brenda knows different. The higher the level of 'scrutiny' (i.e. the more people learn about and get to know her), the more she needs to reinvent herself to avoid labelling and defy easy understanding. As Dawn observes, this activity also denies any possibility of pinpointing who she is as a woman; she fervently resists being stereotyped.

Nathaniel and Isabel: 'You mark my back, I'll mark yours'

Locating a narrative to counter the coherent version of her 'Charlotte' self is not a recent phenomenon. As a child, she and her brother Billy lost themselves in the fictional world of *Nathaniel and Isabel*. Described by their mother as 'quite dark', these storybooks are about 'two orphans who had adventures. They ran away from an orphanage. There was a malevolent nurse who was always hunting them down. But they always managed to outsmart her' ('An Open Book', 1:5). Given that Brenda feels as though she was 'handed over' to 'strangers, experts...[and] academic fucks' as a child, and given her constant attempts to 'outsmart' their plans to assign an identity for 'Charlotte', it is no surprise that she is drawn to these stories. Brenda's penchant for changing identities can be read as a symbolic attempt to escape the evil nurse – or, more accurately, her mother. The books not only provide an escape narrative, but also supply her with an ally. Unlike her experience with the doctors, here she is not left struggling alone: Nathaniel and Isabel – Billy and Brenda – are united against the world. Brenda read the books to her brother, three years her junior, for hours; the siblings thus became allies against the 'malevolent' forces engulfing them.

Brenda and Billy continue their identification with the characters of Nathaniel and Isabel into adulthood. So obsessed are they with the story that they have the characters' names tattooed onto their bodies. Significantly though Brenda has 'Nathaniel' branded onto her lower back and Billy has 'Isabel' marked on his – the identity of Isabel exists only in concert with Nathaniel – one without the other is meaningless. Their codependence is evident: 'He's my brother,' says Brenda. 'And he needs me. This is who I am. This is what you get' ('Brotherhood', 1:7). Meaning: she knows who she is only in relation to Billy (and her later crisis, precipitated by the supposed completeness she admires in Trevor and Dawn, occurs after she has Billy committed and the siblings separate). Brenda is not saying 'this is who I am for now' but that her relationship with Billy gives her a sense of identity, a feeling of completeness – the light to her dark.

In addition, Billy's bipolar disorder means that he needs Brenda as a protector as much as she needs to care for him. Even as Billy's mental illness worsens and Brenda begins to distance herself from him and shift her alliance from brother to boyfriend ('The Trip', 1:11), in the final analysis she insists on taking sole responsibility for his well-being. Her parents propose that Billy should be institutionalised, and Nate, having been terrorised by Billy's antics, insists she follow her parents' suggestion. Brenda however finds it almost impossible to extricate herself from her brother. 'This is so not how I need you to be right now,' she says to Nate ('A Private Life', 1:12), pushing him away for suggesting that Billy might be dangerous.

Eventually, as predicted, Billy becomes violent and destructive, breaking into Dr Feinberg's office, stealing the files relating to 'Charlotte' and scrawling 'Nathaniel and Isabel' on the wall. This is a bizarre, futile and misguided attempt to protect his sister from the *Charlotte Light and Dark* narrative, as well as an effort to supplant the *Charlotte* story with that of *Nathaniel and Isabel*. Given the pointlessness of his actions, Billy suffers a complete breakdown and physically cuts out the mark that connects him to his sister. The final solution, to his unstable mind at least, is to remove her brand as well. Brenda arrives home to find Billy, dripping with blood, claiming he knows 'how to fix it'. 'We can bury them and be new people,' he says to a terrified Brenda. She replies: 'I don't want us to be new people. I like us the way we are.' Her attempt to reason with Billy reveals ambivalence over the separation while, at the same time, the realisation that he could harm her. Refusing to see how potentially dangerous her brother really is hides a more terrifying truth – that she is somehow implicated, somehow responsible for his unstable mental state, somehow like him. She saw herself and Billy as lost, misunderstood, persecuted and orphaned; however, this new reality reluctantly forces her to move beyond *Nathaniel and Isabel*, beyond the dysfunctional sibling relationship – as Billy tells her, 'our relationship is really toxic' ('Someone Else's Eyes', 2:9). Billy's actions not only compel her to resign as caregiver and have him committed, but the elimination of the tattoo severs her tie to *Nathaniel and Isabel* and the narrative they constructed together. Seen for what it is – fucked-up, unhealthy and codependent – the *Nathaniel and Isabel* narrative will never function in the same way for her again.

Brenda: In her Own Words

Freed from past narratives with the destruction of the *Charlotte* research and the hospitalisation of Billy, Brenda falls into depression. She is cut adrift without a narrative. Soon she stumbles on the idea of writing her own story ('The Invisible Woman', 2:5). Nate is enthusiastic: 'I think this is great. Charlotte finally speaks! The story of your fucked-up childhood, but from your point of view! People'll want to read that!' But Brenda has other ideas.

After staring at her computer and absent-mindedly typing, we see Brenda's thoughts on-screen. 'Go ahead, write. What exactly do you have to say that hasn't been said before? All you do is observe yourself. You are incapable of anything real.' Once again, Brenda realises that she has no authentic voice. Her journey from one version of her 'self' to another continues despite the fact that her quest is obviously futile. She will never be able to create a satisfactory counter-narrative to *Charlotte Light and Dark* or locate the 'real' Brenda. She does, however, keep on trying.

Absolutely fascinated with the discovery that one of her clients, Melissa (Kellie Waymire), is a call-girl, Brenda begins to act out sexual fantasies – fantasies that provide her with just the right amount of information to begin writing her novel. When asked by Melissa whether her book is fiction or non-fiction, Brenda replies that 'it's still trying to work itself out' ('Back to the Garden', 2:7) – her reality is only tolerable when she is pretending to be someone else. This allows her to sexually experiment and operate outside the traditional relationship she so admired in Trevor and Dawn. But once she finishes describing her most recent sexual escapade, she must find a new experience – a new onanistic encounter to write about. Each act seems to be more extreme than the last – from the voyeuristic excitement of watching Melissa give a client a blow job, to giving a 'happy ending' to a Shiatsu client and attending swingers' parties, to engaging in anonymous sex with numerous strangers (surfer boys, married men, a self-help guru). Brenda's frustrating journey continues unfettered. Though she might get '12 pages' of writing out of an encounter, she is never content. She just needs to keep writing.

Brenda attends a reading of the self-help book *The Lie of Romance*, by Louis Winchell (Tim Murphy), highlighting her continued search for a complete identity. Perusing the shelves finds Brenda imagining books with titles that identify dilemmas in her life – *Living with Life-Threatening Illness, I Hate You, Don't Leave Me, Charlotte Light and Dark* and *Damaged Beyond Repair: Your Brother's A Wacko And Your Fiancé is Going to Die* – each book offering a complete narrative for her problems.

She listens intensely to Winchell's tirade against romance: 'Of all the lies we're fed on none is more insidious than the lie of romance, the seductive but infantile notion that somewhere there exists someone to complement us in every way – someone who will make us complete ... this illusion keeps us from ever being complete in and of ourselves' ('Someone Else's Eyes', 2:9). In Winchell's words, Brenda recognises the false journey that she has embarked upon in terms of becoming 'one' with Nate through love and marriage.

Winchell acknowledges the futility of looking to others for fulfilment and suggests that individual completeness is possible – but he then ends up having sex with Brenda in the bookstore washroom. Casual sex is most certainly not romantic and it does not allow Brenda to become 'complete in and of [herself]'. Maybe she gets only a momentary buzz and a few more pages for her book, but it reveals a complete lack of control over her narrative after separation from her brother and the destruction of the *Charlotte* files.

Brenda's obsessive/compulsive sexual adventures make her increasingly uneasy; she has had enough therapy to know that she is out of control here. In an imagined conversation with Ruth, she blurts out her confession ('The Secret', 2:10): 'I thought, now, this would be crossing a line. Which I seem to be doing more and more these days. Because, you know what? The lines are only in our heads. In actuality, there are no lines at all, which is really fucking terrifying, if you think about it.' Indeed, the lines, the boundaries, the narratives are, as Lyotard says, actualised and given authority when they are '[put] into "play"' (1997: 23) by people. Resisting socio-cultural positioning as well as patriarchal definitions results in Brenda consistently crossing lines. But, once you cross those lines and dismiss patriarchal language, what rules can you then apply? Brenda is convinced that she will be able to find a stable, un-contaminated identity somewhere that she alone constructs without patriarchal interpretation. Instead, her search for new meaning and her experimentation with various female identities and sexual relationships ends up leading her to face up to what she already knows – the 'fucking terrifying' reality that no narrative is authoritative. Narratives are 'legitimated' for no other reason than the fact that 'they do what they do' (Lyotard 1997: 23).

Brenda's quest to locate, understand and record a satisfactory 'real' self, is therefore endless. She recognises this, and though the third season presents her as pursuing a new identity – she is part of a 12-step programme for sex addicts, and attempts to remake herself by moving to a new apartment and approaching relationships in a new way. Therefore, through Brenda, the viewer of *Six Feet Under* is drawn into an awareness of the innumerable possibilities of female representation. It is not, however, just placing one's finger on a single story that the show reveals to be a problem. It is the entire process of self-construction and the necessity of narrativisation.

Brenda exists in reality, the show tells us, but she will always be involved in the search for the 'real' Brenda. In a show dominated by death and decay, Brenda's exploration of the process of self-construction provides insight into the ever-adapting nature of both self and life. It presents us with various narratives for woman in order to challenge these very narratives.

Through Brenda, we experience how attractive a static, reliable identity is, but we also recognise, as she does, the fallacy of this desire, especially in a post-feminist, post-patriarchal age. Her struggle with both the comfort as well as the restrictiveness of narrative definitions demonstrates that a coherent self is nothing but a fiction. However, the process of working through issues of identity opens up possibilities and allows for new opportunities for viewing the self. By observing Brenda, as a woman or simply as a storyteller, we are encouraged to acknowledge the ever-changing nature of what it means to be a woman, and to challenge the comforting belief that 'it's all in the book'.

Part 4

Post-patriarchal
dilemmas (II):
masculinities
reconsidered

Nathaniel Samuel Fisher, 1943–2000

I'm dead right here. At first he looks aghast
(I'm naked, playing cards), but phasmophobia goes:
my *eminence* is more flowered shirt than *grise*,
the drollery of death much more my gist.
He rifles through my double life and fast
finds out the self I hid in things I chose:
I'm dead right here.

'We'll deal you in next hand': the son I lost,
who turned his back in an unfilial freeze,
now looks askance. It's high time to disclose
about death's afterlife and life's less boring past.
I'm dead right here.

We're in a kind of touch. I'm his consultant ghost,
an apparition that appears to him at ease,
but dry bravado's just the way I pose:
the bus I'm on has fares that really cost.
This time it's personal, buddy boy's harassed:
dead meat, a cheap old box, black crows.
I'm dead right here.

The news from Limbo is that nothing's missed,
but he won't know, till it's his turn. The breeze
of death blacks out life's foolish cameos,
the garbage can of vanities laughs last:
I'm dead right here.

Peter Wilson

twelve

Fisher's sons: brotherly love and the spaces of male intimacy in *Six Feet Under*

Introducing the Fisher Boys

The 'Pilot' episode (1:1) of *Six Feet Under* contrasts two ways of expressing emotion through the conflict of its central protagonists, brothers Nate and David Fisher. At the burial of their father, Nathaniel, the elder complains that his family's grief is 'like surgery – clean, antiseptic, business'. Refusing to use the ridiculous 'salt shaker' filled with dirt, Nate thrusts his hand into the soil that will soon swallow his father. He passionately expresses his feelings – he wants people to see just how 'fucked up and shitty' he feels about the death of the father he barely knew. Younger brother David, however, stands solemn and unmoved, as if officiating a stranger's funeral. He resists Nate's fervour, insisting that restraint is the proper way to deal with grief: calmly, quietly and without public eruptions of emotion.

From the beginning, the Fisher brothers are positioned on opposite sides of an emotional abyss. Their different engagement with the emotional realm and their conflicting responses to the burial of their father establishes the distance existing between them. How that abyss is negotiated and breached is the central question of this chapter. On the surface, David appears uptight, closed and in control of his emotional life. In contrast, Nate is introduced as sensitive and psychologically open. The chasm between them has developed over many years in the context of family tensions, personal resentments and unspoken anger; what we observe across the series is a resolution of what keeps the brothers apart.

This chapter argues that the intimacy which develops between Nate and David is central to the ways in which *Six Feet Under* represents the inner lives of its characters. In particular, its first season focuses on the ties that bind fathers to sons, and brothers together. While the Fisher boys initially deal with tensions that have been building for years, they move beyond hostilities in favour of brotherly love. This chapter will trace the ways in which the brothers move from distance and secrecy to closeness and openness, from detachment and anger to self-disclosure and intimacy. This process is facilitated by their proximity to women and the feminised space in which they live and work: the funeral home. Eve Kosofsky Sedgwick notes that the space in which men bond affects the form and expression that bonding takes (1985: 1). And here the Fisher and Sons Funeral Home is a space that encourages sensitivity and compassion – both a public and a private space, where carefully demarcated borders between the feminine and masculine collapse. Here public rituals and personal pain collide. Faced daily with the vulnerabilities of others, Nate and David's intimacy takes root within this unconventional gendered space.

Nate and David's bonding is predicated on a reversal of the conventional expectations attached to heterosexual and homosexual masculinities. Straight Nate is the sexually promiscuous and irresponsible one. A free spirit, he is represented from the outset as commitment-phobic. Gay David, on the other hand, is emotionally restrained but capable of making traditional choices and sticking with them. He is committed to family, work and God – all those things that are idealised as the province of the heterosexual male. While he is in a relationship with Keith Charles, David struggles to share his inner life with him.

The ideal American man is one in total control of his emotions: stoic, silent, disengaged and not prone to moments of self-disclosure. As Milette Shamir and Jennifer Travis explain (2002:1), the old truisms about masculinity persist: 'White, heterosexual, middle-class, Protestant, northern, urban ... it connotes total control of emotions, that it mandates emotional inexpressivity, that it entraps in emotional isolation, that boys, in short, don't cry.' Hegemonic masculinity is produced in opposition to the feminine world of emotions. Sharon Bird goes further, to suggest that male bonds centre on an unspoken pact between men to emotionally detach themselves from other men, to compete with one another, and to sexually objectify women (1996: 122). Emotional detachment, or the refusal of intimacy between men is necessary to maintain a stable border between the heterosexual and homoerotic – a border always under pressure when men appear to be 'too close'. Further, self-disclosure is often perceived to be a sign of weakness that undermines the competitive nature of male bonds.

Male bonding is a key component to quintessential American generic forms, like the Western or gangster film. Furthermore, the buddy narrative reinforces dominant meanings of masculinity. Television too is a productive site through which to trace similar gender imperatives. Writing about American TV's representation of male bonds, Lynn Spangler suggests that television 'plays a role in our notions of what it is like, or what it should be like, to be male and female, including how each gender behaves in relationships' (1992: 93). Although we have long seen men bond on disparate programmes from *Bonanza* to *The Andy Griffith Show*, Spangler notes that, throughout American TV history, it was taken for granted that audiences simply 'understood' what men were feeling without them ever saying anything (100–101). Male bonds are forged around shared activities, not shared emotions. In contrast, women build ties around vulnerability and openness. As Drury Sherrod explains: 'Women seem to look for intimate confidantes, while men seek partners for adventure' (1987: 217). Spangler points to the highly acclaimed drama, *thirtysomething*, as an important shift in images of vulnerable men. The relationship between Michael Steadman (Ken Olin) and his brother, Brad (Danton Stone), is a precursor to Nate and David's own negotiation of the gulf existing between brothers with differing expectations of family ties. Although reversing the loyal son remaining at home (David)/ returning prodigal son (Nate), Michael and Brad must deal with burning resentments and long-standing difficulties existing between them as they come to terms with their father's sudden death and arrange the family business.

Because the narrative focuses on two brothers, *Six Feet Under* resolves traditional homoerotic tensions arising from close male friendships. The bond that ultimately develops between the Fisher boys is striking for the depth of its disclosure and the ease with which they come to communicate. If masculinity as we know it equals emotional restraint above all else, *Six Feet Under* works against this ethos. Here, boys *do* cry – often. Released from traditional constraints, we are treated to an innovative representation of how intimacy between two men grows. Other contemporary representations of brotherly love, like those on *Frasier* and *Everybody Loves Raymond*, routinely engage with emotional intimacy by virtue of family. But the comedic form contains the difficult emotional terrain, as brothers deal with 'serious' family issues like divorce and ageing parents by diffusing complex emotional pain/disappointments through smart one-liners. Of these, *Raymond* is notable for constructing a strong bond between brothers Ray (Ray Romano) and Robert Barone (Brad Garrett) that is loving while mired in petty jealousies and resentments stretching back to childhood. Such a relationship has a dialogue with *Six Feet Under*'s own complex bonds.

Six Feet Under's absent patriarch contests the conventions of American television repeatedly constructed around a version of the nuclear family in which patriarchal authority is reinforced. The new 'head' of the family is the widow Ruth, and in varying times of crisis this position is shared between her and the brothers. In many ways, this nuanced reconfiguration liberates *Six Feet Under* from a narrative that places various masculinities in constant competition with each other. Instead, we see the real complexities of blood relationships; while there is love, there is also jealousy, guilt, isolation and dependence. Revealing the centrality of sibling ties to a family's emotional life – also evident in the complex bond between Brenda and Billy Chenowith – *Six Feet Under* surpasses any representation of television brotherhood before it.

In Place of Anger

Nate and David are at odds over more than the family business. Peter Krause suggests: 'Nate and David grew up discovering the world together…Nate's leaving home at seventeen created a sense of abandonment in David' (Kilday 2002: 43). Similarly, Michael C. Hall suggests that David has a deep wound: 'Growing up, Nate was probably the more serious one, David was a lot more animated. And then Nate left and David changed' (45). Throughout season one, we are treated to images from Super 8 home movies of the brothers as young boys. These images open a romanticised window to the past – a tenderness missing from Nate and David's initial reunion, but one that the brothers attempt to reclaim.

The abyss between Nate and David is also a result of who they are as men. In 'Knock, Knock' (1:13), David tells Ruth that Nate has always distinguished himself by his frankness. Nate is willing to expose his flaws. David, on the other hand, keeps his vulnerabilities – like his sexuality – hidden; he is on a private journey of self-acceptance. At his father's viewing ('Pilot', 1:1), David incurs Keith's wrath: 'What is this? We can fuck each other, but I can't be a shoulder to cry on?' David's fear of weakness is an effect of well-rehearsed family roles. As he tells Keith during this crisis: 'I'll be the strong one, the stable one, the dependable one. Because that's what I do. Everyone else around me will fall apart because that's what they do.' When David *does* fall apart, it is in the privacy of Keith's apartment – a secret space that allows his public façade to go on.

Nate's openness encourages others to open up around him. When he considers returning to Seattle, Nathaniel's ghost reminds him: 'You have a gift. You can help people' ('The Foot', 1:3). Later Brenda concurs: 'You channel other people's pain' ('Familia', 1:4). Telling Adele Swanson (Tracy Middendorf) that she can use the 'Titan' coffin for her late husband's viewing, despite the fact that she can no longer pay for it and regardless of his forthcoming cremation, Nate reveals how he operates according to his heart, not his head ('The Will', 1:2). His compassion is tangible from their first meeting. She cries inconsolably, and Nate's ability to instinctively reach out is contrasted with David's detached professionalism. Where David silently pushes the tissue box towards her, Nate does not hesitate to physically bridge the distance between them: he gets up and puts a comforting arm around her.

The family business is a point of contention between Nate and David. 'The Will' brings such contestation to the fore, whereby long-buried resentments, disappointments and frustrations come to the surface. When it is revealed that their father has left the family business in equal parts to his sons, Nate is bemused and David feels angry and betrayed. Without a father to attack for this slight, David tells Nate: 'Thanks for making it so clear to me that my choice to dedicate myself to this business and to this family was really stupid. Because, apparently, I would have been rewarded just the same for wasting my life.' Thinking Nate is his enemy, David is too wounded to accept his brother's offer of help and fraternity.

But the will also facilitates the healing of emotional wounds. As their dead father explains, 'It's Fisher and Sons. That's got to continue.' For Nate, who has always run from responsibility, his inheritance provides an opportunity to reconnect with David. In 'The Foot' (1:3), after deciding to reject an offer to join the Kroehner Corporation, Nate reminds David that Fisher and Sons is *more* than just a business. He wants to reinstate the 'human touch' in their work, and, by extension, in family interactions. As he explains: 'This is what I'm supposed to do, which is why I've spent so much time running away from it. My whole life, I've been a tourist. Now I have the chance to do some good, instead of sucking up air.' While initially sceptical, David agrees to their partnership. Nate has sold it to him with the right terms: 'You and me. Together. *Brothers*. Like we used to be.'

The Foundation of Intimacy is Truth

Lillian Rubin explains that intimacy requires the disclosing of emotions and problems (1985: 66). But intimacy develops through *more* than just talking about how you feel; as Rubin suggests, it 'requires some greater shared expression of thought and feeling… some willingness to allow another into our inner life, into the thoughts and feelings that live there' (74). In the secretive *Six Feet Under* universe, self-disclosure involves revealing painful truths. But these revelations are more than an exchange of information; they allow characters to move closer together.

Unable to be open about his homosexuality with his family, the Church (and even himself), David's emotional isolation is mired in personal crisis. While a fuller discussion of David's sexuality is beyond the scope of this chapter, his gradual 'coming out' in season one is relevant here as a marker of his journey towards openness with others. David takes the first steps towards accepting his sexuality when he 'comes out' to Nate after accidentally running into Nate at a coffee shop, where David is enjoying Sunday brunch with Keith ('An

Open Book', 1:5). David may start to be more open because of Keith but this is not easy for him. As soon as he 'comes out' to his brother, David scuttles back into the closet as he takes up the position as church deacon and loses Keith in the process. 'Coming out' to his brother while still living a closeted life results in David beginning to confide more and more in Nate. But this is a slow and often difficult process. Confessing to Nate that he failed the funeral director's examination first time leads David to say: 'I fuck up a lot more than you might think. I fuck up a lot.' Yet David is not just talking about professional qualifications here; he is talking about living the gay youth he bypassed, complete with recreational drugs ('Life's Too Short', 1:9) and about being arrested for soliciting a male prostitute in Las Vegas ('The Trip', 1:11). Interestingly, despite introducing Nate at the Independent Funeral Director's Conference as his 'brother and partner', it is to Keith that he turns for help after his arrest. Yet, over the four seasons, David increasingly learns to trust his brother.

While David moves slowly towards bridging the gulf with his brother, Nate wants to overcome the abyss almost immediately. Although he has intimacy issues with women, including his mother, and is to some extent a solitary figure (often seen running alone, or sitting alone on a beach), Nate's desire for closeness with his siblings is always there. Nate repeatedly tells David that he loves him – a phrase rarely uttered between men on American television without being played for laughs. In the seventh episode, it is clear that Nate has finally begun to penetrate David's emotional armour ('Brotherhood', 1:7). Halfway through season one, this episode is a pivotal one. After the burial of Gulf War veteran Victor Kovitch (Brian Kimmet), Nate and David are alone at the cemetery. In a scene that mirrors their angry encounter after their father's funeral in the pilot, Nate again tries to reach out. Where David aggressively pushed Nate away beforehand he now accepts the offer of brotherly love, and they embrace warmly. Both agree that they want a closer relationship than Victor had with his brother, Paul (Wade Andrew Williams). Nate tells David exactly how he feels: 'I love you David. I always will. I could get hit by a bus on the way to the desert tonight. I just wanted to make sure you know that.' Opening himself up further, David replies, 'I love you too.' He then compliments Nate on arranging the military funeral for Victor (it is what he wanted, after all) despite Paul's objections. 'You did the right thing today.' David praises Nate not only for his business acumen but also for showing him the complete emotional dislocation at stake if they do not know each other well.

The Fisher brothers live and work in a feminising space that encourages these disclosures. Specifically, their work involves dealing with people in a time of emotional crisis and grief. And this feeling of extreme vulnerability is something that the brothers experience first-hand after the death of their father. Perhaps without it Nate and David would remain estranged. But, importantly, it reminds them that their time together is finite; that they must make each day of their lives matter. When a client asks Nate why people have to die, he thoughtfully explains that it is 'to make life important' ('Knock, Knock', 1:13). Nate and David's emotional connection is intensified because they are reminded of this on a daily basis.

As Michael C. Hall suggests, David experienced a profound loss when Nate left home as a teenager. By the season one finale, David reveals how delighted he is that Nate is back. Unafraid of his feelings, David tells his brother honestly from his heart, 'Thanks for staying in LA and helping me run the business. Things have been a lot more fun around here since you've been home' ('Knock, Knock', 1:13). Aware by now that he has a potentially fatal brain malformation (AVM), Nate is overwhelmed. He cries and pulls his brother close. As Rico enters the room, they separate and stand side by side – brothers, business partners and friends.

Throughout season two, Nate and David's closeness develops into the intimacy of the everyday. As David resumes his relationship with Keith, he finds it increasingly easy to discuss his personal life with Nate. He becomes noticeably more relaxed throughout season two, and in response to Ruth's incessant questioning David admits: 'Yes, we're having healthy, affection-based sex on a regular basis. Sometimes twice a day' ('It's the Most Wonderful Time of the Year', 2:8). In addition, in 'Someone Else's Eyes' (2:9), he is unashamed by his red and inflamed mouth after being kissed by an unshaved Keith. The subsequent exchange between the brothers illustrates a new ease, with Nate joking that David is a 'big whore' with a rash as 'red as a baboon's ass'. Nate later rewards David's disclosure by asking him to be his best man.

Nate goes to David first when he wants to disclose his possible death from arterial venous malformation. As 'Out, Out, Brief Candle'

(2:2) concludes, the brothers sit silently together. We cannot hear what Nate is saying but we *know* what is being said. We also know, as Nate begins to cry and David comforts him, that this disclosure is both proof of their intimacy and another source for its growth. Although close to his brother throughout his health crisis, Nate remains emotionally estranged from the women in his life, Brenda and his mother, telling them of his condition only when he has no other choice. Nate finally decides to have surgery when a scan reveals the AVM is bleeding into a critical part of his brain ('The Last Time', 2:13). Helping Nate prepare his funeral, David confesses that this is 'very difficult' for him. While he insists that Nate is not going to die, Nate says, 'I have to get ready for it. And I think you should too.' Nate reveals just how scared he is when he tells David, 'I wish you could come with me.' There is an ambiguity in Nate's request that is both heartbreaking and resilient. And David's embrace answers Nate's request. That Nate and David cannot imagine life without each other reveals how far they have come in healing their emotional rift.

Someone Else's Eyes

Season three opens with a walk through a number of possible outcomes for Nate after his surgery ('Perfect Circles', 3:1). One of the first alternative realities finds him confined to a wheelchair after a stroke. David is teaching him to speak. While Nate struggles to repeat the words held up by David on flashcards, David's love and affection for Nate is self-evident as he patiently cares for his disabled brother. While Nate has quite literally shut down, David is the caretaker. The scenario illuminates the significant emotional shift that will take place across season three: Nate now needs David to be emotionally available.

In an almost complete reversal, the younger Fisher boy becomes more open and willing to be intimate than his older sibling. No longer conditioned by his closeted homosexuality, David is openly able to discuss his feelings. His decision to attend couples counselling with Keith indicates how far he is willing to go to promote intimacy with his partner. Where Nate once wondered if David felt *anything*, we now learn that David feels many things, including being 'judged, criticised and inadequate' ('Perfect Circles', 3:1). Although he and Keith continue to spar, David refuses to be a doormat (behaviour learnt from his mother). When Nate expresses concern about his relationship with Keith, David presents seeing the counsellor (Ayre Gross) as a positive development: 'We're just seeking the advice of a trained professional to help us to establish appropriate boundaries and write the rules of our relationship together.' Thus, when David and Keith split again, it is not David's failure to be open about his homosexuality that contributes to the breakdown. It is Keith's failure to reciprocate David's openness. As he tells Keith, 'I want you on my side. I need you on my side, and it's the one thing I never, ever have' ('Twilight', 3:12).

In contrast, Nate *tries* and *fails* to make love work, by committing to his role as husband and father to Lisa and Maya. The demands of marriage and intimacy with Lisa become too much for him, and he shuts down, becoming capable of communicating his fears, frustrations and disappointments only in his dreams ('The Trap', 3:5; 'Making Love Work', 3:6; 'Timing and Space', 3:7). Unable to love Lisa, he withdraws emotionally from her and later turns to Brenda and his old 'bad' habits – smoking (including dope), drinking and sex with strangers. With Lisa missing, Nate's closed-down-ness is contrasted with David's openness ('Death Works Overtime', 3:11). The brothers are seated alone in Nate's room above the garage. Nate declares that he cannot talk about Lisa any more, and asks his brother how things are with Keith. As David proceeds to open up at length, listing personal grievances and relationship flaws, Nate disengages. Staring into the middle distance, he does not hear a word. Unlike the pattern for disclosure throughout season one, here it is Nate, not David, whose inner life has become hidden and closed off.

When Nate calls David in the middle of the night to inform him that he has filed a missing persons report and is 'really starting to freak out', David comes over immediately ('Death Works Overtime', 3:11). Later Nate asks him to watch Maya while he gets some air, pacing and smoking outside. Frustrated with the situation, Nate starts violently thrashing a tree with a rake, until the garden implement shatters. It is David who wakes him from this trance, and it is David rather than Nate who increasingly becomes competent at providing support in a crisis. David, steadily becoming skilled at the feminine work of care, is literally left holding the baby as Nate disintegrates – both physically and emotionally. Confirming *Six Feet Under*'s challenge to a patriarchal family structure, David is now positioned as the head of the Fisher family; as Ruth marries another man, and Claire deals with the aftermath of her abortion, it is queer David who keeps the family business intact and provides (emotional) strength for all.

Throughout season one, Nate was the open brother, encouraging David to see that he did not have to suffer alone. Now, Nate is closing down – his emotional life in crisis. And he is not sure how to deal with his helplessness. When the police locate Lisa's abandoned car, he goes to a nearby motel, alone. He isolates himself from his family and friends; he continues to shut down ('Death Works Overtime', 3:11). But a knock at the door begins to slowly bridge this distance, revealing David with Claire, who is sharing his grief. Nate lets them in; he hugs them tightly and cries. There is some ambiguity, however, about what Nate is feeling, intensified by the violent beating he provokes in 'I'm Sorry, I'm Lost' (3:13). Perhaps he cannot feel *anything*, and wants this to manifest itself, as punishment, on his body. With Lisa's death, it is certain that the Fishers face another test of their intimacy. Equipped with the tools of brotherly love, David might be the one to open Nate up again as season four unfolds.

thirteen

Queering the Church: sexual and spiritual neo-orthodoxies in *Six Feet Under*

David Fisher's headlong descent into sexual self-hatred throughout season one is constructed as a counterpoint to an emerging *Bildungsroman* narrative of self-acceptance. In the final episode ('Knock, Knock', 1:13), after confronting his family with his sexual orientation, David comes out to his Christian congregation, renouncing his shame and self-loathing from the pulpit. David has discovered that the Church is not the haven before heaven that he thought it was, but a political animal that is bigoted and fearful in order to maintain control. At the end of his speech he imagines a round of applause, but this is a moment of wish-fulfilment. The congregation remains silent. His on-off boyfriend, Keith, smiles knowingly at this most public of self-outings, while the church deacons grimace knowingly that David's outburst and deviance from the Scripture that he was supposed to read out is a political act. The choir strikes up as David goes back to his seat at the edge of the congregation. He looks up to a stained-glass window and glances momentarily at the image depicted of two priests in cassocks. A boy is kneeling in front of one of the priests while another bears witness. The priest's hands rest on the boy's head in front of his groin, as David reads benediction as oral sex. David turns away from the window, but the window remains in the frame for us. David blinks and a slight smile spreads over his face in a moment of sexual 'knowingness'. David has not just rejected his self-loathing for being gay, and stood defiant in the pulpit rejecting the biblical reading in favour of his own personal faith and testimony; in that moment of 'knowingness' at the window, David has queered the Church.

David's struggle with his Christian faith mirrors Jesus's own battles with the institutional and state oppression of minorities. The Jesus with whom David is confronted, however, has been transformed through two millennia of reconstruction, first as the Catholic asexual and then reformed into the Protestant (and, in David Fisher's case, Episcopalian) rampant heterosexual. The choice of denomination of faith for David is crucial, as to be a Catholic would permit a closeted-ness masquerading as abstinence. The Catholic represent-atives of God on earth in human form also deny their own sexuality as well as that of Jesus, and therefore David (were he Catholic) would be able to take some homo-social comfort in his outward performance of celibacy. That David is Protestant denies him this comfort of the closet or the excuse of celibacy that constructs the closet. Protestantism denies celibacy in its social and political formation. The Protestant priest performs not only his faith but also his sexuality. Beyond a certain age, the Protestant priest invariably marries and has children. The social order of the Church unit revolves around this family. It is set up as an ideal model, to be imitated throughout the congregation. The irony for the Fisher family, however, is that their church, St Bartholomew's, has a seemingly celibate priest (Father Jack) at its helm. Further, throughout the series it is assumed, as David assumes, that Father Jack (Tim Maculan) is gay. Whether he is or not is irrelevant, as Jack in the final episode denies he is gay. However, his celibacy remains an issue. His non-sexuality is tantamount to a denial of heterosexuality. His non-sexuality queers the Church as a family, since the asexual unmarried priest cannot be the patriarch. Just as the very impetus for the series is the loss of the patriarch, St Bartholomew's as a political institution is as dysfunctional as the Fisher family itself. David comes out of his own personal closet to discover that the institutions that have constructed and controlled him exist in a macro-closet of anxious hatred and fear.

The window of St Bartholomew's stands in opposition to the lack of religiosity in the Fisher funeral home's chapel of rest. The Fishers' stained-glass window has an absence of iconography, but instead features a painted blue sky with clouds. No two-dimensional patriarchal icon stands over the dead, and until this final episode in season one Christ as an iconic figure is completely absent. When we do discover the church window, we still do not see Christ but Christ's representatives in fabricated patriarchy. David's knowing glance emasculates the construction of Christ as heterosexual. This is nothing new in the history of religious painting and iconography. The Christian visual arts are full of homoerotic longing in their depiction of the perfect musculature of many of the saints (and of St Sebastian in particular), as well as that of the near-naked Christ 'penetrated' on the Cross. This homoeroticism is what Robert E. Goss describes as 'Christian homodevotionalism' (2002: 128), in which Christ is not worshipped as a patriarch but as a male lover. This brand of 'queer liberation theology' has its origins in the feminist movement's attack on the patriarchy of the Church in the late sixties and early seventies. Already by this time the Reverend Elder Troy Perry had established (in 1968) the first Metropolitan Community Church in Los Angeles with a specific mission to integrate spirituality with sexuality, and its deliberate targeting of a gay and lesbian congregation. By the eighties, and with the death toll arising from AIDS mounting, the gay/lesbian Christian theology espoused by the Metropolitan churches had taken on the hue of AIDS activism, and the theology, like the theories of sexuality that underpinned it, turned queer. The politics of the theology also found spiritual brothers and sisters in other activist organisations (particularly against racism), which helped to mould the theology into one not only of compassion but also of affirmative action. Christ the champion of the oppressed provides a hero figure for gay men whose Christian faith remains intact despite the Church's attempts to silence and evict them from the 'family'. The homoerotic gaze looks at the suffering Christ, or Sebastian, and sees the literally penetrated male, either by the sword or the arrow. Christ is penetrated for his beliefs and for his work for social justice. His scars are wounds that gape back at the heterosexist masculinity that inflicted them in the first place. Constructing Christ as a penetrated male completely subverts 'heterosexual phallocentrism' (Goss 2002: 137) and denies the Protestant Church in particular its idea of Christ as heterosexual. David's gaze at the church window does not pick out Christ the penetrated male but his representative on earth seemingly penetrating another, younger male. And thus the challenge to Christian phallocentrism is passed on through the generations. David Fisher's newly queered Christianity challenges both homophobia and erotophobia. Through one blink and a flicker of a smile, he subverts the Church's role in the 'strict economy of reproduction' (Foucault 1998: 36).

Subversion, though, is temporary. In the first episode of season two, David reveals to Keith that, after the congratulations for his pulpit speech in the last episode, 'most people wouldn't make eye contact' ('In the Game', 2:1). The fall-out for David is his transfer from St Bart's to St Stephen's as a parishioner and loss of social status as a deacon. In St Bart's, church and state, though having no formal coupling in law, are represented as being 'coterminous' (Boyd 1974: 180). This can be read by the positioning of the national flag beside the pulpit and equal to it in the space it takes up in the frame. Despite the legality of homosexuality, the Church still reads the Bible in the Judaeo-Christian, anti-Hellenic tradition of assuming criticism of homosexuality in the Book of Leviticus (18: 22; 30: 13) because of its attack on the city of Sodom. Reading Leviticus in this way, though ignoring wide-ranging scholarship on the misrepresentation of hospitality as homosexuality, restores a civic function to Church teachings on the subject in the absence of condemnation in law. Placing the flag alongside the pulpit thus layers onto a particular homophobic reading of the Bible a quasi-endorsement by the state.

What St Bartholomew's presents us with, then, is not a set of Christian leaders who are acting as agents of repression in homophobic persecution. Father Jack is not married, like Jesus, of course, but his seeming asexuality is potentially deviant in the heterosexist Protestant institution. The only other priest we see connected to this particular church is Revd Donald Clark, who is being interviewed by David for the position of associate priest ('Brotherhood', 1:7). Clark, too, presents as someone who is gay-friendly, berating 'most Christians' for ignoring 'the gay kid who gets strung up'. His politics are radical and inclusionary of gay issues, and thus he is seen by the conservative lay deacons as liberal and a threat to their middle-class, white, homophobic security. Though Clark is not gay, he is a widower, and thus is placed outside the heteronormative construction of the Protestant priest. Without a wife he is as asexual and emasculated as the Catholic priest. Therein lies yet another danger. The reaction to him comes largely from David's co-deacon, Walter Kriegenthaler (Frank Birney). He is suspicious of the man because he is Father Jack's choice for associate priest. In this episode it is revealed that Walter was the principal opponent of Father Jack's appointment. What is behind all the fears of the Church, of course, is its move to homonormativity, in the form of gay marriages that Clark might be capable of, and of which Jack was accused for having blessed a same-sex union of two lesbians ('Knock, Knock', 1:13). Whether either priest is gay or not is not the issue. The move to the acceptance of homosexuality within the Church is a blow to centuries of theological assertions of Jesus's asexuality and his post-Reformation reincarnation as heterosexual.

Ironically, the reaction of the Church against Clark's potential radicalism and the threat to its heteronormative rituals (such as marriage) is averted by David himself, as his closeted-ness and fear push him to reject Clark: David says no because Clark is honest. For David to be honest would deconstruct his assumed heterosexuality within the social world of the Church and lead to his exclusion, certainly from his deaconship and possibly from the congregation. What happens here for David is a kind of inverted 'homosexual panic' (Sedgwick 1990: 19). Homosexual panic in its forensic sense, according to Sedgwick, is often used in defence of gay bashing by 'legitimising a socially sanctioned prejudice' (20). David panics at Clark's reference to the 'gay kid who gets strung up' and reads it as his 'knowingness' of his own orientation. One can also read into David's question 'were you so honest with all the other deacons?' his assumption that Clark might also be gay, for he firmly believes in the self-recognising and exclusionary subculture of the gay world. David reads Clark's honesty and recognition as a kind of sexual advance. The only way to protect his dishonest closeted-ness is to eliminate the threat by panicking in the same way as Kriegenthaler and rejecting Clark as an associate priest. The rejection is a form of gay bashing which David inflicts on himself.

Nowhere is 'homosexual panic' more in evidence than with the gay bashing of Marc Foster (Brian Poth) at an ATM ('A Private Life', 1:12). He becomes a victim because of his physical intimacy with another young man on the street. Marc's character is very similar to that of the real-life Matthew Shepard, who was left for dead in Laramie, Wyoming, victim of another gay bashing, and subsequently the subject of Moises Kaufman's 1998 play *The Laramie Project* (based on the collective testimonies of the townspeople), a version of which was televised by HBO in 2001. Throughout the episode David conjures up the ghost of Marc to haunt and taunt him about his own sexuality. This ghost, like David, was a Christian who hated his sexual orientation. He says: 'It's not what God intended. God challenges us like this,' as if homosexuality was an original sin to be rejected. David, in this conversation in the mortuary over the dead man's body, adopts the pro-gay stance faced with the neo-conservative Christology of the ghost. Marc's ghost attacks David's assumed position by declaring it 'liberal propaganda to justify your own depravity'. The ghost brings to an end the conversation with a warning of the doomsday scenario facing gay men in heteronormative religion: 'No matter how nice you fix me up, I'm going to hell.' What is interesting in this sequence is that David's internalised homophobia is projected outwards onto another character, albeit one of his own imagination. David then finds space to separate himself from his homophobia momentarily in order to take up a positive position towards his sexuality. The open-air interment of Marc Foster reveals how the 'homosexual panic' has spread throughout the community in the absence of any restorative or retributive justice. There is no mention of a police investigation into Marc's death and the two murderers would appear to have escaped justice. At the funeral, however, the absent murderers are held up as society's heroes as a motley collection of white men (and a few wives) protest at the funeral. They carry placards with inscriptions such as 'No fags in heaven', and 'Homos in Hell'. Perhaps the most interesting of all the placards is 'God's wrath on fags, Gen 19: 1–26'. The reference is to the demands by the men of Sodom for Lot to bring out his visitors so that they might 'know' them, and clearly the southern Californian evangelicals protesting at the funeral have followed the millennial mistake of understanding 'know' as homosexual relations rather than as hospitality (see Boyd 1974: 168–169; Goss 2002: 185–203). The placard title, though, uses the colloquial 'fags' but the biblical 'wrath', thereby using the language of Scripture to endorse prejudice at its very basic level of name-calling and insult. And yet, despite this perverted universalising of the perpetrator of anti-gay violence as victim and the actual lack of justice for the real victim of the crime, all the while using Christian discourses as means of endorsement, David manages to maintain his faith. But this faith and his own struggle with negotiating a path between it and his sexuality is not permitted the outlets of confession through organised religion, and he is reduced at the end of the episode to talking to God directly in a private anguished prayer. In a bout of insomnia following the funeral and a series of encounters in his mind with the dead Marc, David slips out of bed and onto his knees in supplication before God in a desperate attempt to ease his trauma. His invocation runs as follows: 'Please, God. Help me. Take this pain away. Please fill this loneliness with your love. Help me, God, please, help me.' David's faith by means of religion has been eroded by the attack on his sexuality using Scripture. No longer suppressing his inverted homophobia he is beginning to exorcise it, first by having attacked one of the anti-gay protestors at the funeral, and subsequently by his direct communication with God without intermediaries who have been tainted by the appropriation by their religion of the pathologising of sex. David seeks a suffusion of his sexuality with his spirituality.

David's sexuality is emergent throughout season one, characterised principally by his internalised homophobia. Throughout the series, too, David's faith has emerged from the closet of the institution into something more personal and individual. As a schoolboy David was involved in institutional Christianity, first as an altar boy and later as president of the Youth Ministry (as revealed in 'An Open

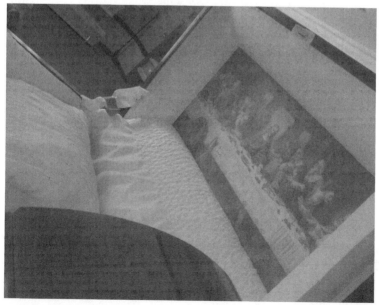

Book', 1:5). When we meet him as a 31-year-old adult he has emerged further embedded in the institution (as a deacon) but has taken on the more socially committed pastoral role of feeding the poor ('The Room', 1:6). The Church, for David, is the principal closet. He can hide behind its heteronormative drives and yet be driven further into the closet because of them. Even when he comes out to Nate, he still wishes it to remain a secret in church. Even when he comes out to his mother, it is the patriarchal Church that remains in the dark about his sexuality. David's self-stigmatised 'secret differentness' (Goffman 1990: 102) spatialises into defined categories his social identity, as well as opening up a space between his competing drives of sexuality and spirituality.

Nowhere is the Church as closet more in evidence than when David looks out from a St Bartholomew's van on its street mission to feed the poor and sees two men walking hand in hand outside a West Hollywood gay club ('The Room', 1:6). In response to David's stare they begin kissing passionately and deliberately. Their aggressive reaction to David becomes clear only when the camera cuts back to David and we see his head framed by the van window. The camera pulls back to reveal the name of his church written on the door underneath the window. The gay kiss is a taunt at the Church (as represented by the van, a church on wheels) as well as at David – ironically, for though he is gay, he can only respond with a shocked stare from within his perambulatory 'church closet'. As Sedgwick says, 'closetedness is a performance initiated as such by the speech act of a silence' (1990: 3). David's silence is even more resonant because of his Protestantism. Had he been born Catholic, David would have been able to engage in the practice of confession, with sex as 'a privileged theme' (Foucault 1998: 61). The Protestant Churches' denial of the godly iconicity of the priest means that David cannot talk about or confess his homosexuality other than internally and therefore in silence. The reformed Church, thus, could be seen to have widened the closet considerably. Its adoption of post-Enlightenment medical and psychiatric theories that nominated homosexuality as a condition turned it into a heteronormative institution, as it rejected its new binaristic 'other' sexuality. St Bartholomew's church thus operates through a culture of silence. The accusation against Father Jack first comes in the form of a fax to the deacons saying 'Father Jack is gay'. No one at first speaks its name. Gay marriages are constructed as a threat circling the Church, though they have not yet penetrated its environs. And so the Church constructs around itself a closet for its own protection. The homosexual who operates within it has to remain doubly closeted, by both Church and himself. Foucault's 'do not appear if you do not want to disappear' maxim (1998: 84) was never more true than in episode 13 ('Knock, Knock', 1:13).

Other than in season one, Father Jack only ever appears again outside St Bartholomew's preaching in the Fisher funeral home for specific services ('The Invisible Woman', 2:5; 'Someone Else's Eyes', 2:9). In the first he is invited by Ruth to offer what turns out to be an 'inspiring' eulogy (Condon 2002: 188) for Emily Previn (Christine Estabrook), who died without friends and family. In the second he turns up to eulogise at the funeral of Dwight Edgar Garrison, who died when hit by a metal lunchbox dropped by a construction worker from a building site. He appears here for a contested funeral, at which the deceased had left specific instructions to be buried with his first wife, much to the chagrin of his living second wife (Dina Meyer). On both occasions he is officiating at funerals for the non-nuclear, the outsiders, those who do not fit into the archetypal model of family. In the Fisher funeral home he has none of the trappings of the Church. There is no raised pulpit, no Christian iconography, no flags. Separated from his Church and his lay phalange of deacons, he preaches non-denominational, liberal humanism. This is very similar to the snippets of sermons heard in St Stephen's in West Hollywood with the inscription near the door 'Everyone welcome'. One can surmise that St Stephen's is an affiliate of the UFMCC (Universal Fellowship of Metropolitan Community Churches) given its post-denominational appearance and doctrinal diversity, as no Scripture is preached (Goss 2002: 33), and its outreach to the gay, lesbian, bisexual and transgendered communities. Officiating at the service is a woman priest (Mary-Pat Green) in a clear sign of this particular church's desire for inclusiveness ('Familia', 1:4). The priest being a woman is an equal act of emasculating phallocentrist Christianity. Two rainbow flags are clearly visible, one standing beside a pulpit that is not used and another draped over the choir stalls. The unmistakeable sign of the acceptance of gays and lesbians in the church also deals a blow to established religion. The inference that the woman priest might also be lesbian is a double blow to phallocentrist doctrine. This brief scene in St Stephen's contests and stands in opposition to the masculinist heteronormativity of services at St Bartholomew's. The sermon is a rethinking of original sin, not as of Eve as the fallen woman, but of assuming that God lies. We return briefly in season two for another sermon of 'God loves us just the way we are' while the camera pans away from the priest and focuses largely on the congregation of mixed races and same-sex couples ('In the Game', 2:1). This is the Christian environment to which David aspires, in which his sexuality and spirituality can be not only embraced under the one roof but also celebrated as neo-orthodoxies. Interestingly, too, the American flag makes a brief appearance in one frame, while the rainbow flags are conspicuous by their absence. Perhaps this is suggestive of a further embrace of sexuality and spirituality with nationality. But it might also be read as a sign of a neo-conservative 'post-gay' Church 'remade into a straight image' (Goss 2002: 73), or of gay sexuality being reined in by a heterosexist 'civic détente' (Johnston 1979: 281).

Previously on prime-time US television the Church as a profession has not featured in terms of gay representation (see Tropiano 2002). ABC pulled an episode of the drama series *Nothing Sacred* in 1998 that featured a gay priest with AIDS. In the theatre, however, Terence McNally's 1998 play *Corpus Christi*, first performed under waves of protests, threats and a fatwa against its author, received extensive media coverage. The play is set in a Texas high school and features a Christ-like figure who has erotic relationships with his disciples. It is the most-cited theatrical queering of Christ to date. The only other media representation of the Church and homosexuality has been in news reports and documentaries about the clerical sex abuse scandals that have rocked the Catholic Church throughout America. By the time season two (2002) was aired the issue of same-sex marriages which to an extent drove the storyline of the Church in season one, had made headline news and had crossed over from an issue of Christian doctrine to one of civil law and civil rights. Apart from the brief scenes in St Stephen's, issues of civil rights and Christianity remain poles apart in representation. These scenes offer an alternative Church to forces of conservatism in both Church and political institutions, and present to us liberal humanism as a form of queering of the Church.

Apart from the scenes in either church, spirituality is still linked strongly to Christianity, although the move is away from organised religion towards individual faith – as seen in David's private prayer. One further form of queering of the Scriptures appears in season one. The featured dead body is that of gang-banger Paco (Jacob Vargas), whom David animates in his imagination after an encounter with a homophobic driver in a parking lot during which Keith reacted violently, using his civic authority as a policeman to protect and bolster his civil right to be gay ('Familia', 1:4). David, on the other hand, stood back without any intervention, while using Keith's violent reaction as an excuse to berate him for being out of control, thus transferring his own internalised anger at the homophobia onto Keith as an act of displacement. Later, while working on Paco's body David's internal monologue places in Paco's mouth a quotation from the Bible (John 18: 25) that recounts how Peter denies being a disciple of Jesus. This is a form of double queering, as it not only displaces Scripture from its exponents (priests) to a gangster (but one who possesses a strict moral code), but also equates a spiritual disciple with a community of sexuality.

Throughout season one, David's struggle to negotiate a path between sexuality and spirituality leads him to rush headlong into a series of encounters with dangerous mind- and body-altering experiences, such as taking Ecstasy ('Life's Too Short', 1:9) and having unprotected sex ('The Trip', 1:11). This might be read as a form of self-loathing based on a death wish (the suppression of sexuality can be achieved only by the erasure of the self). In queer theology, the modern pathologising of unprotected sex in a world of AIDS is a heterosexual construction based as much on fear of anal sex as of AIDS. For a queer Christian, however, according to Goss (2002: 75–79), a post-eighties gay man's equation of sex and death is complicated by both cocaine and AZT, by a desire for a game of Russian roulette and a sense of immortality for having survived AIDS. The sexual act, therefore, provides a moment of spirituality at the point of the utmost vulnerability and trust. David's encounter with unprotected sex, though, does not provide him with spirituality but a deepening of his internalised homophobia constructed as a death wish (see Foucault 1998: 156). His experience with a male prostitute, Brad (Blake Adams), on a trip to Las Vegas also provides him with an opportunity to seek salvation through his own personal saviour – Keith ('The Trip', 1:11).

When David turns to a prostitute to escape the heteronormativity of his profession and the culture that surrounds it, he has lost all the patriarchs in his life. The Church provides no iconographic representation of Christ in pictorial form, and through the quasi-transubstantiated priest (Father Jack) has rendered Christ as asexual. With his own father dead, and the paternalistic community of deacons hovering over issues of his own sexuality, David reads Keith as the only person in his life with a moral authority. Keith does not do drugs, and has no casual sex partners (until season three, of course). He attends church regularly and becomes angry at injustice. He protects the vulnerable against homophobia and domestic violence, and he is made to suffer for it. His rage against injustice (which society around him reads as loss of control) causes him to lose his job. He becomes a martyr crucified for his convictions. And on top of all this David worships him because he is a double minority, both black and gay, in a blue-collar job with a divinely constructed body. When we first meet him wrapping a Christmas gift for David the camera pans over his physique, capturing his police weapon in the process ('Pilot', 1:1). When Claire first encounters him it is to his physicality that she is drawn. Throughout their encounters David is caught observing Keith as a physical icon through glances. And in St Stephen's the camera avoids the priest altogether and all religious iconography (after a swift establishing shot), and views Keith as David sees him ('In the Game', 2:1). At the moment of communion with God, as we experience the visual absence of the patriarch of the Church, David looks at Keith, but Keith shares the frame with his new boyfriend and David's icon falls from grace. David's relationship with Keith mirrors his own relationship with Christ as his sexuality and spirituality struggle for supremacy. His glance at Keith in this sequence replicates the moment in St Bart's when he knowingly interprets the stained-glass window. As the Church swiftly disappears from the narrative, David's homo-devotionalism to Keith goes through as turbulent a process as that of the progression of his sexuality. Keith's un-Christ-like behaviour in season two, in David's eyes, is one cause of his apparent loss of faith. As the Church storyline peters out in season two, David's self-acceptance and his formation of a new social identity begin to materialise. David slowly begins to learn that having a relationship with an icon is actually a relationship with an idealised self. David's new Christ is achingly human and troublingly masculinist. David may have queered Christ into Keith ('It's the Most Wonderful Time of the Year', 2:8), but Keith (and all his post-gay neo-conservatism) needs to be queered as well. In his progression to self-acceptance David's neo-orthodoxies of sexuality and spirituality suffuse at the moment when the storyline erases them. The queer Church disappears (after Foucault 1998: 36) at the moment of its visibility.

fourteen

Revisiting the closet: reading sexuality in *Six Feet Under*

The character of Will Truman (Eric McCormack) from NBC's *Will and Grace* offers a pithy summary of most people's understanding of the closet: 'Coming out of the closet is something you only do once. It's like being born' ('William, Tell', 1:6). This claim turns sexuality into a rigid, binary framework of 'sexual orientation', and it suggests that people who find themselves in the closet must be figuratively reborn as gay through the act of coming out. This singular birth will thereby produce a gay sexual identity for them, which will then persist throughout their lives. Of course, it goes without Will saying it here, but his claim presupposes that only gay people come out. Straight people never need to declare their sexuality at all; all they must do, quite literally, is be born.

The character of Russell Corwin (Ben Foster) from HBO's *Six Feet Under* seriously troubles this view of both the closet and of sexuality, when he unexpectedly says to his close friend and confidante, Claire, 'I'm not gay, you know' ('Nobody Sleeps', 3:4). How do we interpret this claim? What does it reveal about the structures of power and knowledge produced by the closet? What does it tell us about *Six Feet Under*'s representation of sexuality? And above all, in light of a claim such as this, how are we to *read* sexuality?

These are the questions to which this chapter seeks to provoke responses. It builds from an earlier essay in which I defend the claim that *Six Feet Under* is the first show on television to explore the internal workings and political dimensions of the closet. In that essay (2003) I discuss briefly *Will and Grace* and *Queer as Folk* as examples of shows that offer their viewers gay (often *very* gay) characters, but simultaneously erase the politics of the closet. (Writing now, almost four years later, I would certainly add *Queer Eye for the Straight Guy* to such a list.) In these shows, the viewer always *knows* who is gay and who is not, but the problems with presuming (hetero)sexuality or the difficulties of interpreting sexuality are rarely, if ever, raised (and, even then, only for comic effect: see Battles and Hilton-Morrow 2002).

Six Feet Under has been the only show on television to investigate the issue of closeting. Starting with the first few episodes of the series, viewers experience the closet through the life of David: a character who is outed to the viewers in the very first episode, but who remains closeted to family, colleagues and friends for much of the first season. The show thereby explores fundamental epistemological questions (questions concerning the production and limits of knowledge) and crucial political problems (problems of power, identity and representation). This means, finally, that *Six Feet Under* serves to expose the operation of heterosexual norms (what I will call 'heteronormativity') by offering a different perspective on the presumption of heterosexuality.

This chapter will argue that in its third season *Six Feet Under* revisits the closet from a radically different yet still politically salient angle, through the character of Russell. From the pilot episode on, David always remained certain about his sexuality (even if he questioned the morality of it), and he never wavered in his knowledge that he was 'gay'. Thus, while the viewer experiences others' questioning of David's homosexuality (or incorrect presumptions of his heterosexuality), the viewers themselves, like David, still 'knew' he was gay. The viewer is thereby given a certain epistemological privilege in the case of David, and the question of sexuality is always already decided, at least from the viewer's perspective.

With Russell, it does not work that way; he never claims to be gay or straight. And the viewer sees Russell's sexuality through the eyes of Claire, who never attains the certainty about his sexuality that she so desperately (and perhaps phobically) longs for. We can understand or discuss Russell's sexuality only through our (and

Claire's) interpretation of a series of phenomena: his outward signs, his actions and his own denials about his putative homosexuality. Russell's sexuality is *never* fixed because it is never clearly *legible*. I will argue here that it is precisely this illegibility of Russell's character – understood through the storyline that covers the triangular relationship between him, Claire, and Olivier (Peter Macdissi) – that shakes our confidence in the solidity of sexuality, and it troubles the assumptions that a heteronormative society insists on making.

Therefore, despite his refusal to declare a gay sexuality (or, better, *because* of that refusal), Russell proves to be a much more queer character than David. Through Russell's character, the third season of *Six Feet Under* continues the show's unprecedented and still unparalleled tradition of exposing and thereby challenging heteronormativity. I aim to demonstrate that Russell produces for both the characters around him and for the viewers of the show a significant disruption of the terms of modern sexuality; he rejects the offer to claim the modern category of 'the homosexual', while he refuses to play the normative role of 'the heterosexual'. This chapter offers an elucidation of that disruption in the form of a reading of sexuality in the third season of the show; its goal is to reveal the very alterity of those present categories of sexuality and to contest the heteronormativity that preserves, fixes and reifies them.

I. Mappings: Sex, Art and Heteronormativity

Before taking the first steps to build out the logic and provide the evidence to substantiate the above claims, I need to map out a number of terrains. This means sketching a summary of the plot, clarifying my core critical concept and offering a brief overview of the argument to come. For readers who have not recently viewed the third season, I will confine my argument to the relationship between Claire (the Fishers' only daughter, younger by far than her two brothers), Russell (Claire's fellow first-year classmate in art school) and Olivier (their teacher), with occasional references to David (Claire's gay brother, who runs the family funeral home with their brother, Nate). As a triangular relationship, the story of Claire, Russell and Olivier is, almost by definition, complex. Here I will offer only the barest skeleton of the plot, filling in important substance as my argument develops.

Based on their shared status as outcasts in high school and sceptics of the artist ethos now that they are in art school, Claire and Russell bond quickly after meeting. Their friendship appears at least partially founded on Claire's almost immediate assumption that Russell is gay. Claire turns to Russell as a source of emotional support during her brief relationship with Phil (J.P. Pitoc). When things with Phil do not work out, Russell and Claire spend even more time together, with Claire opening herself up to Russell more than she has with any of her boyfriends. It is at this point that Russell, seemingly aware that Claire has taken him for gay up to this point, tells Claire, 'I'm not gay, you know' ('Making Love Work', 3:6). This anti-coming out proves to be the hinge that turns their relationship from friendship to romance, and eventually leads to them having sex (which Russell describes as his first time).

Olivier intervenes in the ostensible happiness of Claire and Russell's relationship; he brings with him manipulation, power games (always filled with sexual undercurrents) and sometimes psychological warfare. Olivier's teaching of art consistently remains thoroughly imbued with sex and power; he insists on conflating all three, both for himself and for his students (at least, his best students). He takes Claire on as his research assistant, but then seduces Russell while Claire is off on an errand ('Tears, Bones and Desire', 3:8). The viewer does not witness this seduction, never seeing Russell and Olivier together in a sexual way, but Russell later confesses to Claire that he and Olivier 'fooled around' ('Everyone Leaves', 3:10). Claire is both shattered and inexpressibly angry at the news; she breaks up with Russell on the spot, and then refuses his repeated efforts to reconcile (and ignores his repeated claims to love her).

This summary lays the framework in which I will forward my argument, but central to that background context is the concept I referred to in the introduction: heteronormativity. The term was coined by Michael Warner (who does much important work *with* the term but very little conceptual or theoretical work *on* the term), but its roots extend back at least to Adrienne Rich's famous argument concerning 'compulsory heterosexuality' (Warner 1993; Rich 1980). Some define heteronormativity as a '*practice* of organising patterns of thought, basic awareness and raw beliefs around the presumption of universal heterosexual desire, behaviour and identity' (Dennis 2003), while other definitions emphasise either 'the *rules* that force us to conform to hegemonic heterosexual standards' ('Guide to Literary and Critical Theory' 2004) or 'the *system* of binary gender' ('Wikipedia' 2004). Heteronormativity certainly involves rules, systems and practices, but to my mind none of these definitions does enough to emphasise the importance of *norms*, which proves so central to the concept. I have therefore tried to distinguish heteronormativity from both heterosexism and homophobia, as the latter terms emphasise individual acts or practices of discrimination in such a way as to neglect the importance of normalising forces. Accordingly, I have argued for the following theoretical articulation of the term (Chambers 2003: 26).

> Heteronormativity means, quite simply, that heterosexuality is the norm, in culture, in society, in politics. Heteronormativity points out the expectation of heterosexuality as it is written into our world. It does not, of course, mean that everyone is straight. More significantly, heteronormativity is not part of a conspiracy theory that would suggest that everyone must become straight or be made so. The importance of the concept is that it centres on the operation of the norm. Heteronormativity emphasises the extent to which everyone, straight or queer, will be judged, measured, probed and evaluated from the perspective of the heterosexual norm. It means that *everyone and everything is judged from the perspective of straight*.

Heteronormativity carries a certain disciplinary power with it. This means that it structures the social, political and cultural worlds not just through its impact on ideas and beliefs but also materially, in the way that it operates through institutions, laws and daily practices. For such practices, we can think of marriage, of course. But we can also think of adoption, immigration and taxes. We can think of gym memberships and car insurance. We can ponder blind dates, bathrooms and Valentine's Day. And none of this is to mention weddings. Any list of laws, customs and practices like this points to the fact that heteronormativity accrues privilege to those behaviours, practices and relationships that more closely approximate the norm, while stigmatising, marginalising or perhaps rendering invisible those behaviours, relationships and practices that deviate from the norm.

With these two background contexts in mind, I develop my argument as follows. In the second section I explore the problem (both theoretical and practical) that Claire and Russell face so concretely: how does one know one's own, or someone else's, sexuality? 'The problem of knowing' lies at the heart of the operation of heteronormativity, and the Russell/Olivier/Claire relationship reveals new and significant dimensions of that problem. I then pose the question of how to 'read' someone's sexuality, leading me to argue, as a contribution to this debate, that Russell forces both the characters around him and the viewers to experience modern categories of sexuality as somehow alienating or inadequate. This latter claim will be demonstrated through an interpretation (a failed 'reading', as it were) of the illegibility of Russell's sexuality, an illegibility that makes his character so very queer. Finally, I conclude with some brief remarks about the political significance of revisiting the closet through a reading of sexuality in *Six Feet Under*, suggesting along the way that the show makes a crucial contribution to emerging cultural politics.

II. Knowing Sexuality

How do we know if someone is gay (see Miller 1991)? Why does Claire assume Russell is gay? How can she know? She never tells us how she knows, but her assumption can only be based upon her reading of outward signs: the way Russell dresses, the way he wears his hair, the way he talks, or even the mere fact that he is a man in the art world. For a long stretch of modern Western history, the question I ask here had no answer because it had no space in which to be asked. The presumption of heterosexuality – what I have already defined and will continue to elaborate upon as heteronormativity – meant that one simply could not *be* gay. The question could not be asked. The gay liberation movement of the seventies and eighties gave a direct and concrete response to the question 'how to know if a person is gay' through the strategy of coming out. The answer: we know because he or she tells us. But, of course, Russell certainly never *tells* Claire he is gay, so all she has to go on are the signs she reads.

Seen from a certain angle, coming out breaks through the homophobic barriers of heteronormativity by calling into question the very presumption of heterosexually. Put more simply, saying 'I am gay' undermines the heteronormative assumption that everyone is heterosexual. More significantly, the more people who say 'I am gay', and the more often they say it, the more likely that the assumption of heterosexuality needs to be made explicit. In other words, coming out may throw heteronormativity into starker relief *as a norm*, thereby limiting some of its powers – since the power of norms only grows when their status as norms need not be revealed. 'Coming out', then, both gives an answer to the question 'how do we know if someone is gay?' and also increases the urgency of asking the question in the first place.

Neither the gay liberation movements nor mainstream heteronormative society have come up with many *other* responses to the question with which I open this section. Perhaps this is for the best, especially when one considers the phobic nature of the question. That is, why not ask the question instead 'how do we know if someone is straight?'. The first answer here proves to be the same as above: we need not ask, since everyone is always already presumed to *be* straight. But, unlike the first question, we can find no second response to this query. One does not 'come out' as straight, except to the extent that one merely exists in a heteronormative society. Indeed, the presumption of heterosexuality must remain just that, a presumption, since to declare one's heterosexuality is precisely to call it into question. As David Halperin puts it, 'As all the world knows, there's no quicker or surer way to compromise your own heterosexuality than by proclaiming it. After all, if you really were straight, why would you have to say so?' (1995: 48).

In one sense, then, we can answer the question 'how does Claire know Russell is gay?' with the response '*because he tells her he's not gay*'. Russell tries to do precisely what Halperin says one cannot do: declare a heterosexual identity. But heterosexuality is the identity that need not – indeed, should not – be declared. Thus Halperin reverses the famous claim about 'the love that dare not speak its name' (1995: 48) by applying it to heterosexuality rather than homosexuality. What happens to our understanding of sexuality – of Russell's in particular, but of all of those around him as well – when he says 'I'm not gay, you know'? How do we read this claim?

Trying to read this claim alerts us to the political and theoretical importance of both the questions 'how do we know someone is gay?'

and 'how do we know someone is straight?'. Folded together, these questions reduce (or add up) to the following: how do 'we' 'know' the sexuality of another person or persons? The multiple sets of quotation marks here serve to mark off the problematic of *knowing*: how can sexuality even be something to *know*, and who is placed in the position of knower and known (see Sedgwick 1990: 70; cf. Chambers 2003: 25)? If sexuality cannot be presumed (and, out from underneath the weight of heteronormativity, it cannot) and if it is not always clearly declared, then how do we come to terms with it? Without a guiding framework that makes sexuality a given, and without a clear declaration, then sexuality must be interpreted. It must be *read*. Claire and the viewers are pushed into the position of reading Russell's sexuality, both before and after he declares he is not gay. This logic suggests that the epistemological question (how do we know?) must be rewritten as an interpretive question: how do we read sexuality?

III. Reading Russell

> We are unknown to ourselves, we men of knowledge – and with good reason. We have never sought ourselves – how could it happen that we should ever find ourselves?... So we are necessarily strangers to ourselves, we do not comprehend ourselves, we *have* to misunderstand ourselves (Nietzsche 1967: 451).

Like just about any other first-year 18-year-old art student, Russell is unknown to himself. This distanciation of self from self is mediated by Russell's own sexuality, about which the only thing that can be said clearly is that Russell himself is trying to come to terms with it. I use the phrase 'come to terms with' to distance myself explicitly from notions of acceptance and recognition. Russell finds his own sexuality illegible to himself, but this is not because he is 'denying the truth' of that sexuality. It is the inadequacy of the modern, binary framework homosexual/heterosexual that makes his sexuality illegible, not the fact that he 'really is gay' but cannot accept it. Just as we are, Russell is attempting to *interpret* his sexuality, not *define* it. Russell therefore engages in a practice of reading his own sexuality, but so far as we can tell it makes no sense to him. Russell's sexuality remains thoroughly, stubbornly unclear when read through the modern categories of homosexuality and heterosexuality. In other words, Russell seems to experience those categories themselves as *other* than what he takes his own sexuality to be; or, perhaps better, he takes his own sexuality to be 'other' than the categories available to him. In distinct ways, Russell refuses both available categories of modern sexual identity.

First, Russell insists (more obstinately before, and less adamantly after, his encounter with Olivier) that he is not gay; he engages in repeated acts of *not* coming out. As Eve Kosofsky Sedgwick has shown, to maintain an openly gay identity in a heteronormative society requires and depends upon continued acts of coming out. The presumption of heterosexuality repeatedly reasserts itself, and consistently and tacitly forces even the most 'out' individuals back into the closet. Coming out is never a singular act. The character Will from *Will and Grace* thus makes a truly *awful* (in its full etymological sense) statement when he claims that 'coming out of the closet is something you only do once. It's like being born.' Here Will somehow manages to assimilate coming out, an act of potential resistance to heteronormativity, into the term heteronormativity. To be born in a heteronormative society is precisely *to be born straight*. And being born also proves to be the only singular act that determines one's sexuality; in other words, it is all you have to do to be straight. Norms cannot be overturned, replaced or erased by singular acts. Coming out reveals the functioning of heteronormativity and it may offer a real challenge to that norm. But it cannot undo it. And an individual who comes out in one context will almost immediately find him- or herself under the presumption of heterosexuality in another. I am not sure how else to say it: coming out is something you must, by definition, do a great deal more than once; it is absolutely nothing like being born.

It is easy to be straight then – unless, of course, one *appears* queer. As will become clear when I discuss some of the literature of queer theory below, I do not take 'queer' to be a synonym for 'gay'. While 'gay' denotes a sexual identity centred on same-sex desire, 'queer' suggests a type of sexuality at odds with, and often resistant to, regimes of normalised sexuality. 'Homosexuality' proves to be a category produced historically in the nineteenth century, a category of identity fixed on a certain essence of desire. Queer 'is an identity without an essence' (Halperin 1995: 62).

Perhaps because he rejects the essence of desire that freezes in place a 'homosexual' identity, Russell finds himself in the rare position of feeling the need to declare a non-gay sexuality, to come out as straight. I have already mentioned that Russell makes such a declaration to Claire, but I have also quoted Halperin to the effect that such a claim actually *undermines* the authority of the speaker and calls into question the statement that he or she makes. But perhaps I am wrong to say that Russell 'comes out as straight', since Russell never asserts any sort of heterosexual identity either. He does not pick one essence (heterosexual) over another (homosexual); all he rejects is the notion that he is gay. The fine distinction in terms proves significant, since it means that Russell never actively *identifies* with heterosexuality, even as he makes his *disidentification* with homosexuality quite clear. Indeed, the power of hetero-normativity and the narrowness of modern categories of sexuality intervene at precisely the point that Russell says 'I'm not gay, you know'; it intervenes in such a way as to *determine for others* that Russell must be straight. To deny being gay will always be taken, under the power of heteronormativity, as an implicit declaration of being straight. Heteronormativity tries to determine readings of sexuality *for us*.

Russell may reject those readings, but as viewers of the show we also take up the practice of reading Russell's sexuality. We do so, however, in a way that remains disconnected from, and outside, Russell's own hermeneutic. We view Russell's sexuality mostly through the eyes of Claire; yet we are aided as we do so by the writers and directors who engage us in that process, leaving all sorts of hermeneutic clues, signs for us to try to decipher. Claire interprets those signs in line with the binary choices offered by modern categories of sexuality, and in a way that remains constrained by the influence of heteronormativity. Her reading of Russell's sexuality traces the following path:

1. presuming he is gay, because of his outward performances of gender and desire;
2. assuming he is straight, not because he says he is, but because he denies being gay;
3. coming to question that very declaration, when Claire feels a variety of jealousies toward Olivier;
4. reverting to the previous assumption that he is gay, again, not

because he says so, but because his having sex with Olivier prohibits recourse for him (in Claire's understanding) to the category of heterosexuality.

At the beginning of their friendship, Claire tells herself and others that Russell is gay. This starting point begs a very significant question that I will not have the time or space to address here: why does Claire presume, against the normative presumption of heterosexuality, that Russell is gay? One place to begin an answer to this question might lie with generational differences in presumption of sexuality. Older generations often still operate under the assumption that unless a person is engaged in an intimate act with a person of the same sex, or appears with a sign identifying themselves as gay, then that person must be straight – or, better, the person just 'is', since heterosexuality remains utterly assumed and completely unmarked, and therefore not remarkable. Younger generations have a much greater tendency to 'read' people for their sexuality. To put it crudely, 'gaydar' is not the possession only of folks who are gay. Thus, we see that Claire reads Russell as gay, right from the start. (In terms of television, I am reminded here of a scene from *My So-Called Life*: Angela's mum, Patty Chase (Bess Armstrong), expresses concern about Angela's new friend Rickie Vasquez (Wilson Cruz), saying: 'I find Rickie a little confusing,' and Angela (Claire Danes) says, 'Okay, so maybe he's bi.' Angela's mum, never considering the possibility of his sexuality, blurts out 'What! He is what?' And Angela's ten-year-old sister, Danielle (Lisa Wilhoit), then explains: 'It means bisexual' ('Pilot', 1:1).)

Taking Russell as her gay male friend may provide Claire with a sense of security and safety: she feels she can build a strong friendship with Russell, and that he can be her sounding board for her boyfriend troubles. Declaring to others, as she does with David, that Russell is gay may help to secure for her those very notions, by reflecting them to a family member. Of course, this very act comes back to haunt Claire, since David later mentions that he thought Russell was gay. Claire reacts very defensively, as she assumes that David has come to this conclusion through his own reading – potentially more 'authentic', since he himself is gay – of Russell's sexuality. David reminds Claire that it was she who called Russell gay in the first place, and he makes fun of the very notion of 'gaydar'. Her agitated reaction here betrays the extent to which she may *still* be reading him as something other than straight ('Making Love Work', 3:6).

That agitation is only exacerbated when Claire hears from Billy that he and Olivier once had a sexual relationship. Certainly, Claire had already sensed that Olivier's intense interest in the life and work of both her and Russell also extended to sex, but the confirmation that Olivier's sexual encounters with his students also includes guys puts her more on edge. Billy, in a sense, tries to reassure her, saying: 'It was a sex thing. Not a gay thing' ('The Opening', 3:9). Yet, under the terms of heteronormativity, there is no non-normative sexuality that is not in some sense 'gay'. Or, to put it in other terms, the sexual tension between Russell and Olivier may not represent a future 'gay relationship', but it further erodes Claire's confidence in the notion – derived from his refusal of a gay identity – that he is straight. (Along the same lines, one sees no reason to conclude that Olivier is gay, but he is certainly not simply straight.)

Claire is discomfited by the fact that Russell's sexuality stubbornly remains so hard to read. She insists with some urgency that Russell declare precisely whether he is gay or not, ignoring along the way the plain fact that Russell himself does not seem to know. After the revelation of his encounter with Olivier, his claim to be uncertain about his own sexuality only angers Claire all the more ('Everyone Leaves', 3:10). And she will not allow such confusion to stand in tandem with Russell's positive and forceful declaration of his love for her. For Claire, still reading Russell through modern heteronormative categories, Russell cannot love her and be confused at the same time. Claire's insistence not just to read but *to define* Russell's sexuality probably has much to do with the way she understands her own sexuality. She can reconcile her current feelings for Russell and his past feelings for her only when she 'knows' the 'truth' about his sexuality. If he is gay, then their relationship was a front. If he is straight, then his feelings for her may have been real and their sexual encounter would be validated. But his queerness queers their seemingly heterosexual relationship (Williford 2004).

If we use the crib of heteronormativity, then it seems easy (though still confusing) to read Russell's sexuality: he is either gay or straight, and he just cannot figure it out for himself. Once he does, it will be incumbent upon him either to a) come out, or b) begin to live a consistently and thoroughly heterosexual life. If, instead, Russell merely denies a gay identity once again, or if he tries to claim a straight one, he will find himself back in the third modern category: 'confused'. To reconcile oneself to modern categories requires a recognition that one cannot come out as straight: one can either *be/act/perform* straight or come out as gay. One could complete this line of logic as follows. Russell refuses to commit to a heterosexual identity while remaining committed to a relationship with Claire. His refusal of identity, however, causes Claire to reject him. His very queerness halts their heterosexual relationship because of the fact that his sexuality cannot be clearly *defined* by his actions or feelings. For Claire, Russell's sexual ambiguity precludes the possibility of a relationship with him. For Russell, being with Claire does not affirm a sexual identity; their 'heterosexual' relationship does not really consolidate heterosexuality for Russell. For this very reason, it constitutes an extreme threat to heteronormativity. In other words, their relationship proves to be 'more queer' than a homosexual relationship because of its challenge to those categories themselves.

If we read Russell against the grain of heteronormativity, then we come to a completely different conclusion from the 'gay or straight' options found within the terms of heteronormativity. *We cannot read Russell's sexuality*. Interpreted through the framework of modern categories, his sexuality remains *illegible*. Russell experiences his own sexuality as 'other' than the modern categories, and his presence on the show can serve to denaturalise those categories for us (something much easier for us to do than for Claire, because we are not in love with Russell). Russell's refusal to come out or to effectively perform heterosexuality leads to a rejection of the terms of heteronormativity; he refuses the only things he possibly can be, gay or straight. His sexuality, then, remains in a state of *becoming*. The resistance to static identity and the embrace of becoming lies at the centre of the meaning of queer, as Halperin defines it (1995: 62).

> Unlike gay identity, which, though deliberately proclaimed in an act of affirmation, is nonetheless rooted in the positive fact of homosexual object-choice, queer identity need not be grounded in any positive truth or in any stable reality. As the very word implies, 'queer' does not name some natural kind or refer to some determinate object; it acquires its meaning from its oppositional relation to the norm. Queer is by definition *whatever* is at odds with the normal, the legitimate, the dominant. *There is nothing in*

particular to which it necessarily refers. It is an identity without an essence. 'Queer', then, demarcates not a positivity but a positionality vis-à-vis the normative – a positionality that is not restricted to lesbians and gay men but is in fact available to anyone who is or feels marginalized because of his or her sexual practices.

Russell's queer identity emerges precisely through his refusal to claim an identity with an essence. The illegibility of his sexuality produces a queer positionality, and his rejection of his only hetero-normative options constitutes his resistance to heteronormativity.

IV. The Cultural Politics of *Six Feet Under*

Six Feet Under first reveals the operation of heteronormativity by showing its viewers the workings of the closet. In watching the character of David negotiate the parameters of heteronormativity, viewers experience the power of the presumption of heterosexuality. Yet it seems crucial to note that the system of heteronormativity continues to marginalise even 'out' individuals – now not despite but because they are out. The discourse of 'tolerance' operates by way of the same epistemological privilege as 'discrimination'. In other words, that discourse says we as a society will tolerate you but we insist on *knowing* whether you are gay or not. It is unacceptable, however, for your sexuality to remain an undecided. And this means that trans-gender identities are erased whenever possible, while bisexuality either means a transit point on the way to being truly gay or a lifestyle option of sexy younger women.

The power of heteronormativity to co-opt even the discourse of gay rights points to the continued significance of *Six Feet Under* as a show that participates in cultural politics (see Atkinson 2004). With the character of Russell we witness a more radical form of resistance to heteronormativity (even though Russell could never serve as a poster child for the mainstream gay movement). As if we needed another way of putting it, Russell reveals the ludicrous nature of the claim that 'coming out … is like being born'. The reading of Russell's sexuality shows us exactly how alienated we can be from our very own categories of sexuality. It shows us that our sexual practices and identities are both specific and 'othering'. Indeed, it is not Russell who is weird in his sexuality but the very presumptive categories of sexuality that are bizarre in their heteronormative expectations. Those expectations and their attendant coercive capacities are heightened and strengthened through proclamations like 'National Defense of Marriage Week', and (it almost goes without saying) through President Bush's endorsement of a 'Federal Marriage Amendment'. Resistance here must emerge both electorally – as a fight against disenfranchisement for lesbians and gays – and also through cultural politics. In its continued ability to undermine the power of heteronormativity, *Six Feet Under* remains a valuable asset in this latter battle.

Part 5
Reflections:
music and
melancholia

S&D @ HBO (TR for *SFU*)

A death for starters, a main course of sex:
desire or rigor mortis makes that smile
we watch uneasily. These lives, these wrecks

laid out, vile bodies mended, made less vile:
the ones who undertake to view might gag
if there was nothing done mortician-style,

if no incision let the gas out of the bag,
no satin covered the serrated slash
of muscles that once shuddered to a shag.

A fuck's around the corner, so's a crash:
the body biker-sex once dirtied down
gets cleaned for stardom at a funeral bash.

The heart (to some the soul) must also drown
in sex to stem the ghostly father's ache,
his heard voice visualised: death's not a noun

declined with a deliberate mistake.
At family teas dysfunctionally they find
that life's not just a piece of grassed-up cake,

more of a soup they're swimming in, half-blind,
uncertain who to touch or kiss or curse.
Ecstasy is met with undesigned

and paranoia makes plain love perverse
until the penny drops: life's more complex
than sucking off a loser in a hearse.

A lifted casket lid, a mourner checks
for faults, berates foul-mouthed mortality:
we watch uneasily these lives, these wrecks
(a death for starters, a main course of sex).

    Peter Wilson

fifteen

I'm dead, wow, cool: the music of *Six Feet Under*

The success of the first season *Six Feet Under* in 2001 included much critical appreciation for the music. Caryn James, in her *New York Times* article, comments on the musical connections between *Six Feet Under* and other TV shows (James 2001, E25). Her article not only highlights the way soundtracks are increasingly becoming a focal point of popular US TV series, but also serves to remind me of similarities between *Six Feet Under* and *Twin Peaks*, maybe its most direct ancestor. Not only are both shows strongly marked by their creators (Alan Ball and David Lynch) but their filmic pedigrees, the originality of their underscores and innovative use of such, distinguishes their use of music. In this chapter I will chart the complex musical territory of *Six Feet Under* by identifying its historical pedigree which, I will argue, is rooted in movies and popular culture. I will then provide an analysis of the main title music of *Six Feet Under* and discuss how music is used, generally, in 'The Pilot' episode (1:1). The chapter concludes with an interview with Richard Marvin, who composes the original weekly underscore for the series.

The History

Since the late 1940s, American dramatic television music, due to fore-shortened drama lengths, shorter post-production schedules, format obligations and smaller budgets, has curiously reflected the music of feature films. As the larger radio networks took on television, they retained the familiar radio formats, themes and act-ins and -outs, clarion calls acting as a musical curtain opening and closing, creating an imagined separation between the diegesis and the commercial announcements that paid the bills. This created an identifying aural brand for each show, capable of going through doors and reaching around corners, alerting the viewer that their favourite show was about to begin.

HBO makes use of a different type of musical signature in its original programming. As it is supported by paid subscriptions there is no need to stop the diegesis for commercials and station identification. The constant musical reminders, the curtain closings and openings are absent, making the shows feel more like feature films. Starting with *Sex and the City* and followed by *The Sopranos*, it was discovered that a lack of musical underscore lent verisimilitude. The places where music was used in the HBO scores were as source (diegetic), both because music happens in real life and also because it adds quickly readable sociological/psychological signs about the people playing or listening to the music. All non-diegetic underscore was minimalised for fear of exposing any intentional, emotional manipulation to the audience. 'Trust me, this is real life', the absent underscore lied.

The Music of *Six Feet Under*

The music of *Six Feet Under* can be split into three distinct departments overseen by executive producers Alan Ball and Alan Poul – although it is reported that music is Ball's domain. The three departments are: the main title composed by Thomas Newman (while the pilot was still in post-production); the licensed (pre-existing) music, which is suggested, researched and licensed by Thomas Golubic and Gary Calamar (of the firm SuperMusicVision); and the original underscore, composed and performed for each episode by Richard Marvin. As I shall argue, it is Alan Ball's strong awareness and appreciation of these three branches that contribute to the success of the final product.

Thomas Newman

Thomas Newman was an obvious choice for Alan Ball when he was deciding on a composer for his new TV series about a dysfunctional family of undertakers. The two men had previously worked together on *American Beauty* to critical acclaim and commercial success. Newman picked up the Anthony Asquith Award for Film Music at the BAFTA Awards, the BMI Film Music Award and the 2001 Grammy for Best Score Soundtrack Album for a Motion Picture, as well as receiving nominations for Best Original Score at the Academy Awards and Golden Globes. Television producers have long turned to well-known composers to score music for the main titles. But the practice has fallen out of favour because of the high expense involved. In addition, many feature composers do not want to tarnish their reputations by working in television. Two recent exceptions are James Newton Howard, who composed the main theme for NBC's hit hospital drama, *E.R.*, and Mark Isham for its CBS rival, *Chicago Hope*. Newman had worked on television before, composing the main title of *Boston Public*.

One would hope not to have to mention Newman's family background in writings such as this but for its Hollywood pedigree. Newman's father, Alfred Newman (1901–1970), came to Hollywood in 1930 straight from a successful career on Broadway. He scored hundreds of movies, including *Captain from Castile* (1947), *The Robe* (1953), *The King and I* (1956), *South Pacific* (1958), *How the West Was Won* (1962) and *Airport* (1970), and was nominated for over 40 Academy Awards, of which he went on to win nine. He was later music supervisor for Goldwyn, a job he held for ten years before moving to Twentieth-Century Fox, with whom he worked for the next 20 years. His influence on film music during the heyday of the studio system was considerable. Alfred was not the only musical success in the family. His siblings, Lionel and Emil, have hundreds of scores to their credit, and Lionel ended up as head of Twentieth-Century Fox's music department following Alfred's departure. The second generation include three of Alfred's children, David, Thomas and Maria, all of whom are successful composers, as well as their cousin, singer-song-writer Randy Newman, who is also known for composing music for motion pictures (he picked up an Academy Award for the song 'If I Didn't Have You', from *Monsters, Inc.*, in 2001). And a third generation, Lionel's grandson Joey, is already gathering credits.

Thomas Newman has a dual musical identity. One is as a worthy descendant of a musical line that goes from Charles Ives to Aaron Copeland and the Elmer Bernstein of *To Kill A Mockingbird* (1962). He utilises a strong yet simple 'American' (read folk, triadic, modal) style that is closely crafted to the emotional key points. Examples from Newman's work in this style include *The Shawshank Redemption* (1994), *Little Women* (1994), *How to Make an American Quilt* (1995) and *Road to Perdition* (2002). He is a master of this style, bringing an emotional strength and accuracy to these scores.

The other is a more idiosyncratic style, defined by an amalgamation of 'world music' rhythms and instrumentation (perhaps the 'classical' music of our time (Ling 2003)) with an ambivalent, almost improvisational new age harmony and melodies. Fully realised in *American Beauty*, this style can be heard strongly hinted in *Desperately Seeking Susan* (1985), and makes noticeable appearances in films including *The Rapture* (1991), *The Player* (1992) and *Flesh and Bone* (1993). Its strength is the accuracy of colour with minimal elements, balancing ambivalence and emotion.

This second style requires a different composing technique from the traditional. It does not presume the Western orchestra and disrespects traditional associations, so that an Indian tabla and a tropical marimba can accompany the story of white, middle-class Americans as in *American Beauty*. Newman says of his approach to scoring (Newman 1996):

> My approach normally is to start from a point of colour, meaning do I hear woodwind sounds or do I hear plucking sounds or bell sounds, and I try to build up. I normally start from a point of colour as opposed to a point of melody, and that's probably because I figure at some point I'll have to write melody anyway, so it's kind of a given, whereas colour is just fun to think about. What would happen if I did this or that, and what would happen if I used this kind of instrument?

In the 'featurette' on the making of the main title sequence (on the DVD of season one), it is revealed that both Ball and Newman share a working style of aesthetic management that I label 'the patient shopper'. They might not know what they want but they know it when they hear/see it. In this spirit, one of Newman's techniques is to use a group of instrumentalists specialising in making 'out of the ordinary' sounds on their instruments, either through their playing techniques or through physical and/or electronic modification. Newman will describe a sound he might like, and when this group creates their varied responses he decides how and where he might use these 'found objects'.

The Main Title

The main title of *Six Feet Under* enjoys a strongly symbiotic relationship between picture and music. The music was written first (more often not the case) and the graphic team then created the visuals to match the music, resulting in something more akin to a music video than a television main title. As a result of this process, both visual and musical accent points are highly synchronised, reducing the cognitive work required to reconcile the two elements and creating a strong impression of musical/visual 'appropriateness' (a phenomenon noticed in practice and confirmed in empirical studies (Lipscomb and Kendall 1994)). This particular example of a marriage between the visual and musical resonates with symbolic synergy.

Ching! Right on the downbeat. A chord that the high piano and icy synthesiser patch chime together. In one beat the public is alerted. It is the musical brand for *Six Feet Under*, instantly recognisable to the viewer. The raised fourth (a B sharp) makes this dominant seventh chord special. It is bright, almost cheerful; its attack sharp, like something breaking, and yet extremely restless and harmonically, ambiguously unstable. Visually, we are looking at the sky crossed by a crow. There is no sense of how far down the ground might be. The chime fades into an ethereal, high sample/synthesiser note (the resolution of the raised fourth to a major third), as the camera pans down to a tree and a hill. The harmonic resolution seems to happen as the ground is localised. We are 'grounded' both harmonically and visually.

The major third is amusing for at least two reasons: a) this style normally relies on not committing to any third (the scale degree that defines the major from the minor), but, in a gentle way, it does so here; and b) Newman has consciously put a major third here. This is, after all, a show about a family working in the mortuary trade, and one thing musicians and non-musicians alike know about funeral music is that it is slow and minor. But here it resolves to almost 'happy', at least in the beginning. This tonal allusiveness is part of what makes the title music feel dreamlike and unsettled. And the tempo is perky, almost allegro.

This ethereal vocal/string-like sound, which the initial chime/piano dissolves into, contains a burble of what might be the high partials of an automobile hubcap spinning loose on the pavement. This is a subtle foreshadowing of the jingly-jangly percussion to come. Four bars of four – neat and even. When it repeats with pizzicato strings, as the hands are broken apart by the chime, the basses play a jaunty dance rhythm, a syncopation of the second attack in each bar. The major third is then lost to the ambivalence of the root under the hand washing. The low violins/violas start a figure that somehow finds the line between energetic and stately. Everything falls into neat pairs of twos, building up, but first a stop for a bar of six to contemplate the idea with that hubcap spinning, like the sky above, in slow motion.

The gurney wheel spins and we are off. Various tickings add a mix of someone tapping his watch to show you time is getting on, and a jaunty enjoyment of the ride. The soprano saxophone/oboe d'amore leads (although, not being typical Newman instruments, it could just be a cor anglais) and aspires to the spiritual by reaching up to the note but always falling back. It feels mediæval, but there is also a jazzy, sensual cockiness.

The gurney continues along the corridor: a loose bearing in the wheel, a soft pointillistic cloud of higher string plucks teasing the major third again and creating an eccentric lightness of air effect. Instead of the obvious death tradition of gloom and despair, Newman and Ball have decided to go with the always present opposite tradition. Death is a ride in a clown car with a bunch of wild and weird party people: Nino Rota might approve.

The embalming fluid dances its six-beat dance with the jolliness of Balinese shadow puppets, the sliding bass pushing the very last drop out. A rest. We needed that. A brow is wiped. But then a brazilian *quica* (a squeaky percussion instrument) bird laughs at the folded hands! Nature doesn't stop when we die. Then a two-bar surrealistic break to honour human hope and to set up a repeat of the main theme – as the flowers wilt, the music solemnly resolves and lifts up its eyes to the master. The reversed, backwards-sounding amplitude envelope adds to the surreal effect of the time-lapse photography.

There is an urban myth that the nursery rhyme 'Ring-a-Ring-a-Roses' is about the fourteenth-century plagues; the lyrics list the pathology of the illness, ending in death, and are sung as a cheerful chant. It is to this mediæval tradition that the *Six Feet Under*'s main theme belongs. Harmonically, it functions as a drone, hurdy-gurdy-like, while the pizzicato strings keep trying to trick us otherwise. The only true harmonic movement is at the hopeful turnaround (the flowers wilting) and at the end of the second statement of the melody.

The visuals in the second iteration of the melody are impressive, although lacking the same kinetic connection to the music as before. The slow-moving coffin masks the flying clouds that would otherwise carry the energy. The still pictures of gravestones and old photographs seem simply unwilling to dance. The basses get a little more rumbustious in encouragement. But at the end we are finally set right. The very last note of the second and last iteration of the melody slips down to the minor third, the bass sliding with it. 'This is about death after all', the image of the crow seems to rasp, although the echoes of the chirping accompaniment have not yet got the message. The crow flies away, knocking Alan Ball's third credit off the screen with one last 'ching', as if to say 'enough of this human malarkey'. The tree squeaks out its concurrence, and *Six Feet Under*, the ground humming low, awaits us all.

The Licensed Music

Licensed music fills an important function in *Six Feet Under* at a time when music is meta-symbol of culture and lifestyle choices. It acts as a knowing wink from programme makers to the viewer, whether through actual lyrics or the cultural currency associated with the song. Licensed music has also usurped many traditional underscoring purposes, either reflecting a character's interior state, altering the sense of time passing or quickly telling us what the images cannot. This is because, as the licensed music can be perceived as having a legitimate place in the diegesis, it can bypass many of the modern viewer's sensitivities to emotional manipulation that a similar underscore would trigger.

Much great thought and work goes into the licensed music of the show. It is the job of musical supervisors Thomas Golubic and Gary Calamar, who have for years been DJs at KCRW (Santa Monica), a radio station known for its cutting-edge, eclectic music appreciation. They bring not only a vast knowledge of different styles of music to the show but a 'finger on the pulse' awareness of contemporary musical tastes. In consultation with Alan Ball, they develop identifying styles for various characters (such as Brazilian bossanova sophistication for Brenda's parents, rock for Claire or classical for Ruth), and establish the culture of the various locations (nightclubs, restaurants).

Licensing a piece of music can be an expensive business. There are two rights that must be licensed. One is with the owner of the song for the right to synchronise the underlying musical conception to picture. The other is with the owner of the recording. Each requires negotiating lawyers and contracts. You might have the perfect song for a scene but if either party decides they want a large amount of money, or do not want their song connected with the production, you can be out of luck. Sometimes the owners cannot be located, which causes additional problems. Although the budget for licensed music on *Six Feet Under* started small, it has burgeoned to six figures per episode over the four seasons.

Golubic and Calamar start by reading the script and listing possibilities while discussing ideas with Ball. By the final day, on the dubbing stage where the audio is mixed together, they may have assembled a handful of possibilities for each cue, edited so that starts, ends and possibly pertinent lyrics are properly placed. Each possibility has had to be researched in terms of copyright and permission acquired. Alan Ball reviews the choices and picks the one to use. To demonstrate their particularly creative use of licensed music, as well as some of its usual functions, I will use the pilot episode as a guide ('Pilot', 1:1).

The first piece starts right after the main title, a *faux* commercial for a 'Millennium Edition' hearse. The music used to accompany the commercial is the operatic aria 'L'Amour est un Oiseau Rebelle', from *Carmen* by Bizet. Since the music is out of copyright (Bizet died in 1875) there is no need for it to be licensed, and the recording could be from an inexpensive music library. Few will recognise the melody; fewer still will know the opera and its association with bullfighting. Almost all will recognise the sound as opera – elegant and glamorous. Exactly the message the advertiser is outlining in the voice-over. This cue also shows the conscious editing of the music with the perfect ending line, throttled by the collapsing of the picture and audio when the power is turned off.

Right into the next example, 'I'll Be Home for Christmas', sung by Bing Crosby and written by Walter Kent, Kim Gannon and Buck Ram. It is used to introduce the doomed father of the Fisher family, Nathaniel, as it plays on the car radio in the brand new 'Millennium Edition' hearse driven by him. The song is also playing on the radio in the Fishers' kitchen, where Ruth and David hear it. Although originating from World War II, it is a Christmas song played each year over the holidays; it thus establishes the time of year for us. Moreover, identified with fifties pop and light jazz, it says much about Nathaniel and his tastes: he is more a smoothie than a rebel. There are several examples of cognitive dissonance here that ironically comment on what we are seeing. It is contemporary times but the song is old; it is a Christmas tune but we are in snowless, sunny southern California. Another emotional frisson occurs when the sweet song plays on over the image of the bus colliding with the hearse and killing Nathaniel. We intuitively know that radios can play on in such situations, inviting us to suspend our disbelief, but we take note of the incongruence of the song and the situation. As the lyric 'if only in my dreams' wafts through the street after the fatal accident, back inside the house Ruth cuts her finger. The song's lyrics concern a wartime soldier's promise, and are filled with nostalgia and longing – everyone will be nostalgic for Nathaniel for the rest of the series. He will continue to appear, if only in the dreams of the other Fishers, and often he will be accompanied by fifties pop and light jazz.

Another interesting aspect of this cue is how it shifts between diegetic/source and non-diegetic/score. There is little concern for the realities of music here. It shifts from radio to commentator to score to represent the characters' emotions with such skill that it disarms any resentment for the obvious manipulation. Notice how the cue starts out on the street; it is score, since the people on the street cannot hear it, only us. We cut into the hearse. Nathaniel is singing along; it is source. He turns down the radio when the phone rings, confirming it is diegetic sound. He picks up the phone and answers. We cut to the exterior of the Fisher Funeral Home and family residence, while the music level stays the same; it is non-diegetic. It is also un-effected. This means that the myriad qualities our brains use to judge the source of a sound, including amplitude level, frequency content and phase and time anomalies such as reverb, remain unchanged. If it was diegetic a dubbing mixer would try to change these qualities from cut to cut to match up with what might be expected in the visible space; in this case it has not been done. We cut to the interior of the Fisher house, through a window between the kitchen and living room at the big music console, telling us the music is now coming from there; it is diegetic/source again. This demonstrates how much of this clever working of music is conceived early on. Here it is already in the shooting script. When the song finishes, no radio announcer comes on and there is no new music segue. It is score/ non-diegetic again. Much can happen, and much can be learnt about a family and the depth of its love for each other, in the two minutes and ten seconds that it takes this song to play.

One can compare this with the much more traditional use of source in the cue that follows. This cue intercuts with the interior of Claire's car. On her car radio is a barely distinguishable piece of aggressive rock, identified as 'Attitude' by a group called Hardknox. We hear it only when we are in the car with Claire, which solidly attaches it to the car's stereo, and additionally it has been 'effected' to sound as though it is playing in a car. Although this appears to be library music it immediately notifies us that teenager Claire is a bit of a rebel. Spylab's 'Celluloid Hypnotic' does double duty in the next scene, as it diegetically conveys some of the musical tastes and cultural aspects of Claire and her friends while they smoke crystal meth. At the same time it has a hallucinatory effect that helps us to identify with the internal state of the group, and, moreover, when Claire learns her father is dead and is momentarily speechless, the music becomes her internal state. When she utters the words 'he's dead' to her friends the drums kick in and she panics.

Then there is the diegetic piece of baroque music by Albinoni, which, although particularly appropriate and tasteful for a funeral service at the Fisher and Sons Funeral Home (and even commented on, appreciatively, by someone at the service), is completely inappropriate for what Nathaniel's son, David, is feeling. This is a sophisticated reversal, successful because of the amount of visual signals provided by the director and actor. We fairly explode with

David in relief when he finally screams, and then giggle at ourselves because it was a fantasy. The same, particularly gentle phrase is looped, repeating its cloying rightness. We cut to another scene, and then back to where a mourner starts, aggravatingly, bearing down, camera zooming in and filling the screen with the tormentor's face, music pulled down to heighten the reality. This time David really screams, the music flooding back with the other sounds of the room to heighten the sudden shameful awareness, its appropriateness now seeming a stern comment on the inappropriateness of David's scream.

For ten minutes of the episode there is a piece of music playing that is identified, in the on-line music list, as Mozart's Divertimento no.1, Andante. This is a tremendous understatement. Ten minutes is a long time for one piece of music in this medium, and Alan Ball himself reportedly put this section together. It is minutely and specifically worked in, both in the editing and the mixing, and is one of those great works of craft the effectiveness of which is measured by its seeming invisibility. At first glance it is just another use of appropriate funeral music for Nathaniel's wake. Closer inspection reveals that it also works as the 'zombie world' score for Nate's heartfelt admission to his sister; it is also an Italian movie soundtrack to accompany the surreal story of the Sicilian funeral that Nate recounts on his travels; a distant sadness for Ruth's breakdown and the admission of her infidelity; and the score to a host of other vignettes involving the extended family, which range from comic to tragic.

The last song in 'The Pilot', 'Waiting' by The Devlins, is another unique kind of music use and the last example from this episode. Personal to Alan Ball (who wrote it into the script) and not bothering to masquerade as source, it functions as Nate's inner voice when he sees his father board the bus. The lyrics seem to be about something important; one can hear that the person will always be waiting. But this essentially trite paean to self-pity is masked by the earnest seriousness of the vocal performance and musical accompaniment. As in the main title, the music and images are very carefully intercut so that one does not consciously notice the intentionality behind the dramatic musical break just before the bus moves, the space artfully filled with the rhythmic and emotional punctuation of the bus's air brakes sighing. This is key to much of the music used in this style, and, as used in *American Beauty*, it implies importance but never tells you the significance of it.

The Underscore and Interview

Richard Marvin's more lyrical take on Thomas Newman's eclectic style is another case of good casting by the producers. Although there is less underscore in this show than in most other television dramas, the licensed music fulfilling many of its traditional roles, it is still called upon for the most specific and important emotional moments. The three cues that Marvin used to audition for the job worked so well that they remained in the pilot and are used as the music for the DVD menus.

One of these, during Nate's nostalgic dream of his family in younger days ('Pilot', 1:1), shows the prescience to foreshadow the theme's string/vocal ethereal note. A high, muted guitar tremolo note adds a pointillistic cloud not unlike the high pizzicato strings in the theme. The lack of diegetic sound and the incongruent tempo tell us that we should perceive this from someone else's perspective. When the B flat chord (bVI) shows up *sans* third, it feels all of a sudden warm; only a promise, though, as the harmony moves to the C chord (bVII), but always thwarted by melodic appoggiaturas or harmonic suspensions. In the end it just barely fizzles back to the tonic D as we see Nate awaken.

A minute later we are presented with another non-committal, if a hair more sprightly, Celtic whisper as Nate satisfies Ruth's desire that he stay. But the more prominent thirds and final resolution over Nate's running provide just enough colour to tell us this is good. Both of these cues show a careful and sophisticated knowledge of the emotional/musical language.

*   *   *

I interviewed Richard Marvin in July 2004 at his studio in Studio City, California.

PK: So, how did you come to be scoring *Six Feet Under*?

RM: My former agent, Seth Kaplan, told me about it and submitted a tape, and then we got a call back. There were four finalists and they asked if I would be interested in doing three scenes as a demo. I said, 'Sure.' I did that and it got down to two of us, and then we had an interview with Alan Poul and Alan Ball. I hit it off with the Alans, and they liked my music.

PK: Had they given you the theme, or any instructions?

RM: No, the theme hadn't been done yet. They gave me three scenes from the pilot. No instructions. I knew Alan Ball was from *American Beauty* so I had an idea that the direction would be minimal, ambient and piano-based.

PK: How long later did you start, considering the theme wasn't done yet?

RM: It might have been a couple of months. The first episode was really easy as they just used my demos in the show. They liked them so much they put them into the 'temp' [a temp track is a music track that is put in just for viewing when editing]. To be replaced with the final music. And then there were just a couple of extra ones.

PK: When did Thomas Golubic and Gary Calamar come into the picture?

RM: They were already there, and we had a lot of interaction at that time because it was a low-budget show for HBO, so we made a deal for me to do the music editing as well as the composing, which was a complete disaster. They have a very unique [sic] way of working. They give many, many, many choices for each selection, and each choice has to be cut up so that certain parts of the song land a certain way. So that was my job to do, and I lasted only seven episodes.

PK: It seems in the first season there was more an attempt to have the songs comment on the drama.

RM: I think that has kinda gone away in subsequent seasons. They still cut it very carefully; even on source you barely are going to hear.

PK: So, spotting; where does it start with each show?

RM: Now, Gary and Thomas have a session with the Alans. First because it takes longer for them to clear stuff. And then we have a spotting session with sound and score later – a week and a half in front of the dub.

PK: Do they make you score everything and then just make you one of the choices?

RM: No. Alan Ball, who is totally in charge of where the music goes, he oversees everything. He has got a really incredible knowledge of bands and music. Fortunately for me, he and I sort of relate to music in the same way.

PK: You don't seem to get asked too much to score the traditional places, like transitions?

RM: I don't think he knows what one is. He likes the show to be a little shocking. Not shocking, but when you go from one scene to the next he wants you to notice it. He doesn't want to smooth out the show like other TV guys. And, also, he has such great performance that he's not trying to fix something.

PK: Who are the people commenting and coming up with the ideas – the directors? As I think I've noticed a musical difference between episodes directed by Alan Ball and others.

RM: The directors, in general, do not have much to say about the music. The writers have more impact on the music; because Alan Ball, being a writer, makes sure they have a lot of say in what goes on. Especially in the first season, there would be references to specific songs in the scripts. There still are.

PK: Some of these can be expensive, but you say it is a low-budget show?

RM: It's not any more.

PK: The licensed songs are listed on the Website. But I often hear source music that isn't listed. I have assumed that this is you?

RM: There is some I do. I do a lot of the classical, pseudo-classical music – for the slumber room. I often have to do source that needs to change.

PK: Yes, I have noticed that Ruth seems to listen to classical music. But is not really a cognoscente?

RM: I think Alan, in particular, wants to promote that she is in a little box, trying to be sophisticated and intellectual. I would say his point on most music is that it is projecting something about the character. Everyone has their kind of music to which they listen.

PK: The emotions you play are very carefully specific. Is this your spotting or does Alan point these out in spotting?

RM: He is very specific. I would think, in the first couple of years, it was pretty clear what he was going for. He would say, 'This is surreal,' or 'This is incredibly sad' or 'This is just a heightened awareness with just a taste of sadness', and I would have to say there is a tad of sadness in everything in the show. I have been accused, by other directors, of having a tad of sadness in anything I do, which I think has helped me a lot in this show, a sort of melancholia, so I can relate to it.

PK: But a lot of the time the music feels emotionally non-committal. It allows the audience to be more emotional, while you pick your spots – avoiding thirds, or using them at very specific moments?

RM: There are more thirds in the last couple of seasons than the first two. That's interesting... We are very careful we are not commenting on the emotions. We are trying to provide an environment where the emotion becomes slightly more moving or enhanced.

PK: So, when he says 'this is incredibly sad', that doesn't mean he wants you to weep all over?

RM: No, whenever I try something, like in the fourth season, when Nate buries his wife. To me, it was so emotional, so operatic that I wrote this, like, Puccini-esque string thing. I thought it was great. I played it for them and they just sat there and said, 'It's killing the scene. It's just too emotional.' So I went back to what I know works for them, which is the suspended stuff, non-committal piano, a lot of false cues building up to something and not going there, and they're weeping on the couch, saying: 'Now you're letting the characters do it, you're not commenting on how sad this is.'

PK: It seems towards the end of shows there is almost always a reunion, a sense of resolution between two members of the family that have been at odds, and there you bring a quality of hope in the music.

RM: I always try to make it … as bleak as some of these situations are. Intrinsically, I think this is just life. And there is courage that people have. To me this show has tons of love in it. These characters all love each other, and that's when you go to that major chord in a low register, that is what you are saying: that this is life.

PK: Does Alan talk about trying to delineate the characters, musically, through your underscore, as opposed to the source?

RM: Well, we have had some character themes. Ruth has a theme. It started out, in the pilot, when she is opening the kitchen cabinets and asking Nate if he had to leave. That has recurred at times: Ruth feels lost and the family is leaving her. There is also 'Nate remembering his dad' theme, from the pilot, where he is going down the stairs to the prep room. And in the pilot, when Nate is on the bus remembering his dad squirting him with the hose. This nostalgia Nate feels for his dad happens a few times through the first two seasons. There is no David theme, or Claire.

PK: And there are times where the music seems to be about time flow, sense of time moving.

RM: I always think of it as trying to suspend time.

sixteen

Playing in the deep
end of the pool

Like David Fisher in the new HBO series, *Six Feet Under*, when my
father died I embalmed him. My brother Pat assisted. We dressed
him, put him in a box and soon thereafter buried him. Tim did the
obits and drove the hearse. Eddie called the priest and did the printing.
Mary handled the florals and disbursements. Julie organised the
luncheon that would follow. Brigid got the pipers and the soloist.
Christopher called the sexton and stonecutter. Colonel Dan, the
eldest of us, flew in from his army post in Seattle and assumed
command. We all were pall-bearers.

It's what we do – family and funerals. It is what our father had
taught us to do.

Like David Fisher, I have siblings – alas, four times as many –
and a funeral home. In fact, we have four of them. Lynch and Sons
is what we call them. And, unlike David and his brother Nate, we're
not just 'on' one night a week for an hour. Like the venerable London
firms of Leverton and Sons (now eight generations old) or A. France
and Sons (who buried Lord Nelson), we are always 'on'. Whenever
someone calls, we answer. Round the clock and round the calendar
we're at the ready. Dinners and Christmases, holidays and family
outings, days off and the night's sleep – every imaginable intimacy
has been interrupted by a death in the family, someone else's family,
be they royalty or regulars. Of course, the Levertons are in Camden

Town and the Frances are in Holborn, and the Lynches are, in fact, in Milford, Michigan – real places where the cameras aren't running and the characters aren't acting and the corpses aren't manufactured by the prop makers. The Fisher brothers are in, well, Hollywood. And it shows.

Six Feet Under is a caricature – deftly sketched; a cartoon, in the best artistic sense, of life and death and the undertaking trade. As such it traffics in hyperbole and lampoon – a purposeful distortion that helps us see the truth. Still, it is more than just another smart, hip, sure-fire hit show. Beyond the weekly belly laughs and heartbreaks, between which viewers are run up and back the emotional register and are thereby 'entertained', there seems a deliberate effort to probe a deeper question: *what should we do when someone dies?*

Before Alan Ball, the prevailing version of matters mortuary, four decades old, was Mitfordian: death as non-event; the undertaker as obsequious ghoul, an extremely unctuous predator with an inordinate interest in dead human bodies and an overpriced box for every occasion. Jessica Mitford's *American Way of Death*, published in 1963 and again in 1998, made much of the sales pitch and oddments of the funeral biz, most of which she pulled from the pages of *Mortuary Management* – a trade magazine still being read in *Six Feet Under*.

Of course, Mitford's own experiences of death in Britain and America – her first daughter's death in infancy of a fever, her first husband's death in World War II, and the death of her first son, Nicholas, killed at age 10 in a horrible accident in Oakland, California – were never mentioned in either the original or revisited text. Indeed, Nicholas, who was delivering newspapers on a bike when the bus ran him down, is never even mentioned in the two volumes of Mitford's autobiography. His death was simply 'disappeared' from the story of her life. Decca, as she was known to friends, preferred the stiff upper lip, a good laugh to the good cry and the talk of money to the talk of mourning when it came to deaths in the family. On the maths of caskets she was a good read and reliable source. On the deeper meanings of life and death she seemed, sadly, to have no clue.

Nathaniel Fisher, Sr, is also killed by a bus in California. He's driving his new hearse to the airport to pick up his first son, Nate, who is coming home for the holidays from Seattle and who, at the moment of his father's death, is having vigorous and blissfully anonymous sex with a fellow pilgrim in an airport broom closet.

Like Shakespeare and the book of Genesis, Alan Ball has a knack for getting sex and death, the good laugh and the God-awful, the ridiculous and sublime, in the same scenes.

On the matter of bodies, Ball offers a version that is more fleshy and recognisable. While Mitford preferred the dead kept out of sight and out of mind, Ball brings them front and centre, with all their wounds and foibles and post-mortem scars, to be dealt with before they are disposed of, and afterwards. Every episode begins with an end – a death from usual to not so usual causes – and a stone with names and dates cut in. And this damaged but not entirely dysfunctional family of funeral directors – Fisher and Sons – is not so ghoulish as they are ordinary neurotics, made extraordinary by living under the one roof with the constant procession of the dead and bereaved.

When Alan Ball was 13, his sister died in a car accident, and his mother's abject grief was hushed and over-buffered by the fashions in funerals then – to treat grief as a structural weakness, by which people were forever 'breaking down' or 'falling apart' or 'going to pieces'. Ball recognises that both the undertakerly tendency to prettify death, with cosmetics and euphemism and warm-fuzzies, and Mitford's instructions to dispose of them by hasty cremation in the name of convenience and cost efficiency are equally misguided efforts to get around rather than through the difficult business of mortality. Disguise and disappearance are both denials. So is diversion.

What Alan Ball so clearly 'gets' is that the funerals are about the living *and* the dead – the talk and the traffic between them. In his show, they constantly confront one another. He lets them occupy the same space, often the unlikely 'space' of the Fisher and Sons mortuary, where the living look the dead in the face. Not because we need answers but because, in the face of mortality, we need to stand and look, watch and wonder, listen and remember. Alan Ball presses us to examine the difference between the fashions and the fundamentals in the business of death.

And it is time we did.

With the erosion of religious, ethnic and social connections and the rituals and metaphors they provide to confront mortality and bereavement, more and more of us must reinvent, from the leftovers and borrowings of our various traditions, the wheel that works the space between the deaths that happen and the deaths that matter. This is what we do funerals for; not only to dispose of our dead, but to bear witness to their lives and times among us, to affirm the difference their living and dying makes among kin and community, and to provide a vehicle for the healthy expression of grief and faith and hope and wonder. The value of a funeral proceeds neither from how much we spend nor from how little. A death in the family is an existential event, not only or entirely a medical, emotional, religious or retail one.

I came up burying Presbyterians and Catholics, devout and lapsed, born again and backslidden Baptists, Orthodox Christians, an occasional Zen Buddhist and variously observant Jews. For each of these sets, there were infinite subsets. We had right old Calvinists who drank only single malts and were all good Masons and were mad for the bagpipes, just as we had former Methodists who worked their way up the Reformation ladder after they married into money or made a little killing in the market. We had Polish Catholics and Italian ones, Irish and Hispanic and Byzantine, and Jews who were Jews in the way some Lutherans are Lutheran – for births and deaths and first marriages.

My late father, himself a funeral director, schooled me in the local orthodoxies and their protocols, as I have schooled my sons and daughter, who work with me. There was a kind of comfort, I suppose, in knowing exactly what would be done with you, one's ethnic and religious identities having established long ago the fashions and the fundamentals for one's leave-taking. And, while the fashions might change, the fundamental ingredients for a funeral were the same: someone who has quit breathing for ever, some others to whom it apparently matters, and someone else who stands between the quick and dead – priest or shaman, rabbi or imam – and says something like 'behold, I show you a mystery'.

'An act of sacred community theatre', Dr Thomas Long, writer, thinker and theologian, calls this 'transporting' of the dead from this life to the next. 'We move them to a further shore. Everyone has a part in this drama.' The dead get to the grave or fire or tomb while the living get to the edge of a life they must learn to live without them. The transport is ritual, ceremonial, metaphor and reality, process and procession, witness and participation.

Late in the last century there was some trending towards the more home-grown doxologies. Everyone was into the available 'choices'. We started doing more cremations – it made good sense. People seemed less 'grounded' than their grandparents, more 'portable', 'divisible', more 'scattered' somehow. We got into balloon releases and homing pigeons done up as doves to signify the flight of the dead fellow's soul towards heaven. 'Bridge over Troubled Water' replaced 'How Great Thou Art'. And if Paul's Letter to the Romans or the Book of Job was replaced by Omar Khyyam or Emily Dickinson, what harm? After great pain, a formal feeling comes, rings as true as any sacred text. A death in the family is, as Miss Emily describes it, First – Chill – then Stupor – then the letting go.

Amidst all the high fashions and fashion blunders, the ritual wheel that worked the space between the living and the dead still got us where we needed to go. It made room for the good laugh, the good cry and the power of faith brought to bear on the mystery of mortality. The dead were 'processed' to their final dispositions with a pause sufficient to say that their lives and their deaths truly mattered to us. The broken circle within the community of people who shared blood or geography or belief with the dead was closed again through this 'acting out our parts', as Reverend Long calls it. Someone brought the casseroles, someone brought the prayers, someone brought a shovel or lit the fire, everyone was consoled by everyone else. The wheel that worked the space between the living and the dead ran smooth.

Lately I've been thinking the wheel is broken or gone a long way off the track or must be reinvented every day. The paradigm is shifting. Bereft of communities of faith or family, the script has changed from the essentially sacred to the essentially silly. We mistake the ridiculous for the sublime.

Take Batesville Casket Company, for example. They make caskets and urns and wholesale to funeral homes all over the globe. Their latest catalogue is called 'Accessories' and includes suggested 'visitation vignettes' – the stage arranged around neither Cross nor Crescent nor Star of David, but around one of Batesville's 'life-symbols' caskets featuring interchangeable corner hardware. One 'life-symbol' looks like a rainbow trout jumping from the corners of the hardwood casket, and for dearly departed gardeners there is one with little plastic potted mums. There is the 'sports dad' vignette, done up like a garage with beer logos, team pennants, hoops and hockey skates – and, of course, a casket that looks a little like a jock locker gone horizontal. There's one for motorcyclists and the much-publicised 'Big Mama's Kitchen', with its faux stove, kitchen table and apple pie for the mourners to share with those who call. Instead of Methodists or Muslims we are golfers now; gardeners, bikers and dead bowlers. The bereaved are not so much family and friends or co-religionists as fellow hobbyists and enthusiasts. And I have become less the funeral director and more the memorial caddy of sorts, getting the dead out of the way and the living assembled within a theatre that is neither sacred nor secular but increasingly absurd – a triumph of accessories over essentials, of stuff over substance, gimmicks over the genuine. The dead are downsized or disappeared or turned into knick-knacks in a kind of funereal karaoke.

Consider the case of Peter Payne. Dead at 44 of brain cancer, his wife arranged for his body to be cremated without witness or rubric, his ashes placed in the golf bag urn, the urn to be placed on a table in one of our parlours with his 'real life', which is to say 'life-sized' golf bag, standing beside it for their son and daughter and circle of friends to come by for a look. And, if nobody said 'doesn't he look

by kind permission of T. Cribb and Sons

natural?' several commented on how much he looked like, well, his golf bag. The following day the ensemble was taken to the church, where the minister, apparently willing to play along, had some things to say about 'life being like a par-three hole with plenty of sand traps and water hazards' – to wit, all too short and full of trouble. And heaven was something like a '19th hole', where, after 'finishing the course', those who 'played by the rules' and 'kept an honest score' were given their 'trophies'. Then those in attendance were invited to join the family at the clubhouse of Mystic Creek Golf Course for lunch and a little commemorative boozing. There is already talk of a Peter Payne Memorial Tournament next year. A scholarship fund has been established to send young golfers to a PGA training camp. Some of his ashes will be scattered in the sand trap of the par five on the back nine with the kidney-shaped green and the dog-leg right. The rest will remain, for ever and ever, perpetual filler for the golf bag urn.

Whether this is indeed a paradigm shift, the end of an era, or, as Robert Pogue Harrison (2003) suggests, an 'all too human failure to meet the challenges of modernity' is anyone's guess. But we are nonetheless required, as he insists, to choose 'an allegiance – either to the post-human, the virtual, and the synthetic, or to the earth, the real and the dead in their humic densities'.

In the albeit virtual world of Six Feet Under, the allegiance is clearly pledged to the 'the earth, the real and the dead in their humic densities'. Ours is a species, as Ball portrays it, that deals with death by dealing with the dead – actually, physically, hands-on – the palpable, loveable, corruptible corporeality of the dead in the flesh. Paraphrasing Wallace Stevens (1990), the show insists that we deal with not only 'the idea of the thing', but with 'the thing itself'. This is why the dead are everywhere in Ball's version – because for generations, now, they've seemed to be nowhere. Much of the attraction to Six Feet Under is that it puts the bodies back in funerals. In Britain and America, for half a century now, they've been hidden under coffin lids in the name of 'good taste' or dispatched to the retort or the grave unceremoniously in the name of convenience and cost efficiency.

The tastefully upmarket, emotionally neutered, socially ambiguous 'memorial service' that Mitford peddled, to which everyone but the dead guy gets invited, where the chit-chat and finger-food are determinedly light-hearted and, needless to mention, 'life-affirming', and after which 'closure' is predictably proclaimed (often just before the Merlot runs out), is no more authentic than the junk-mailed, telemarketed, prepaid, pre-planned commemorative 'events', heavy on warm-fuzzies and merchandise that the multi-national 'death care' conglomerates have been peddling, by quota and commission, for the past two decades now. Both miss the mark. Both confuse merchandise with meaning, fashions with fundamentals, accessories with essential elements. The mortuary moguls insist that a good funeral is about what you buy. The new century Mitfordians insist it is about what you don't. Ball seems to be arguing that it is neither what we spend nor what we save. Good funerals are about what we *do*.

Can they be done without coffins and gladioli? Without limousines and morning suits? Without flags and anthems and processionals? Of course. But can we do them without the dead?

When the Fisher family gathers at the graveside to bury their dead man, in the opening episode of *Six Feet Under*, the cleric says the prayers then passes a canister of sand for the family to sprinkle on the casket. The dutiful David observes the protocol; his wide-eyed sister Claire follows suit. But Nate, the blow-in elder brother from Seattle, refuses, protesting loudly that it is like 'salting the popcorn'. He won't have the experience 'sanitised'. He searches for a clump of 'real' dirt because it better represents his 'real' grief – the untidy business of anger, love, guilt, pain and loss. His prim but apparently passionate mother follows suit, unwilling to go gently into the good night of widowhood. David gets his reality in the embalming room, conversing with his dead father gone horizontal, and argues for tradition, ceremony, decorum and calm. Claire sees her father's ghost, propped on the hearse parked at the kerb, smiling widely. Nate shows his mother how to dirty her hands in her husband's burial, while her wrenching, whole-body sobs remove any pretence of ease. They all leave with their separate longings for the dead – the sons still fighting for their father's approval, the daughter still hungering for attention, the wife wanting him back long enough to forgive her for her clumsy infidelities.

By the opening of the fourth season, the widow Fisher is re-married, David remains in furtive, fitful love with Keith, Claire has been investigating her broadening sexual options and sad internal life, and Nate is, as his mother was, the guilt-tinged widower. When his dead wife Lisa's badly done and putrefying corpse is found in the ocean, Nate and David go to collect the body. Once again, *what to do* becomes a dense embrangle of love, grief, duty and desire. Lisa's parents want her cremated and her ashes installed in the family niche 'back home'. Nate wants her buried, *sans* box, *sans* embalming, in keeping with her stated preferences. A quiet conspiracy of the Fisher brothers allows both sides to get a bit of what they want when Lisa's parents are given an urn full of ashes and Nate drives out into the desert to do the needful thing for his dead wife and for himself. He deals with the notion of her mortality by dealing with the gruesome, decomposing 'remains' of her. Nate's is a large-muscle, 'shovel and shoulder work', 'dark night of the soul' kind of keening that leaves him, at daybreak, covered with the dust and dirt from which we humans come, quite literally a voice crying in the desert.

It is Ball and Company at their very best, avoiding the temptation for happy endings, easy maths or tidy metaphors. We are given, instead, humanity – aching, uncertain, ragged and struggling, weeping and giggling at the awkward facts of life and facts of death. If Nate's whole-body immersion in his wife's disposition is too much for most mourners, the no-body obsequies of the Mitford set seem like too little to do, lacking any witness and rubric any 'humic densities' or human duties.

Ball and his team 'get' what funeral directors have always understood: that, once you put a dead body in the room, you can talk about anything. Next to a corpse, everything, anything is possible and possibly remedial. It ups the existential, emotional, and spiritual ante in a way that virtual or symbolic memorials fail to do. On the evidence, it will be a wide-ranging conversation on sex, death, drugs and religion, love and money, heartbreak and desire, funerals and family.

Like the Levertons and Lynches and A. France and Sons, the brothers who inherit Fisher and Sons find themselves playing in the deep end of the pool, among the verities and uncertainties that are the human condition.

Sometimes Nate and David hear their dead father speak to them. The air is full of ghosts, who both instruct and disturb us. It was ever thus. I hear my father still, these long years since he died. 'We serve the living', he was fond of saying, 'by caring for the dead.'

Like the living, the dead are everywhere.

Unlike Mitford or the mortuary moguls, unlike anything else on TV now, *Six Feet Under* plays – sometimes tongue in cheek, sometimes casting the cold eye – for the most part in the deep end of the pool.

EPISODE GUIDE

Season One (2001): US premiere on 3 June.

1. 1:1 *Six Feet Under* (Pilot).
    w. Alan Ball.
    d. Alan Ball.
    Deceased: Nathaniel Samuel Fisher (1943–2000).
    Final moments: killed when a city bus ploughs into his hearse.

2. 1:2 The Will.
    w. Christian Williams.
    d. Miguel Arteta.
    Deceased: Chandler James Swanson (1967–2001).
    Final moments: dives into his swimming pool and sustains a fatal head injury.

3. 1:3 The Foot.
    w. Bruce Eric Kaplan.
    d. John Patterson.
    Deceased: Thomas Alfredo Romano (1944–2001).
    Final moments: chopped into pieces by an industrial dough mixer while cleaning it.

4. 1:4 Familia.
    w. Laurence Andries.
    d. Lisa Cholodenko.
    Deceased: Manuel Pedro Antonio (aka Paco) Bolin (1980–2001).
    Final moments: shot by rival gang members.

5. 1:5 An Open Book.
    w. Alan Ball.
    d. Kathy Bates.
    Deceased: Jean Louise McArthur (aka Viveca St John) (1957–2001).
    Final moments: electrocuted when cat knocks heated rollers into her bath.

6.   1:6 The Room.
         w. Christian Taylor.
         d. Rodrigo Garcia.
     Deceased: Mildred 'Hattie' Effinger Jones (1922–2001).
     Final moments: passes away peacefully in her sleep.

7.   1:7 Brotherhood.
         w. Christian Williams.
         d. Jim McBride.
     Deceased: Victor Wayne Kovitch (1971–2001).
     Final moments: dies in a military hospital after losing his
     battle with Gulf War syndrome.

8.   1:8 Crossroads.
         w. Laurence Andries.
         d. Allen Coulter.
     Deceased: Chloe Ann Bryant Yorkin (1959–2001).
     Final moments: skull shattered in collision with an overhead
     traffic light after standing up through a limo sunroof.

9.   1:9 Life's Too Short.
         w. Christian Taylor.
         d. Jeremy Podeswa.
     Deceased: Anthony Christopher Finelli (1994–2001).
     Final moments: accidentally shoots himself in the face while
     playing with a gun found under his mother's bed.

10. 1:10 The New Person.
         w. Bruce Eric Kaplan.
         d. Kathy Bates.
     Deceased: Jonathan Arthur Hanley (1946–2001).
     Final moments: murdered at breakfast by his wife hitting him
     over the head with a frying pan.

11. 1:11 The Trip.
         w. Rick Cleveland.
         d. Michael Engler.
     Deceased: Dillon Cooper (2001–2001).
     Final moments: dies in his sleep, a victim of cot death (SIDS).

12. 1:12 A Private Life.
      w. Kate Robin.
      d. Rodrigo García.
      Deceased: Marcus Foster, Jr. (1978–2001).
      Final moments: beaten to death by two homophobes.

13. 1:13 Knock, Knock.
      w. Alan Ball.
      d. Alan Ball.
      Deceased: Lilian Grace Montrose (1939–2001).
      Final moments: struck on the head by a stray golf ball.

Season Two (2002): US premiere 3 March.
14. 2:1 In the Game.
      w. Alan Ball.
      d. Rodrigo García.
      Deceased: Rebecca Leah Milford (1980–2001).
      Final moments: overdoses on cocaine while attending her
      movie premiere party.

15. 2:2 Out, Out, Brief Candle.
      w. Laurence Andries.
      d. Kathy Bates.
      Deceased: Joshua Peter Langmead (1981–2001).
      Final moments: dies of heat stroke during try-outs for the
      California state football team.

16. 2:3 The Plan.
      w. Kate Robin.
      d. Rose Troche.
      Deceased: Michael John Piper (1952–2001).
      Final moments: dies in hospital after a long battle with cancer.

17. 2:4 Driving Mr Mossback.
      w. Rick Cleveland.
      d. Michael Cuesta.
      Deceased: Harold Mossbank (1932–2001).
      Final moments: passes away while on a coach trip to Seattle.

18. 2:5 The Invisible Woman.
    w. Bruce Eric Kaplan.
    d. Jeremy Podeswa.
Deceased: Emily Previn (1954–2001).
Final moments: chokes to death on a TV dinner.

19. 2:6 In Place of Anger.
    w. Christian Taylor.
    d. Michael Engler.
Deceased: Matthew Heath Collins (1959–2001).
Final moments: drunkenly falls overboard the company yacht
and is chopped by propellers.

20. 2:7 Back to the Garden.
    w. Jill Soloway.
    d. Daniel Attias.
Deceased: Jeffrey Marc Shapiro (1963–2001).
Final moments: accidentally strangles himself while
attempting autoerotic asphyxiation.

21. 2:8 It's the Most Wonderful Time of the Year.
    w. Scott Buck.
    d. Alan Taylor.
Deceased: Jesse Ray Johnson (1944–2001).
Final moments: collides with a truck on his Harley-Davidson
while riding to work as a department store Santa.

22. 2:9 Someone Else's Eyes.
    w. Alan Ball.
    d. Michael Cuesta.
Deceased: Dwight Edgar Garrison (1945–2002).
Final moments: skull shattered when a metal lunchbox,
dropped by a construction worker, falls on his head.

23. 2:10 The Secret.
    w. Bruce Eric Kaplan.
    d. Alan Poul.
Deceased: Benjamin Srisai (1935–2002).
Final moments: sustains heart attack while taking out the
rubbish.

24. 2:11 The Liar and the Whore.
    w. Rick Cleveland.
    d. Miguel Arteta.
    Deceased: Edith Kirky (1929–2002).
    Final moments: dies after complaining of extreme pain in the nursing home where Vanessa works. Rico later pulls out a sausage from her oesophagus.

25. 2:12 I'll Take You.
    w. Jill Soloway.
    d. Michael Engler.
    Deceased: Leticia Perfect Perez (1922–2002).
    Final moments: passes away while underneath a hairdryer in a beauty salon.

26. 2:13 The Last Time.
    w. Kate Robin.
    d. Alan Ball.
    Deceased: Aaron Buchbinder (1976–2002).
    Final moments: dies in Nate's arms after losing his battle with pancreatic cancer.

Season Three (2003): US premiere 2 March.

27. 3:1 Perfect Circles.
    w. Alan Ball.
    d. Rodrigo García.
    Deceased: Nathaniel Samuel Fisher (1965–2002/?)
    Final moments: blood vessel erupts during surgery to deal with his AVM but this is only one possible outcome.

28. 3:2 You Never Know.
    w. Scott Buck.
    d. Michael Cuesta.
    Deceased: Matthew Clark Hazen (1962–2003); Martin Jacobs (1978–2003); Andrew Wayne Milne (1952–2003).
    Final moments: each is shot by Daniel Showalter, a disgruntled ex-employee of the telemarketing company where they work.
    Deceased: Daniel Showalter (1978–2003).
    Final moments: commits suicide by shooting himself after his killing spree.

29.   3:3 The Eye Inside.
   w. Kate Robin.
   d. Michael Engler.
Deceased: Callie Renee Mortimer (1984–2003).
Final moments: knocked down by a car after running into the road fearful of a group of boys following her; they turn out to be her friends.

30.   3:4 Nobody Sleeps.
   w. Rick Cleveland and Alan Ball.
   d. Alan Poul.
Deceased: Robert Lamar Giffin (1955–2003).
Final moments: passes away, after battling a congenital heart problem, surrounded by friends enjoying a late-night showing of that classic chiller *The Bad Seed* on television.

31.   3:5 The Trap.
   w. Bruce Eric Kaplan.
   d. Jeremy Podeswa.
Deceased: William Aaron Jaffe (1951–1975).
Final moments: found by the Bickerson in Griffith Park some 16 years after his car came off the road, killing him.

32.   3:6 Making Love Work.
   w. Jill Soloway.
   d. Kathy Bates.
Deceased: Karen Postell Pepper (1964–2003).
Final moments: queuing with her friends to see a recording of Dr Dave, her nose starts to bleed and she collapses; Rico later identifies that damage caused by cosmetic surgery is responsible for the bleed.

33.   3:7 Timing and Space.
   w. Craig Wright.
   d. Nicole Holofcener.
Deceased: Bernard Asa Chenowith (1939–2003).
Final moments: dies of stomach cancer surrounded by his family – Margaret, Brenda and Billy.

34. 3:8 Tears, Bones and Desire.
  w. Nancy Oliver.
  d. Daniel Attias.
Deceased: 'Daddy' (1940–2003).
Final moments: dies in his deckchair after concluding a home schooling mathematics lesson with his numerous children.

35. 3:9 The Opening.
  w. Kate Robin.
  d. Karen Moncrieff.
Deceased: Melinda Mary Bloch (1965–2003).
Final moments: commits suicide by asphyxiation from carbon dioxide fumes.

36. 3:10 Everyone Leaves.
  w. Scott Buck.
  d. Daniel Minahan.
Deceased: Jeanette Louise Bradford (1928–2003).
Final moments: dies from allergic reaction to a bee sting while on a picnic with her family, the Charles's (Keith's parents).

37. 3:11 Death Works Overtime.
  w. Rick Cleveland.
  d. Daniel Attias.
Deceased: Dorothy Kim Su (1945–2003).
Final moments: shot in the face during a convenience store hold-up.

Deceased: David Raymond Monroe (1971–2003).
Final moments: suffers a fatal heart attack while exercising at the gym.
Deceased: Edward Tully (1955–2003).
Final moments: electrocuted while fixing an overhead power line during a minor earthquake.

38. 3:12 Twilight.
  w. Craig Wright.
  d. Kathy Bates.
Deceased: Carl Desmond Williman (1948–2003).
Final moments: state execution by lethal injection.

39. 3:13 I'm Sorry, I'm Lost.

    w. Jill Soloway.

    d. Alan Ball.

Deceased: Anahid Hovanessian (1951–2003).

Final moments: huge chunk of blue ice (from an aeroplane) falls from the sky and crushes her skull.

Deceased: Lisa Kimmel Fisher (1967–2003).

Final moments: unknown (but possibly drowned); the ocean washes up her badly decomposed and half-eaten body.

Season Four (2004): US premiere 20 June.

40. 4:1 Falling Into Place.

    w. Craig Wright.

    d. Michael Cuesta.

Deceased: Bruno Baskerville Walsh (1951–1972).

Final moments: jumps from a roof high on acid before falling to his death (ashes remain uncollected).

41. 4:2 In Case of Rapture.

    w. Rick Cleveland.

    d. Daniel Attias.

Deceased: Dorothy Sheedy (1954–2003).

Final moments: gets run over while caught in the rapture of confusing inflatable (and pornographic) dolls for angels rising to heaven.

42. 4:3 Parallel Play.

    w. Jill Soloway.

    d. Jeremy Podeswa.

Deceased: Kaitlin Elise Stolte (1989–2003).

Final moments: after making a prank phone call falls off the bed laughing so hard that she breaks her neck.

43. 4:4 Can I Come Up Now.

    w. Alan Ball.

    d. Dan Minahan.

Deceased: Lawrence Henry Mason (1938–2003).

Final moments: struck by lightning while carrying an umbrella.

44. 4:5 That's My Dog.
   > w. Scott Buck.
   > d. Alan Poul.

   Deceased: Anne Marie Thorton (1966–2004).
   Final moments: slips in the shower after celebrating her thirteenth wedding anniversary with a romp in the hot tub.

45. 4:6 Terror Starts at Home.
   > w. Kate Robin.
   > d. Miguel Arteta.

   Deceased: Robert Carol Meinhardt (1962–2004).
   Final moments: bound and then shot in the head by two unknown assailants.

46. 4:7 The Dare.
   > w. Bruce Eric Kaplan.
   > d. Peter Webber.

   Deceased: Joan Morrison (1939–2004).
   Final moments: dies from stomach cancer after visiting the doctor's surgery and hearing nothing more can be done.

47. 4:8 Coming and Going.
   > w. Nancy Oliver.
   > d. Daniel Attias.

   Deceased: James Dubois Marshall (1923–2004).
   Final moments: pulls up into the Fishers' driveway before dying at the wheel.

48. 4:9 Grinding the Corn.
   > w. Rick Cleveland.
   > d. Alan Caso.

   Deceased: Lawrence Tuttle (1969-2004).
   Final moments: fatally reaching for his collectable comic, muttering how he will be buried with it before he sells it, Lawrence is killed when the shelf falls back onto him.

49. 4:10 The Black Forest.
   > w. Jill Soloway and Craig Wright.
   > d. Peter Care.

Deceased: Robert Duane Wething (1958–2004).

Final moments: dies after a fatal kicking administered by his wife, Suzanne.

50. 4:11 The Bomb Shelter.
    w. Scott Buck.
    d. Nicole Holofcener.

Deceased: Edward Gorodetsky, (Coco Gorodetsky); (Michael Gorodetsky); (Amanda Gorodetsky).

Final moments: the Gorodetskys perish in their state-of-the-art car when confusion reigns over the directions given by the On-Star facility and Edward, the father, makes a bad turn.

51. 4:12 Untitled.
    w. Nancy Oliver.
    d. Alan Ball.

Deceased: Kenneth M. Henderson (1954–2004).

Final moments: chopped in half as he tries to effect a rescue when he and others get trapped in a lift.

FILM AND TV GUIDE

FILM

Airport (George Seaton, 1970).
American Beauty (Sam Mendes, 1999).
American President, The (Rob Reiner, 1995).
Analyse This (Harold Ramis, 1999).
Badlands (Terrence Malick, 1974).
Bad Seed, The (Mervyn LeRoy, 1956).
Blair Witch Project, The (Daniel Myrick and Eduardo Sánchez, 1999).
Blue Velvet (David Lynch, 1986).
Captain from Castile (Henry King, 1947).
Citizen Kane (Orson Welles, 1941).
Desperately Seeking Susan (Susan Seidelman, 1985).
Flashdance (Adrian Lyne, 1983).
Flesh and Bone (Steven Kloves, 1993).
Gladiator (Ridley Scott, 2000).
Godfather, The (Francis Ford Coppola, 1972).
Harold and Maude (Hal Ashby, 1971).
How the West was Won (John Ford, Henry Hathaway, George Marshall and Richard Thorpe, 1962).
How to Make an American Quilt (Jocelyn Moorhouse, 1995).
King and I, The (Walter Lang, 1956).
Kissing Jessica Stein (Charles Herman-Wurmfeld, 2001).
Kiss Me Deadly (Robert Aldrich, 1955).
Little Women (Gillian Armstrong, 1994).
Looking For Mr Goodbar (Richard Brooks, 1977).
Loved One, The (Tony Richardson, 1965).
Monsters, Inc. (Peter Docter, David Silverman and Lee Unkrich, 2001).
My Girl (Howard Zieff, 1991).
My Girl 2 (Howard Zieff, 1994).
Ordinary People (Robert Redford, 1980).
Parting Glances (Bill Sherwood, 1986).

Philadelphia (Jonathan Demme, 1993).

Player, The (Robert Altman, 1992).

Psycho (Alfred Hitchcock, 1960).

Rapture, The (Michael, Tolkin, 1991).

Road to Perdition (Sam Mendes, 2002).

Robe, The (Henry Koster, 1953).

Shawshank Redemption, The (Frank Darabont, 1994).

Shining, The (Stanley Kubrick, 1980).

South Pacific (Joshua Logan, 1958).

To Kill a Mockingbird (Robert Mulligan, 1962).

2001: A Space Odyssey (Stanley Kubrick, 1968).

Virus Knows No Morals, A (Rosa von Praunheim, 1985).

TV

Ally McBeal (David E. Kelley Productions/Fox Television, 1979–2002).

And the Band Played On (Roger Spottiswoode. Odyssey Entertainment/HBO, 1993).

Andy Griffith Show, The (Mayberry Enterprises/CBS, 1960–1968).

Angels In America (Mike Nichols. Avenue Pictures Production/HBO, 2003).

Beverley Hillbillies, The (Filmways TV/CBS, 1962–1971).

Bonanza (NBC, 1959–1973).

Boston Public (David E. Kelley Productions/Twentieth-Century Fox Television/Fox Network, 2000–2004).

Boys from the Blackstuff (Philip Saville. BBC, 1982).

Blackadder (BBC, 1983).

Buffy the Vampire Slayer (Mutant Enemy Inc./Twentieth-Century Fox Television, 1997–2003).

Carnivale (HBO, 2003).

Casualty (BBC, 1986–).

Charmed (Spelling Television/WB Television Network, 1998–).

Chicago Hope (David E. Kelley Productions/Twentieth-Century Fox Television/CBS, 1994–2000).

Cracker (A&E TV Network Inc./Granada/ITV, 1993–1995).

Cybill (Carsey-Werner Company/River Siren Productions Inc./CBS, 1995–1998).

Dawson's Creek (Columbia TriStar Television/Sony Pictures Television/WB Television Network, 1998–2003).

Deadwood (Roscoe Productions/HBO, 2004–).

Diagnosis Murder (Viacom Productions Inc., 1992).

Dream On (MTE/HBO, 1990–1996).

E.R. (Constant Productions/Amblin Entertainment/WB Television Network/NBC, 1994–).

Everybody Loves Raymond (Talk Productions/HBO, 1996–2005).

Frasier (Paramount/NBC, 1993–2004).

Grace Under Fire (Carsey-Werner Company/NBC, 1993–1998).

Inspector Morse (Carlton UK Productions, 1987–2000).

Joan of Arcadia (Sony Pictures Television/Barbara Hall Productions, CBS, 2003–).

Knots Landing (Lorimar Television/CBS Television, 1979–1993).

Laramie Project, The (Moisés Kaufman Cane/Gabay Productions/Good Machine/HBO, 2002).

Larry Sanders Show, The (Columbia Pictures Television/HBO, 1992–1998).

Murrow (Jack Gold. TAFT Entertainment Pictures/HBO, 1986).

My So-called Life (ABC Productions/Bedford Falls Production, 1994).

Nearly Departed (NBC, 1989).

Nip/Tuck (Shephard/Robin Productions, 2003–).

Northern Exposure (Universal TV/CBS, 1990–1995).

Office, The (Ricky Gervais and Stephen Merchant. BBC, 2001–2003).

Oh Grow Up (Greenblatt Janollari/ABC, 1999).

One Foot in the Grave (BBC, 1990–2000).

Oz (Rysher Entertainment/The Levinson/Fontana Company/HBO, 1997–2003).

Partridge Family, The (Screen Gems TV/ABC, 1970–1974).

Queer as Folk (Cowslip Productions/Showtime Networks Inc., 2000–).

Queer Eye for the Straight Guy (Scout Productions, 2003–).

Real Sex (HBO Documentaries, 2000–).

Sex and the City (Sex and the City Productions/HBO, 1998–2004).

Silent Witness (BBC, 1996–).

Singing Detective, The (Jon Amiel. Australian Broadcasting Corp./BBC, 1986).

Sopranos, The (Brad Grey Television/Chase Films/HBO, 1999–).

Stalin (Ivan Passer. HBO, 1992).

Survivor (Castaway Television Productions/CBS, 2000–).

Talking Heads (BBC, 1987).

Taxicab Confessions (Harry and Joe Gantz. HBO, 1995).

thirtysomething (Bedford Falls Productions/ABC, 1987–1991).

Topper (Charles S. Dubin. Cosmo Productions/ABC, 1979).

24 (Imagine Entertainment/Twentieth-Century Fox TV, 2001–).

Twin Peaks (Lynch/Frost Productions/ABC, 1990–1991).

Will and Grace (KoMut Entertainment/NBC Studios, 1998–).

Wire, The (Blown Deadline Productions/HBO, 2002–).

You Are There (CBS, 1953–1957).

BIBLIOGRAPHY

Adams, Parveen. 'Mothering'. Parveen Adams and Elizabeth Cowie, eds. *The Woman in Question*. London and New York: Verso, 1990: 315–327.

Adler, Alfred. *The Practice and Theory of Individual Psychology*. Huber Heights, OH: Littlefield, Adams & Co., 1959.

Altman, Rick. 'Television Sound'. Tania Modleski, ed. *Studies in Entertainment: Critical Approaches to Mass Culture*. Bloomington: Indiana University Press, 1986: 39–54.

Ariès, Phillippe. *Western Attitudes Toward Death, from the Middle Ages to the Present*. London: Marion Boyars, 1976.

Atkinson, Ted. 'Cultural Politics in *Six Feet Under*'. Unpublished manuscript.

Atkinson, Ted. Personal e-mail to Samuel Chambers. 10 March 2004.

Bakhtin, Mikhail. *Rabelais and His World*. Trans. Helene Iswolsky. Cambridge, MA: MIT Press, 1968.

Ball, Alan. 'Afterword'. *American Beauty*: The Shooting Script. New York: Newmarket Press, 1999: 113–114.

Ball, Alan, and Alan Poul, eds. *Six Feet Under: Better Living Through Death*. New York: Melcher Media/HBO, 2003.

Barthes, Roland. *The Pleasure of the Text*. Trans. Richard Miller. New York: Noonday Press, 1990.

Bataille, Georges. *Erotism: Death and Sensuality*. San Francisco: City Lights Books, 1986.

Battles, Kathleen, and Wendy Hilton-Morrow. 'Gay Characters in Conventional Spaces: Will and Grace and the Situation Comedy Genre'. *Cultural Studies in Media Communication*. 19.1 (2002): 87–105.

Bauman, Zygmunt. *Mortality, Immortality and Other Life Strategies*. Cambridge: Polity Press, 1992.

Beecher, Henry Ward. *Royal Truths*. Boston: Ticknor and Fields, 1866.

Berlant, Lauren. *The Queen of America Goes To Washington City: Essays on Sex and Citizenship*. Durham, NC, and London: Duke University Press, 1997.

Bhabha, Homi. 'Introduction: Narrating the Nation'. Homi Bhabha, ed. *Nation and Narration*. London and New York: Routledge, 1990: 1–7.

Bianculli, David. *Daily News* (New York). 1 March 2002: 123.

Bird, Sharon R. 'Welcome to the Men's Club: Homosociality and the Maintenance of Hegemonic Masculinity'. *Gender and Society* (April 1996): 120–132.

Blum, David. '*Six Feet Under* Finds Its Footing'. *Wall Street Journal.* 28 February 2003: 15.

Borges, Jorge Luis. 'Kafka and His Predecessors'. Eliot Weinberger, ed. *Selected Non-Fictions.* New York: Viking, 1999: 363–365.

Boulous Walker, Michelle. *Philosophy and the Maternal Body: Reading Silence.* London and New York: Routledge, 1998.

Boyd, K. 'Homosexuality and the Church'. J.A. Loraine, ed. *Understanding Homosexuality: Its Biological and Psychological Bases.* Lancaster: MTP Press, 1974: 159–186.

Braidotti, Rosi. 'Becoming-Woman: Rethinking the Positivity of Difference'. Elisabeth Bronfen and Misha Kavka, eds. *Feminist Consequences: Theory For the New Century.* New York: Columbia University Press, 2001: 381–413.

Brod, Harry, ed. *The Making of Masculinities: The New Men's Studies.* Boston: Allen & Unwin, 1987.

Brown, Keely. 'Deep Down'. *New York Blade News.* 8 June 2001: 22.

Carpentier, Alejo. 'The Baroque and the Marvellous Real'. Lois Parkinson Zamora and Wendy B. Faris, eds. *Magical Realism: Theory, History, Community.* Durham, NC: Duke University Press, 1995: 89–108.

Carson, Tom. 'The Most Overrated Show on TV: *Six Feet Under*'. *Esquire.* March 2002: 64.

Carter, Bill. 'On Television'. *New York Times.* 2 July 2001: C8.

Castronovo, Russ. *Fathering the Nation: American Genealogies of Slavery and Freedom.* Berkeley: University of California Press, 1995.

Chambers, Samuel. 'Telepistemology of The Closet; Or, the Queer Politics of *Six Feet Under*'. *Journal of American Culture.* 26.1 (2003): 24–41.

Cherniavsky, Eva. 'Real Again: Melodrama and the Subject of HIV/AIDS'. *GLQ.* 4.3 (1998): 375–402.

Chodorow, Nancy. *The Reproduction of Mothering: Psychoanalysis and the Sociology of Gender.* Berkeley, Los Angeles and London: University of California Press, 1978.

Cixous, Hélène. 'The Laugh of the Medusa'. Elaine Marks and Isabelle de Courtivron, eds. *New French Feminisms.* Trans. Keith Cohen and Paula Cohen. Brighton: Harvester, 1980: 245–264.

Cixous, Hélène and Catherine Clement, *The Newly Born Woman.* Minneapolis: University of Minnesota Press, 1986.

Clemetson, Lynette. 'Oprah on Oprah'. *Newsweek.* 8 January 2001: 38–48.

Condon, Paul. *Six Feet Under: The Unofficial Guide.* London: Contender Books, 2002.

Craig, Steve, ed. *Men, Masculinity and the Media.* Newbury Park: Sage, 1992.

Creed, Barbara. 'A Journey through Blue Velvet'. *New Formations.* 6 (Winter 1988): 97–117.

Creed, Barbara. 'Alien and the Monstrous Feminine'. Annette Kuhn, ed. *Alien Zone: Cultural Theory and Contemporary Science Fiction Cinema.* London: Verso, 1990: 128–141.

Crimp, Douglas. *Melancholia and Moralism: Essays on AIDS and Queer Politics.* Cambridge, MA: MIT Press, 2002.

Cuddon, J.A. *The Penguin Dictionary of Literary Terms and Literary Theory.* Fourth Edition. New York: Penguin, 1998.

Curti, Lidia. *Female Stories, Female Bodies: Narrative, Identity, and Representation.* New York: New York University Press, 1998.

Danow, David K. *The Spirit of Carnival: Magical Realism and the Grotesque.* Lexington: University of Kentucky Press, 1995.

Dennis, Jeffery. 'Heteronormativity'. Michael Kimmel, ed. *Men and Masculinities: A Social, Cultural, and Historical Encyclopaedia.* New York: ABC-CLIO, 2003.

Doty, Mark. *Still Life With Oysters and Lemon.* Boston: Beacon Press, 2001.

Douglas, Susan J. and Meredith W. Michaels. *The Mommy Myth: The Idealization of Motherhood and How It Has Undermined Women.* New York: Free Press, 2004.

Dubois, W.E.B. *The Souls of Black Folk.* Toronto: Dover, 1994.

Farrell, James J. *Inventing the American Way of Death, 1830–1920.* Philadelphia: Temple University Press, 1980.

Fiedler, Leslie A. *Love and Death in the American Novel.* New York: Stein & Day, 1982.

Flett, Kathryn. 'Drop-Dead Wonderful'. *The Observer* ('Review' section). 16 June 2002: 20.

Foucault, Michel. *Discipline and Punish.* New York: Vintage Books, 1977.

Foucault, Michel. *The Will to Knowledge: The History of Sexuality.* Volume 1. Trans. Robert Hurley. London: Penguin, 1998.

Free, William J. 'Fellini's I Clowns and the Grotesque'. Peter Bondanella, ed. *Federico Fellini: Essays in Criticism.* New York: Oxford University Press, 1978: 188–201.

Freud, Sigmund. 'The Uncanny (1919)'. *Art and Literature*. London: Penguin, 1985: 335–376.

Freud, Sigmund. 'Femininity (1933)'. *The Essentials of Psychoanalysis: The Definitive Collection of Sigmund Freud's Writings*. London: Penguin, 1986: 412–432.

Freud, Sigmund. 'The Ego and the Id'. 'Three Essays on the Theory of Sexuality'. Peter Gay, ed. *The Freud Reader*. London: Vintage, 1995: 239–292, 628–658.

Freud, Sigmund. *Dora: An Analysis of a Case of Hysteria*. New York: Touchstone, 1997.

Friend, Tad. 'The Next Big Bet'. *The New Yorker*. 14 May 2001: 80–91.

Fromm, Erich. *The Art of Loving*. New York: Harper & Row, 1956.

Gamson, Joshua. 'Death Becomes Them'. *The American Prospect*. 2 July 2001: 36.

Gilbert, Sandra. 'Literary Paternity'. Hazard Adams and Leroy Searle, eds. *Critical Theory Since 1965*. Tallahassee: Florida State University Press, 1979: 486–496.

Glassner, Barry. *The Culture of Fear: Why Americans Are Afraid of the Wrong Things*. New York: Basic Books, 1999.

Goddu, Teresa A. *Gothic America: Narrative, History, and Nation*. New York: Columbia University Press, 1997.

Goffman, Erving. *Stigma: Notes on the Management of Spoiled Identity*. Harmondsworth: Penguin, 1990.

Gorer, Geoffrey. 'The Pornography of Death.' *Encounter*. 5 (October 1955): 49–52.

Goss, Robert E. *Queering Christ: Beyond Jesus Acted Up*. Cleveland: Pilgrim Press, 2002.

Halperin, David. *One Hundred Years of Homosexuality: And Other Essays on Greek Love*. New York and London: Routledge, 1990.

Halperin, David. *Saint Foucault: Toward a Gay Hagiography*. Oxford: Oxford University Press, 1995.

Halperin, David. *How To Do The History of Homosexuality*. Chicago: University of Chicago Press, 2002.

Harrison, Robert Pogue. *The Dominion of the Dead*. University of Chicago Press, 2003.

Hawthorn, Jeremy. *A Concise Glossary of Contemporary Literary Theory*. Third Edition. New York: Arnold, 1998.

Heffernan, Virginia. 'Death Becomes Her, Her and Her: The Women of *Six Feet Under*'. *New York Times*. 30 May 2004: S2, 1, 18.

Hendrickson, Paula. 'How Dare You!' *Emmy*. 24.3 (2002): 112–114.

Hirsch, Edward. *The Demon and the Angel: Searching for the Source of Artistic Inspiration*. New York: Harcourt, 2002.

Hockey, Jenny. 'Women in Grief: Cultural Representation and Social Practice'. In David Field, Jenny Hockey and Neil Small, eds. *Death, Gender and Ethnicity*. New York and London: Routledge, 1997: 89–107.

Hoffman, E.T.A. 'The Sandman (1816)'. *Tales of Hoffman*. Harmondsworth: Penguin, 1982: 91–94.

Horney, Karen. *New Ways in Psychoanalysis*. New York: Norton, 1939.

Horney, Karen. *The Neurotic Personality of Our Time*. New York: Norton, 1964.

Horney, Karen. 'The Dread of Woman'. In H. Kelman, ed. *Feminine Psychology*. New York: Norton, 1967: 133–146.

Huff, Richard. 'Writer Digs Back In'. *Daily News* (New York). 29 May 2001: 72.

Illich, Ivan. 'Medicine is a Major Threat to Health' (Interview with Sam Keen). *Psychology Today*. 9. 12 (May 1976).

Irigaray, Luce. 'The Bodily Encounter with the Mother'. In Margaret Whithard, ed. *The Irigaray Reader*. Oxford: Blackwell, 1991: 34–46.

Johnston, Gordon. *Which Way Out of the Men's Room?* Cranbury, NJ: A. S. Barnes & Co., 1979.

James, Caryn. *New York Times*. 1 June 2001: E25.

Kaminer, Wendy. *I'm Dysfunctional, You're Dysfunctional: The Recovery Movement and Other Self-Help Fashions*. New York: Vintage Books, 1993.

Kaplan, E. Ann. *Women and Film Both Sides of the Camera*. London and New York: Routledge, 1993.

Kaplan, E. Ann. 'Mothering, Feminism and Representation: The Maternal in Melodrama and the Woman's Film 1910–40'. Christine Gledhill, ed. *Home is Where the Heart is: Studies in Melodrama and the Woman's Film*. London: BFI Publishing, 1994: 113–137.

Kaplan, E. Ann. *Motherhood and Representation: The Mother in Popular Culture and Melodrama*. London and New York: Routledge, 2002.

Kenyon, Jane. 'The Stroller'. *Constance: Poems by Jane Kenyon*. Saint Paul, MN: Graywolf Press, 1993: 12.

Kilday, Gregg. 'Brother to Brother'. *The Advocate*. 19 March 2002: 42–46.

Kipnis, Laura. *Bound and Gagged: Pornography and the Politics of Fantasy in America*. New York: Grove Press, 1996.

Kitman, Marvin. 'HBO Is Having a Coffin Spell'. *Newsday*. 3 June 2001: D39.

Kitman, Marvin. 'Digging Up New Love for *Under*'. *Newsday*. 28 July 2002: D35.

Klein, Melanie. 'The Importance of Symbol Formation in the Development of the Ego'. *Love, Guilt and Reparation and Other Works 1921–1945*. London: Hogarth Press.

Kristeva, Julia. *Desire in Language: A Semiotic Approach to Literature and Arts*. Trans. Thomas Gora, Alice Jardine and Leon Roudiez. New York: Columbia University Press, 1980.

Kristeva, Julia. 'Women's Time'. Trans. Alice Jardine and Harry Blake. *Signs*. 7.1 (1981): 13–35.

Kristeva, Julia. *Powers of Horror: An Essay on Abjection*. Trans. Leon S. Roudiez. New York: Columbia University Press, 1982.

Kushner, Tony. *Angels in America: A Gay Fantasia on National Themes*. Part I: *Millennium Approaches*. New York: Theatre Communications Group, 1992.

Lacan, Jacques. 'The Direction of the Treatment and the Principles of Its Power'. *Écrits*. Trans. Alan Sheridan Smith. London: Tavistock, 1977: 226–280.

Lacan, Jacques. *The Four Fundamental Concepts of Psychoanalysis*. Penguin, 1991: 216–229.

Laderman, Gary. *The Sacred Remains: American Attitudes toward Death, 1799–1883*. New Haven, CT: Yale University Press, 1996.

Lavery, David. 'News From Africa: Fellini/Grotesque'. *Post Script*. 9.1/2 (1990): 82–98.

Lavery, David. 'Coming Heavy: The Significance of *The Sopranos*'. David Lavery, ed. *This Thing of Ours: Investigating The Sopranos*. New York: Columbia University Press, 2002: xi–xviii.

Lavery, David, and Robert J. Thompson. 'David Chase, *The Sopranos*, and Television Creativity'. David Lavery, ed. *This Thing of Ours: Investigating The Sopranos*. New York: Columbia University Press, 2002: 18–25.

Lawson, Mark. 'A Slice of Life'. *Guardian*. 12 January 2004: 10.

Leal, Luis. 'Magical Realism in Spanish American Literature'. Lois Parkinson Zamora and Wendy B. Faris, eds. *Magical Realism: Theory, History, Community*. Durham, NC: Duke University Press, 1995: 119–124.

Leonard, John. 'The Big Sleep'. *New York*. 4 June 2001: 93–94.

Lesser, Wendy. 'Here Lies Hollywood: Falling For *Six Feet Under*'. *The New York Times*. 22 July 2001: S2, 28.

Letters. *The New York Times* (Sunday). 5 August 2001: S2, 4.

Ling, J. 'Is "World Music" The "Classic Music" of Our Time?'. *Popular Music*. 22.1 (2003): 135–240.

Lipscomb, S.D., and Kendall, R.A. 'Perceptual Judgment of the Relationship between Musical and Visual Components in Film'. *Psychomusicology*. 13 (1994): 60–98.

Lovece, Frank. 'A Producer's Unusual Undertaking'. *Newsday*. 3 June 2001: D31, D33.

Lynch, Thomas. *The Undertaking: Life Studies From the Dismal Trade*. London: Vintage, 1998.

Lynch, Thomas. *Bodies in Motion and At Rest*. London: Jonathan Cape, 2000.

Lyotard, Jean-François. *The Postmodern Condition: A Report on Knowledge*. Minneapolis: University of Minnesota Press, 1997.

Magid, Ron. 'Family Plots'. *American Cinematographer*. 83.11 (2002): 70–72, 74–79.

Martin, Robert K., and Eric Savoy, eds. *American Gothic: New Interventions in a National Narrative*. Iowa City: University of Iowa Press, 1998.

Menton, Seymour. *Magic Realism Discovered, 1918–1981*. Philadelphia: The Art Alliance Press, 1983.

Miller, D.A. 'Anal Rope'. Diana Fuss, ed. *Inside/Out: Lesbian Theories, Gay Theories*. London and New York: Routledge, 1991: 119–141.

Miller, George C. 'Psychology as a Means of Protecting Human Welfare'. *American Psychologist*. 24 (1969): 1063–1075.

Mills, Nancy. 'The Dying Game'. *Daily News* (New York). 27 May 2001: 11.

Mink, Eric. '6 Feet Stiffs Viewers'. *Daily News* (New York). 1 June 2001: 112.

Mitford, Jessica. *The American Way of Death*. New York: Simon and Schuster, 1963; revised 1978; reprinted London: Virago Press, 1998; 2000.

Modleski, Tania. 'The Search for Tomorrow in Today's Soap Operas: Notes on a Feminine Narrative Form'. Charlotte Brundson, Julie D'Acci and Lynn Spigel, eds. *Feminist Television Criticism: A Reader*. Oxford: Clarendon Press, 1997: 36–47.

Moon, Michael. 'Memorial Rags'. George E. Haggerty and Bonnie Zimmerman, eds. *Professions of Desire: Lesbian and Gay Studies in Literature*. New York: MLA, 1995: 233–240.

Moore, Christopher. 'When *Six Feet Under* Strikes Close to Home'. *The WestSider*. 9–15 May 2002: 9

Morrison, Toni. *Playing in the Dark: Whiteness and the Literary Imagination*. New York: Vintage, 1993.

Mulvey, Laura. 'The Pre-Oedipal Father: The Gothicism of Blue Velvet'. Vic Sage and Alan Lloyd-Smith, eds. *Modern Gothic: A Reader*. Manchester: Manchester University Press, 1996: 38–57.

Munoz, Jose. *Disidentifications: Queers of Color and the Performance of Politics*. Minneapolis: University of Minnesota Press, 1999.

Nardi, Peter M., ed. *Men's Friendships*. Newbury Park: Sage, 1992.

Neale, Steve. 'Melodrama and Tears'. *Screen*. 27.6 (1986): 6–22.

Nietzsche, Friedrich. *The Genealogy of Morals*. Trans. Walter Kaufmann. New York: Vintage Books, 1967.

Nunokawa, Jeff. 'All the Sad Young Men: AIDS and the Work of Mourning'. Diana Fuss, ed. *Inside/Out: Lesbian Theories, Gay Theories*. London and New York: Routledge, 1991: 311–323.

O'Hehir, Andrew. 'The Undertaker's Tale'. *Sight and Sound*. 12.5 (2002): 6.

People. 'Did the Atkins Diet fail Dr. Atkins?' 23 February 2004:71.

Perec, Georges. *Species of Spaces and Other Pieces*. Ed./Trans. John Sturrock. New York: Penguin, 1997.

Peyser, Marc. '*Six Feet Under* Our Skin'. *Newsweek*. 18 March 2002: 52–59.

Poirier, Suzanne. 'On Writing AIDS: Introduction'. Timothy F. Murphy and Suzanne Poirier, eds. *Writing AIDS: Gay Literature, Language and Analysis*. New York: Columbia University Press, 1993: 1–8.

Press, Joy. 'Exquisite Corpses'. *The Village Voice*. 19–25 March 2003: 55.

Reid, Helen, and Gary Alan Fine. 'Self-Disclosure in Men's Friendships: Variations Associated with Intimate Relations'. Peter Nardi, ed. *Men's Friendships*. Newbury Park: Sage, 1992: 132–152.

Rich, Adrienne. 'Compulsory Heterosexuality and Lesbian Existence'. *Signs*. 5 (1980): 631–660.

Rilke, Rainer Maria. 'Death (Der Tod)'. *The Demon and the Angel: Searching for the Source of Artistic Inspiration*. Trans. Edward Hirsch. New York: Harcourt, 2002. 41–42.

Rogers, Mark C., Michael Epstein and Jimmie L. Reeves. 'The Sopranos as HBO Brand Equity: The Art of Commerce in the Age of Digital Representation'. David Lavery, ed. *This Thing of Ours:*

Investigating The Sopranos. New York: Columbia University Press, 2002: 42–57.

Rosenthal, Phil. 'Let Them Blow Your Mind'. *Chicago Sunday Times*. 28 February 2002: 89.

Rosett, Claudia. 'TV: Home Sweet Funeral Home'. *The Wall Street Journal*. 4 June 2001: A20.

Ross, Peter. 'Death Becomes Him...' *Irish Sunday Tribune*. 2 November 2003: 10–13.

Rowe, Kathleen. *The Unruly Woman: Gender and the Genres of Laughter*. Austin: University of Texas Press, 1995.

Rubin, Lillian B. *Just Friends: The Role of Friendship in Our Lives*. New York: Harper & Row, 1985.

Sedgwick, Eve Kosofsky. *Between Men: English Literature and Male Homosocial Desire*. New York: Columbia University Press, 1985.

Sedgwick, Eve Kosofsky. *Epistemology of the Closet*. Berkeley and Los Angeles: University of California Press, 1990.

Shamir, Milette, and Jennifer Travis, eds. *Boys Don't Cry? Rethinking Narratives of Masculinity and Emotion in the U.S.* New York: Columbia University Press, 2002.

Shattuc, Jane. *The Talking Cure: TV, Talk Shows and Women*. London and New York: Routledge, 1997.

Sherrod, Drury. 'The Bonds of Men: Problems and Possibilities in Close Male Relationships'. Harry Brod, ed. *The Making of Masculinities: The New Men's Studies*. Boston: Allen & Unwin, 1987: 213–239.

Sontag, Susan. *Against Interpretation and Other Essays*. New York: Farrar, Straus & Giroux, 1966.

Spangler, Lynn C. 'Buddies and Pals: A History of Male Friendships on Prime-Time Television'. Steve Craig, ed. *Men, Masculinity and the Media*. Newbury Park, CA: Sage Publications, 1992: 93–110.

Starker, Steven. *Oracle at the Supermarket: The American Preoccupation with Self-Help Books*. New Brunswick, NJ and Oxford: Transaction Publishers, 1989.

Stasi, Linda. 'Esprit de Corpse'. *New York Post*. 29 May 2001: 83.

Stern, Lesley. 'The Oblivious Transfer'. *Camera Obscura*. 30 (May 1992): 76–91.

Stevens, Wallace. *The Collected Poems of Wallace Stevens*. New York: Vintage, 1990.

Stevenson, Diane. 'Family Romance, Family Violence, and the Fantastic in *Twin Peaks*'. David Lavery, ed. *Full of Secrets: Critical*

Approaches to Twin Peaks. Detroit: Wayne State University Press, 1994: 70–81.

Sturdivant, Susan. *Therapy with Women: A Feminist Philosophy of Treatment*. New York: Springer, 1980.

Thomson, Philip. *The Grotesque: The Critical Idiom*. London: Methuen, 1972.

Tobin, Robert. 'Six Feet Under and Post-Patriarchal Society'. *Film and History*. 32.1 (2002): 87–88.

Todorov, Tzvetan. *The Fantastic: A Structural Approach to a Literary Genre*. Trans. Richard Howard. Ithaca, New York: Cornell University Press, 1970.

Toynbee, Arnold et al. *Man's Concern with Death*. St. Louis: McGraw-Hill, 1968.

Trockle, Stephan. 'Successful Hybrid *Six Feet Under*'. *ScriptWriter*. 17 (July 2004): 57–58.

Tropiano, Stephen. *The Prime Time Closet: A History of Gays and Lesbians on TV*. New York: Applause, 2002.

Turner, Victor. *The Ritual Process: Structure and Anti-Structure*. Ithaca, NY: Cornell University Press, 1969.

Turner, Victor. 'Frame, Flow and Reflection: Ritual and Drama as Public Liminiality'. Michel Benamou and Charles Caramello, eds. *Performance in Postmodern Culture*. Mikwaukee: University of Wisconsin-Milwaukee Press, 1977: 33–55.

Wade, Nicholas. 'The Bodies are Creepy, but Death Does Us Proud'. *The New York Times*. 14 April 2002: S4, 3.

Walter, Tony. *On Bereavement: The Culture of Grief*. Buckingham: Open University Press, 1999.

Warner, Michael. 'Introduction'. Michael Warner, ed. *Fear of a Queer Planet: Queer Politics and Social Theory*. Minneapolis: University of Minnesota Press, 1993: vii–xxxi.

Warner, Michael. *The Trouble with Normal: Sex, Politics, and the Ethics of Queer Life*. New York: The Free Press, 1999.

Waugh, Evelyn. *The Loved One*. Boston: Little, Brown & Company, 1948.

Weinraub, Bernard. 'An Oscar Winner Returns to TV on New Terms'. *The New York Times*. 4 March 2001: S2, 21, 25.

Weisgerber, Jean. *Le Réalisme Magique: Roman, Peinture, Cinéma*. Lausanne: Editions L'Age d'Homme, 1988.

Whittle, Peter. 'Los Angeles Finally Sees the Funny Side of Death'. *Financial Times*. 19 May 2002.

Williams, Linda. *Hard Core*. Berkeley: University of California Press, 1999.

Williford, Daniel. Personal e-mail to Samuel Chambers. 5 March 2004.

Zamora, Lois Parkinson, and Wendy B. Faris, eds. *Magical Realism: Theory, History, Community*. Durham, NC: Duke University Press, 1995.

Zaslow, Jeffrey. 'Quite an Undertaking'. *Daily News* New York, USA Weekend. 15–17 March 2002: 10.

Websites

Baughman, Rhonda. 'American Beauty'. PopMatters: Film: http://www.popmatters.com/film/american-beauty.html.

Buckman, Adam. 'Death Be Not Proud'. *New York Post* Online Edition. 10 June 2004: http://www.nypost.com/entertainment/22685.htm.

Clinton, Paul. 'Diggin' *Six Feet Under*'. The Advocate. 3 July 2001: http://www.theadvocate.com.

Chocano, Carina. 'Love and Death'. Salon.com. 9 March 2002: http://www.archive.salon.com/ent/tv/diary/2002/03/09/six_feet.

Guide to Literary and Critical Theory. 2004: http://www.sla.purdue.edu/academic/engl/theory/genderandsex/terms/heteronormativity.html.

Havrilesky, Heather. 'Digging Their Way Out'. Salon.com. 3 March 2002: http://www.salon.com/ent/tv/diary/2003/03/03/six_feet.

Havrilesky, Heather. 'One Wedding and Two Funerals.' Salon.com. 2 June 2003: http://www.salon.com/ent/tv/review/2003/06/02/6_feet_finale.

Lavery, David. 'A Religion in Narrative: Joss Whedon and Television Creativity'. Slayage: The Online International Journal of Buffy Studies. 7 December 2002: http://slayage.tv/PDF/Lavery2.pdf.

Magid, Ron. 'HBO's Acclaimed Series *Six Feet Under* Shot by Alan Caso ASC, Bucks Television Conventions'. American Cinematographer. November 2002: http://www.theasc.com/magazine/nov02/six.

Miller, Laura. 'Sex, Death and Other Family Matters'. Salon.com. 5 June 2002: http://www.salon.com/ent/tv/review/2002/06/05/six_feet.

Newman, Thomas. 'Interview'. The Motion Picture Editors Guild Newsletter. 17. 1 1996): http://www.editorsguild.com/newsletter/newman.html.

Nussbaum, Emily. 'Dropping the Ball: The Overrating of *Six Feet Under*'. Slate. 25 July 2002: http://slate.msn.com/?id=2068478.

Rogers, Bruce Holland. 'What is Magical Realism, Really?', 2004. Writing-World.com: http://www.writing-world.com/sf/realism.shtml.

Television Without Pity. '*Six Feet Under*, I'm Sorry, I'm Lost'. 2003: http://www.televisionwithoutpity.com/story.cgi?show=68&story=5246&limit=&sort=.

Vowell, Sarah. 'Please Sir, May I Have a Mother?'. Salon.com. 2 February 2000: http://www.salon.com/ent/col/vowe/2000/02/02/vowell_wb/index.html.

Wikipedia. 2004:http://en.wikipedia.org/wiki/Heteronormativity.

Index